T0330983

The
Idea Chase

Seven Principles for
Breakthrough Innovation

The
Idea Chase
Seven Principles for Breakthrough Innovation

Albert H. Segars

University of North Carolina at Chapel Hill, USA

 **World Scientific**

NEW JERSEY · LONDON · SINGAPORE · BEIJING · SHANGHAI · HONG KONG · TAIPEI · CHENNAI · TOKYO

Published by

World Scientific Publishing Co. Pte. Ltd.

5 Toh Tuck Link, Singapore 596224

USA office: 27 Warren Street, Suite 401-402, Hackensack, NJ 07601

UK office: 57 Shelton Street, Covent Garden, London WC2H 9HE

Library of Congress Cataloging-in-Publication Data
Names: Segars, Albert H., author.
Title: The idea chase : seven principles for breakthrough innovation /
   Albert H. Segars, University of North Carolina at Chapel Hill, USA.
Description: New Jersey : World Scientific, [2024] | Includes bibliographical references and index.
Identifiers: LCCN 2023008268 | ISBN 9789811267789 (hardcover) |
   ISBN 9789811268281 (paperback) | ISBN 9789811267796 (ebook for institutions) |
   ISBN 9789811267802 (ebook for individuals)
Subjects: LCSH: Creative ability in business. | Creative thinking. |
   Technological innovations. | New products. | Organizational change.
Classification: LCC HD53 .S445 2024 | DDC 658.4/063--dc23/eng/20230223
LC record available at https://lccn.loc.gov/2023008268

British Library Cataloguing-in-Publication Data
A catalogue record for this book is available from the British Library.

For any available supplementary material, please visit
https://www.worldscientific.com/worldscibooks/10.1142/13183#t=suppl

Desk Editors: Sanjay Varadharajan/Kura Sunaina

Typeset by Stallion Press
Email: enquiries@stallionpress.com

Printed in Singapore

This book is first and foremost dedicated to my wonderful family. My wife Barbara Patton Segars as well as my children Kristen Leigh Segars and Joseph Keith Segars. They are God's Blessings.

I also want to thank the many people who gave me the precious gift of their time. Their explanations of things I did not understand but needed to know were life changing. I was not always an easy, patient, or willing student. So, in some instances, the time and patience given to me by friends, teachers, coaches, and mentors were a kind demonstration of sacrifice, perseverance, and ambitious belief in what I could become, even when I could not see it. Those types of people are the essential ingredients in creating an overachiever.

Albert H. Segars

About the Author

Albert H. Segars is the PNC Bank Distinguished Professor at UNC Chapel Hill's Kenan-Flagler School of Business. He is also the Chairperson of the Board and Faculty Lead of the North Carolina Policy Collaboratory (NCPC), which the North Carolina General Assembly established in 2016 to utilize and disseminate the research expertise across the University of North Carolina System for practical use by state and local government. In May 2020, the NCPC was awarded $39 million from the state of North Carolina for COVID-19 research. Since its inception, the NCPC has managed more than $148 million in research projects. Along with his experience in academe, Segars has led research projects for Apple (iPod project), Disney, Pixar, Bose, Sesame Workshop, Red Hat, and the Defense Research Projects Agency (MSTAR, LOGX). In 2015, he was recognized as one of the top professors in entrepreneurship by a consortium of leading technology-based entrepreneurs. Since 2017, he has been part of the advisory council for CNBC's Disruptor 50.

Dr. Segars' area of research, teaching, and consulting expertise includes innovation, technology management, as well as entrepreneurship. He has written numerous articles on these topics within the context of strategic planning, product innovation, financial investment, logistics, supply chain, and corporate sustainability. His research

SEVEN TECHNOLOGIES REMAKING THE WORLD

An *MIT SMR* Executive Guide

March 09, 2018
by: ALBERT H. SEGARS

has been recognized as "Best in Practice" by *The Financial Times*, *The Wall Street Journal*, the Society of Information Management (SIM), the Society for Logistics Engineers (SOLE), as well as the Association for Computing Machinery (ACM). His recent work, "Seven Technologies Remaking the World" is featured in MIT's *Sloan Management Review*.

"How a Values-Based Approach Advances DEI" appeared as a featured article in *Sloan Management Review* in the summer of 2022. In this work, Segars, along with Anselm Beach, explores how innovative organizations achieve transformative impact through their Diversity, Equity, and Inclusion initiatives. It is a story about building a workplace that is attractive to diverse communities and using those diverse perspectives to successfully frame tough challenges.

Contents

Introduction

The definition, expectation, and execution of chasing big ideas are different today than they were just five years ago. It is impossible to mark precisely when it all changed. I would guess that it began after 2010, escalated in 2015–2017, and manifested itself completely right after the pandemic of 2020. The change was not initially dramatic, it was subtle. However, it quickly gained dramatic momentum. Those of us working in the world of innovation were being shaped and guided by a new set of principles. There were different ways of chasing ideas and different stories of success. Old ways that had worked were no longer working as well. New avenues that were once unavailable and costly were now easier and working quite well. As a researcher, I kept hearing the phrase *You know, things are different now* from leaders, scientists, designers, and innovators of the world's most creative organizations. Like most people, I looked *outside* first. The world was a different place. There were different challenges, exciting new technologies, and lots of new frontiers to explore. All of that was true. However, what I was being told and, at first, had difficulty hearing, is that things are also different on the *inside*. There is a revolution inside innovative organizations that is as dramatic as the changes on the outside. There is a new way to think about ideas and innovation, new principles to apply, a new way to organize to achieve success, and new expectations about what is worth chasing. Finding the breakthrough in today's sea of noise is clearly challenging. However, there are organizations and leaders that are riding this new wave and finding remarkable success. This book is about this new wave of

innovation as well as the people and organizations that are riding it. It is active, it is dynamic, and it coexists with the emergence of new workplaces that are built as a network rather than a hierarchy. So, we will use terms like "idea chase" and "innovation" to describe today's new approach in finding ideas that are bigger, more impactful, and novel. Just keep in mind that the art of chasing ideas has been reinvented and there is a place for you in that story.

Of course, it is tempting to believe that reinvented innovation wipes everything we know about chasing ideas off the map. Not true. Like most things, innovation responds to new revolutions in technology and society through evolution. It reshapes itself to be more effective, to do its job better, and to serve as a guide for directing resources. It carries with it the attributes of the past that are valuable, subtracts those that are not, and adds new ones that meet the challenges ahead. That is what has happened. So, to tell the story, we will follow the same script. We will explore *schools of thought* around innovation, examine the path of great innovators, and extract from these lessons the things that are critical for today's idea chase. We will also leave some things behind. We will add things that are now available to us because of new technology, knowledge, and reinvented workplaces. We will then frame today's new landscape as a "Universal Revolution". From this, we will clearly see the triggers of our new age and how the best organizations are responding. Finally, we will take the things retained, left behind, and added to develop seven principles of breakthrough innovation that capture critical aspects of discovering and implementing big ideas.

Things are different; I will show you *Why*. Chasing ideas has changed; I will show you *How*. There are new places to look for breakthrough ideas; I will show you *Where*. Your task is to walk into this new world with a fresh perspective, new expectations, and an open mind. What's ahead in terms of new ideas and innovation is spectacular. However, it will take a different set of eyes and a reinvented approach to fully see its potential. No book can fully create this for you. In fact, I send this book to you incomplete. You will complete the story by imprinting your brand of innovation, your insights, and your style of chasing ideas within the framework of the principles presented. That's the way it should be because now it's possible.

Chapter 01

Chasing Big Ideas: Stars, Constellations, and Breakthrough Innovation

Great things are done by a series of small things brought together.

— Vincent Van Gogh

There are few things more exciting than a chase. To track, hunt, run after, or pursue something is exhilarating. It might be the story of our lives; we chase our dreams, we seek to be more than we are, we help others in their quest, and we marvel at those whose chase ends in something fantastic. To chase is to engage with the knowledge that success will be sweet, but failure is a possibility. However, to decline the chase might lead to lasting regret or, at best, a bittersweet memory. So, we choose our chases carefully. Perhaps we choose those with little risk. Or, we take our chances and shoot for the moon. Most likely, we do some of both as our story unfolds. Those outcomes, good and bad, are the times of our lives.

For the purpose of this book, let's narrow the field of chases and chasing just a bit. First, let's confine it to the field of commerce, science, or government. The chase is part of our professional life. Second, let's consider the object of the chase, a novel or "big" idea. An idea that is very important, yet, it goes unnoticed by everyone else. Perhaps an alignment of conditions that reveal some new perspective or opportunity, yet is not obvious. Such a chase would likely involve interlocked activities of search, discovery, evaluation, and refinement. All together, we can think of these activities as our way of chasing the "hard-to-find" idea. It is the process of innovation. If we are chasing bigger game, then it is "breakthrough innovation". All of the conditions are the same. We might win, we might lose. If the task seems daunting, we might choose to alter the chase so that success is guaranteed. We limit our search space, discover only what is safe, and use evaluation to comb out anything risky. Or, if we are ambitious, we might take our chances and venture into the risky frontier. Our search frontier widens, we discover new ideas, and our evaluation encourages riskier "bets". Clearly, how we choose to innovate will determine what we find! Now, having said that, think about it for a moment. There are few incentives for anyone to chase the fantastic. This is particularly true if you believe big ideas and breakthrough innovation are the playground of only extraordinary individuals. It is magic, it is inexplicable, it happens randomly. The chase is only for the talented or insightful. Yet, think further; the world is full of big ideas revealed through breakthrough innovation. How can this be if only a selected few can innovate? The jets we fly, the trains we ride, the medicines we take, our corrected vision, the lighting that replaces darkness, clean drinking water, the surgery that saves our life, the artwork, the music, the sugar in our coffee were all novel and undiscovered ideas at some point. There are many, many more that we encounter every single day. We literally live in a world of breakthrough innovation! So, statistically, there must be something more than unique enlightenment behind it all. These things can't be accidents and they cannot be the result of musing or messy collisions of chance. Maybe this magic is something we can define. Maybe it is something we can learn. Maybe it is something that we can manage. Maybe it is a form of innovation that is inclusive rather than exclusive. Maybe chasing big ideas is not as risky if we know the path for breakthrough innovation.

That is the purpose of this book — to show you a new path for breakthrough innovation that is followed by teams in some of the most amazing organizations and projects of today. Surprisingly, it is a well-worn path. Yet, it is also a very different path. Innovation began changing in the late 2010s and changed even more after the pandemic of 2020. That's because the world radically changed. Still, we can learn a lot from the innovation stories of individuals such as Van Gogh, Mozart, Bach, Prince, Steve Jobs, the Wright Brothers, and the Rolling Stones. We can also learn from the experiences of great organizations such as Apple, Google, Genentech, Sesame Workshop, Pixar, and the Event Horizon Telescope (EHT). It takes courage to walk the path; it also takes courage to recognize that now the path is different. That said, keep in mind that the great innovators all began their journey as ordinary people who wielded a form of unconventional innovation. Plus, every innovative organization most likely started as something that was unconventional or perhaps ridiculed. It is the journey along with their talent (or collective talents in the case of an organization or team) that turned the ordinary into the extraordinary. The main lesson of those breakthrough innovators is this: *A person or organization must be motivated to chase ideas by the expectation of success rather than the fear of failure.* That is the path to the extraordinary. It requires you to accept the notion that you are in control of creativity and innovation, not some inexplicable force of nature or some messy process. This is particularly true in today's complex world. So, to begin our quest, let's look at some "schools of thought" around ideas and breakthrough innovation. These are the explanations and rationale of how the magic happens. Perhaps you are a believer in one of the schools. Most of us are. That is not a problem. The purpose of this discussion is not to choose one over the other; all of the "schools of thought" contribute something. They all offer clues to solving the bigger mystery of how novel ideas are found. Yet, no school seems to offer a complete or perfect story for today's new frontier. This is particularly true as the challenges become bigger, more noise distorts the signal, organizations become more complex, and technology continues to expand possibilities. So, with that in mind, let's take a somewhat humorous but insightful look at some of the more prominent schools of thought around chasing breakthrough ideas.

Breakthrough Innovation: Schools of Thought

The theories that explain the "give and take" between innovation (how you chase) and ideas (what you chase) are numerous. There are many ways to categorize them, describe them, apply them, and evaluate them. However, if you have been around organizations and teams that "do" this and if you have been around writers that describe this activity (I have done both), you realize that the stories and theories tend to fall on a continuum as illustrated in Figure 1. The continuum is anchored on one extreme by "inspiration". This is the unexplainable. The intuitive and ultra-creative phenomena that "just happens". We could even go a little beyond that extreme and say that it is random or accidental. It is a situation or context that is unplanned, yet it occurred and everyone was extremely fortunate. On the other extreme is grit, hard work, muscle, method, tenacity, and experimentation. We can call this extreme "discipline". It is not an accident, it is a tenacious effort, led by determined people, guided by engaged leaders, and driven by methods. Of course, we can populate the continuum with examples and say that some follow the inspirational path and others the path of discipline. But, as we will see, it's not quite that simple. Before we go there, let's examine the "schools of thought" with an eye toward extracting the unique and important contributions of each to chasing ideas in today's world.

Figure 1: Breakthrough Innovation: Major Schools of Thought

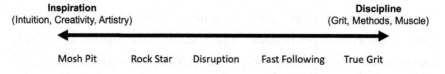

The Mosh Pit

A popular school of thought around finding ideas is that of an undisciplined, messy, and chaotic set of activities that cannot be managed. In fact, any attempt to manage this "organic" collision of talent, collaboration, and conversation will likely kill the supernova of an idea that will likely result.[1] It is analogous to a *mosh pit* and it lives in the inspirational neighborhood of the continuum. A mosh pit is an area in front of the stage of a rock concert where physical, uncontrolled dancing and celebration occur. *Moshing* is intended to be lively, energetic, but totally uncontrolled. So, the story goes, leaders in an organization should accept the randomness and unmanageability of innovation, particularly breakthrough innovation. Orderliness is the enemy; instead, create a mosh pit where the ideas can flow, the spirit can soar, and the chaos can reign. This perspective of uncontrolled or semi-controlled chaos is often personified by high-profile "design thinking" consulting firms and further stoked by TED Talks, popular articles, and documentaries. Like mosh pits and the band Nirvana, it hit its high-water mark in the 90s and early 2000s. Then, it reappeared in force around 2015. The message is clear, and it spreads like wildfire: discipline kills innovation. Plus, most organizations are way too disciplined.

To be fair, there is nothing completely wrong with this perspective, that's why it appears and reappears; maybe it works for some organizations. Plus, it brings a seemingly new and exciting perspective to the practice of innovation. However, it also begs the question of whether such an approach is well suited for big or complex challenges. Plus, this school of innovation clearly implicates discipline as a problem rather than any potential contributor. Let's face it, the story is very attractive. Yet, imagine a medical team taking this approach in deciding what procedure is required for your heart or lung operation. Should an organization such as Genentech use this approach in developing new vaccines? Can Pixar or Marvel

---
[1]Chuck Swoboda, Leading Innovation Is Messy, So Get Over It, *Forbes*, June 15, 2020.

Studios really bring together its talent in a timely fashion with a mosh pit approach to innovation? Is this how SpaceX develops its technology? Can government use this approach to address critical infrastructure needs? Can we achieve Diversity Equity and Inclusion through a messy innovation process? Of course, the answer to these questions is a resounding "NO". In fact, a closer examination of innovation that is typically classified as chaotic proves that it is not complete "freestyling". It may look that way, but behind the toys, foosball tables, resort wear, and sandals is something a bit more organized and analytical. So, while the chaotic approach to innovation is a great story, it is not a complete story. That said, this school of thought did give us some novel contributions that are important now. Community, collaboration, enthusiasm, creativity, and playfulness are all important attributes of this perspective. They are also critical elements of the most successful idea chases in today's world. The *mosh pit* also reminded us that the "know-it-all" leader is more myth than fact. It's impossible for a leader to do it all. Communities innovate and these communities form, evolve, and improvise based on the challenges faced. Also, there are preconditions such as flexible workspaces, absence of titles/hierarchy, and inclusivity that help the process along. All of these notions are very important today for breakthrough innovation and the discovery of big ideas.

A Rock Star

Another school of thought around breakthrough innovation is the "rock star". This is the de-facto school of many MBA classrooms, consultants, and Executive Education seminars. The story goes like this: The key to big ideas is to find the one person who "gets it". Quite likely that person will be an "outsider" to the organization. Someone who is ultra-creative, edgy, and has the right instincts. Find that "one" creative spirit and they will conjure up the big idea, change the organization, lead the charge, and everything in the kingdom will be safe and sound. In some sense, the rock star and the breakthrough innovation are one. Of course, the rock star story transcends many endeavors such as invention, politics, sports, and leadership. Business Leaders, Coaches, and Politicians are fired and hired routinely based on faith in the rock star perspective. It is a quick fix to a perceived innovation problem. Again, it is a great story, something that is fantastic and similar to a fairy tale. Because of that, the legend grows, and over time rock stars are credited with feats, insights, and superpowers that are beyond their actual achievements. In turn, belief in the school is reinforced and amplified. It is very human and very satisfying to attribute superhero feats to a magnanimous personality or persona. Plus, some of it is true, just not all of it.

Again, my purpose here is not to diminish the importance or achievements of rock stars. However, most of these styled innovation warriors will quickly note other aspects of their organizations (people, technologies, assets) and situations (new frontiers, shifts in marketplaces, the complacency of competitors) that helped them to lead and succeed. So, there is nothing completely wrong with this school of innovation. It sells books and it excuses the non-magnificent members of the organization from the rigors and risk of breakthrough innovation. However, some of the organizations led by rock stars eventually fell on hard times. Or, when their management teams or key players disappeared, so did the magic. In other instances, the organizations continued to innovate, sometimes more effectively, after the rock star was gone. So, it is apparent that the rock star story is not complete. There are often teams of people working "behind the scenes" to bring the idea to life. There are existing and perhaps underperforming labs or other resources that the rock star cleverly leveraged or revitalized. Perhaps the rock stars are great leaders and perhaps they helped personify innovation, but the fairy-tale story of simply finding such people and watching the magic happen is too good to be true. There is a context and there are capabilities that help the rock star and those things do not exist in every organization. In fact, it is likely true that a bona fide rock star or two failed when placed with the wrong band! Would Mick Jagger have been just as great without the rest of the Rolling Stones? I doubt it. Sales of his solo work will confirm my observation. Still, some very important contributions emerged from this school of innovation, namely, the roles of leadership, inspiration, and timely intervention. The guiding hand that creates a predisposition for discovering the big idea is a subtle and important storyline of the rock star perspective. The leader creates a space and conditions for ideas to flourish. In its less hyped form, the rock star school reminds us that innovation is not leaderless chaos. Plus, it tells us that the leader may not be the one that discovers the big idea. Instead, the leader's task is to lead such that the big idea has an improved chance of being discovered. The leader must also encourage and inspire the community when times are tough and success seems very far away. The timing of these leadership interventions can make or break an idea chase. These are the critical contributions that are often hidden in the glitz and glamour of the stories that describe this school. Like the mosh pit, the rock star lives in the inspirational neighborhood of the continuum. Although it does not tell the whole story, it does highlight the subtle magic of leadership and chasing breakthrough ideas.

Disruption

This school of innovation is intricate. It is built on the foundations of organizational behavior and economics. This is how the story goes. Breakthrough innovation is incredibly difficult to achieve for an organization that has a history and a track record of success in playing the game a certain way. For these incumbents, change will be difficult and riskier because a departure might result in outcomes not as desirable as those that have been realized. So, the organization "stays the course" — many times, to their own peril. The Disruptors are not bound by history or success. They see the changes more clearly. They intentionally seek to change the rules so that they can play the game and play it better than the incumbent. In a very aggressive fashion, the disruptive organization applies breakthrough innovation, weaponizes a big idea, and destroys the old guard. The passing of the old ushers in the new and a dazzling new frontier is born.[2] It is very "Star Wars" like in terms of its storyline. A young boy becomes a Jedi and completely destroys a complacent evil empire. Or, similar to the biblical story of David and Goliath, the armed and armored giant is slain by a boy who knows how to use a sling and a stone.

There is a lot to like about the disruption school. It explains so much. In fact, the school became so popular that it took on a life of its own. The concept of "disruption" was applied to anything that shook the foundation of an industry. Therefore, it is sometimes difficult to categorize or understand the effectiveness of strategic responses from both the incumbent and the disruptor. The speed of disruption is frequently cast as immediate and unexpected. Yet, research revealed that such efforts took time, were not always successful, and were not a total surprise to the incumbent. Impatient venture capital firms often abandoned disruptors when times became tough and projects became delayed. In addition, many incumbents successfully took on the persona of the disruptor when needed. Big ideas, it turned out, were not exclusively the playground of entrepreneurs. Interestingly, the researchers and practitioners of this school never really made those claims. However, they did not quell them either. The school itself became a bit bigger than reality. It also overpromised in the development and execution of strategy.

Yet, the school of disruption made an enormous contribution — the role of data in capturing the impact and emergence of a big idea. It told us that disruption is manifest in data, it is measurable. We can see patterns forming that announce the arrival of a new frontier and new opportunities. Therefore, changing conditions should not be a surprise if leaders correctly interpret the disruption through data and respond accordingly. Obviously, this is where the problems begin. Disruptive patterns are the kind of data that leaders have a hard time believing. Plus, they are also very tempted to

---

[2]Clayton Christensen, Michael Raynor, and Rory McDonald, What Is Disruptive Innovation? *Harvard Business Review*, December 2015.

assign false sources of cause and effect. This type of data tells us that things which once worked are no longer working. It tells us that the organizations we ridicule are pioneering new and promising paths of success. Ironically, it tells us that success is not where we want it to be. It is unwelcome, it is a problem, it might require work, we might have to learn something new. So, some organizations throw the lifeline of unwelcome knowledge back to the rescuer and ask for another means of escape. It is the irony of a novel idea; it appears in data as a contradiction or exception and is quickly discounted as an aberration. However, capturing this phenomenon in data moves us away from the inspirational extreme of the continuum to a place nearer the middle that incorporates discipline, intent, and managed action. It is a critical contribution of the disruption school, no matter how unwelcome it may be!

Fast Following

As we continue our journey away from inspiration toward discipline, we encounter the school of fast following. This might be the cleverest of all the schools. It is the strategic and methodological response to disruption. This is how the story goes. Like disciples of disruption, fast followers also believe a novel idea is likely to occur somewhere other than an established organization. However, they also believe that the idea will not appear in a polished or final form. This is a key difference. Therefore, the least risky strategy is to recognize the unpolished idea, improve it, and then move ahead of the initial innovator and the rest of the competition. The organization endures none of the risk yet reaps all the rewards of breakthrough innovation. This tactic is brilliant. It recognizes the disruptive nature of breakthrough innovation but it also allows the non-innovative to play the game. All you have to do is recognize the emerging idea, improve it, move fast, and rake in the glory. All of the heavy risk is taken on by the disruptor. The follower is still innovative since it takes some skill to recognize the rough draft of the initial idea, yet its adoption can be orderly and methodical. Best of all, the new idea can leverage the scope and resources of the established organization. Done well, this can lock others out, particularly the disruptor who came up with the initial idea! After all, no one remembers which horse is leading the race half way through; the important task is to place first.[3]

Again, there is nothing completely wrong with this school. It can be easily recognized by the presence of "innovation czars", "innovation task forces", and "innovation offices" within an organization. Ironically, these outposts of innovation are typically off the main highways of true innovation in the organization. While they play no real role in creating breakthrough innovation, they can provide useful facilitation, intelligence, and signaling. The organization has some recognizable hub of information around innovation. The problems occur when leaders expect such people, offices, or committees to engage meaningfully in breakthrough innovation or find the big idea. They can't; it is beyond their power or resource. However, they can identify trails of opportunity that have been pioneered by others, perhaps better than participants outside the committee or task force. So, in their best form, they remain a very useful tool of the fast followers.

It is easy to find examples where fast following worked well. Even innovative organizations such as Apple, Microsoft, Google, and others have applied it successfully. So, it may also be thought of as a path of innovation that accompanies riskier "first-mover" paths when conditions warrant. It is likely that every organization plays "fast follower" at some point. However, there are just as many stories of disaster. First and foremost, first movers are given more "slack" by the marketplace. Mistakes are forgiven and missteps are counted as the price of being innovative. Followers often do not enjoy this dynamic. Second, a key assumption of fast following is that an organization or leader can act fast. This is not often the case. If one is a follower, then by definition they are not likely to be decisive or ready to commit resources when the breakthrough is revealing itself. In addition, committees, czars, and task forces are easily ignored if they have

---

[3]Scott Anthony, First Mover or Fast Follower, *Harvard Business Review*, June 14, 2012.

no real organizational authority. So, the school appears easy in theory but becomes far more difficult in execution. Plus, there are followers waiting to follow you after you yourself have followed! Most importantly, it is very risky to rely on this school as the sole foundation for finding the next big idea. In a sense, you are outsourcing breakthrough innovation to others. There is no guarantee that conditions will avail themselves favorably to the follower in terms of timing, opportunity, and acceptance.

All that said, there is an incredible contribution made by the school of fast following. It is looking beyond the boundary of your familiar frontier for changing conditions and the next big idea. The best followers look ahead, laterally, behind, above, and below their own trajectory for new ideas. So, while they may not be the pioneer, they may be more equipped to develop a fuller story of what is working and what will work better in the future than the pioneer. Many avenues of innovation involve finding that unconventional influence, that new way of doing things, or creatively combining something new with something old. To do this, it is important to keep our eyes and the eyes of the organization focused on a broader frontier, not just a space of predefined or limited scope. It is the act of "borrowing" other perspectives and other influences that creates the incredible combination of something novel yet familiar. This is often the very best attribute of breakthrough innovation, and something seen in the makeup of today's most innovative organizations.

True Grit

This is the least attractive, dismal, and ugliest school of breakthrough innovation. This perspective frames the idea chase as muscle, hard work, grit, tenacity, experimentation, setbacks, and heartbreak. In the extreme, this school frames the chase as a "science" that is built around disciplined design principles. The backbone is a goal-oriented activity that progresses from identifying a problem to developing and deploying a solution. To achieve non-incremental outcomes, a "convergent" approach is recommended. Insights from diverse fields such as strategy, economics, entrepreneurship, systems of systems, design, policy, anthropology, sociology, education, engineering, and technology are used to frame more holistic and innovative solutions. As argued by disciples of this school, such an approach is critical to solving complex problems.[4] On a less extreme level, the school of *true grit* casts the journey as one driven by a scientific approach. This requires observation, forming a hypothesis, making a prediction, conducting an experiment, and then analyzing the results. This process repeats as many times as needed to determine the "truth" underlying some phenomena that are not perfectly observable. It is a structured and replicable activity that can be described, measured, and managed. So, while it is not the most exciting of the schools in description, it is inherently the least risky. Plus, this school implicitly rewards scale, resources, as well as slow, methodical progress. This is great news for organizations with lots of history and a long record of success. The end result is a bigger idea that is vetted, tested, and fully understood.

Again, there is a lot to like about the school of true grit. It harkens images of space exploration, mathematical proofs, anatomical discoveries, and architectural wonders. All of these are big ideas and life changing. And, all of them are products of very disciplined innovation paths. However, critics of the approach frequently point out the lack of velocity in overly methodical innovation. Sometimes, the very strength of the approach hampers the timely revelation and development of the idea. This is popularly termed "analysis paralysis". It is a fair criticism. It is easy to become too accomplished in a disciplined approach. It becomes a prized capability and leaders may lean on it to kill or temper something that threatens the status quo. Plus, some say that the approach yields mostly incremental achievements, nothing truly inspirational. Like science itself, the cumulative results of a true grit approach form a "bubble" of inquiry. If one lives in the bubble too long, then it becomes hard to identify new or emerging paths that are more promising. In fact, it might

---

[4]Peter F. Drucker, The Discipline of Innovation, *Harvard Business Review*, 2002.

leave the innovative door open for a rock star or a disruptor that is not bound by a linear, rigorous methodology. Yet, there is an enormous set of contributions from this school. First, this perspective acknowledges the challenge of breakthrough innovation and the amount of effort, sacrifice, and perseverance needed to find great ideas. Second, it shapes the activity as something manageable, measurable, and visible. This is great news for those in leadership. The focus becomes finding methodologies rather than esoteric paths of pure inspiration. Tools, techniques, data, and methods are used to structure something that is cast as inexplicable and unmanageable by other schools. Finally, in its most recent form, a perspective of "convergent science" is applied. Rather than working in silos, solutions are envisioned as emerging from across silos. Interdisciplinary teams, multiple sciences, and diverse methodologies are united by an approach that is scientific, visible, and predictable.

So, now we have a context for how breakthrough innovation has been cast. Along with the schools described here, I am sure there are many others. Quite likely, they also fall somewhere along the "inspiration" and "discipline" continuum. That's the salient point. The continuum is a unifying model of bringing together different schools of thought about how big ideas are revealed. Now that we have this important perspective, let's take a "behind-the-scenes" look at the idea chase of some extraordinary people, teams, and organizations. Importantly, let's do this with an eye toward reconciling the schools of breakthrough innovation and developing some principles for launching and successfully completing an idea chase in today's environment. Making what was once invisible, visible; what was once unexplained, explained; and what was once exclusive, inclusive.

The Symbiosis of Inspiration and Discipline

So, let's circle back to our key question. Is breakthrough innovation primarily a function of inspiration? Is it creativity, intuition, artistry, ingenuity, a lightning strike? Something imbedded in a unique individual? Or, is it discipline? Is it grit, methods, data, experimentation, orderliness, and muscle? If it is purely inspiration, then managing it will be luck. In fact, to manage it might be to damage it. We just need to find that genius and make the grand hire. Although many idea chases are described this way in books, articles, and talks, we will soon see that the lofty legend does not quite match the reality. In contrast, if it is purely discipline, then it is nothing more than a method. It's mechanical and if we turn the wheel enough we will get that "hard-to-find" innovation. It can be managed precisely, it can be mastered, it can be codified, and it can be replicated. We will also soon see that this extreme is often glamorized beyond its capability. What we will *not* see in the following stories is a total reliance on either inspiration or discipline. In fact, it is hard to find any process of breakthrough innovation that does not contain some combination of the two. As we will see, this is true in today's post-pandemic context of innovation. So, what at first seems like a dichotomy of either inspiration or discipline is actually a very intricate form of symbiosis. Inspiration and discipline live in very close proximity to each other and are mutually beneficial. The leadership mandate is to design and manage this combination so that the advantages of each perspective are magnified and the disadvantages are minimized. This is critically important as the challenge that is faced becomes bigger in scope and more complex in possible solutions. So, with that in mind, let's take a closer look at how some famous innovators and innovative organizations created the perfect symbiosis of inspiration and discipline for chasing their big ideas.

Vincent Van Gogh

Vincent Van Gogh is certainly a genius of artistic expression. He was able to collect and combine multiple influences then express them in works that are highly innovative in style and technique. It might be tempting to explain this innovative behavior as simply "inspiration". In fact, this is often how it is described. A person such as Van Gogh is "gifted" with enormous talent and therefore his path of success is not explainable. It is his talent or insight that is unique to him that explains the breakthrough outcomes in his paintings and drawings. Certainly, some of this is true; no one wants to take away the notion of his artistic genius. However, there is another story about his journey that points to something different than just unbridled inspiration. Van Gogh's journey and his process of creating art were as rigid and disciplined as the biological principles of science. It was muscle, grit, and a very methodical work ethic. His achievements were not an accident or a "lightning strike" of luck. Van Gogh himself noted in a letter to his brother that there were artists who were more talented than he; however, those artists were not willing to work persistently to develop their craft. Van Gogh worked tirelessly every day to improve as an artist.[5] There was also a passion, an ambition, a stubborn perseverance, and an awareness of other artists' work that provided the inspirational fire to his work. Along with his innate talent, there was a very disciplined set of behaviors and a spirit of curiosity that elevated Van Gogh's artwork from mere paintings to masterpieces. This combination applied at that moment in time made his work legendary.

So, if we recast Van Gogh's story, we might say that his innate talents and insights were amplified by a methodical approach, grit, a spirit of inquisitiveness, and pure muscle. Through this combination, he was able to capture an emotional and impassioned "breakthrough idea" in his art, again and again — something very different from that of other artists and something not seen before. Van Gogh began with a vague idea captured in a rough sketch, the sketch then became a rough drawing, the rough drawing then became more formal, and finally a painting exploded from the canvas. All through this methodical process, the vague idea is refined, reconsidered, and reshaped through a more playful dose of curiosity, imagination, and improvisation. There is forward momentum and a disciplined undercurrent in the process coupled with an inspirational spirit for achieving more. The innovative outcome emerges out of the effort and is not fully conceived or shaped at the beginning. There is "space" for the breakthrough idea to emerge as the journey unfolds. In some sense, the result is "earned" through hard work and timely insights. In the mind of

---

[5]David Sweetman, *Van Gogh: His Life and His Art*, Crown, 1st Edition, 1990, New York, NY.

Van Gogh, art does not rise suddenly from the flame of inspiration as a polished and recognizable form. Instead, it is an elusive idea that becomes more recognizable and revealed as the process of innovation unfolds. Clearly, Van Gogh did not wait for "perfect moments" to paint or draw, he was always working, always improving, always thinking. He viewed the blank canvas as an opportunity, not a threat. Beginning his career in art in his mid-20s, Van Gogh produced roughly 2000 works between 1880 and 1890. His work is timeless as evidenced today in the Immersive Van Gogh exhibits around the world. These exhibitions combine modern technology with music to create an experience that is engaging, immersive, and accessible to everyone. His work remains as innovative and breakthrough today as it did in the past.

Wolfgang Mozart

In a similar manner, Wolfgang Mozart found success in a way that was unconventional for its time. Mozart left his benefactor to achieve success away from the formal and stifling court of Salzburg. Unlike his peers, he organized piano concertos with smaller orchestras in venues such as restaurants and apartment buildings. He also composed music that was simple but elegant. It appealed not only to the aristocracy but also to all classes. The audiences grew and Mozart continued to write and perform. Mozart's productivity and new musical ideas enabled him to outwrite and outperform the contemporaries of his day. Like Van Gogh, Mozart was well aware of other artists and other forms of art. He had traveled Europe extensively. Doing so allowed him to create unique compositions that integrated German and Italian influences. He was able to absorb these different influences and combine them with his own ideas to create something unique yet familiar to a wide range of audiences.

Again, it is very easy to cast the story of Mozart as one of inspiration. The genius is granted insights and achievements through some mysterious and unexplainable force of nature. *How could Mozart's music be anything but a divine gift?* This beautiful point of view has been embellished and amplified in movies and multiple writings about Mozart. It is very appealing, it is inspiring, we want to believe it. Such a viewpoint excuses us from pursing the extraordinary. It also allows us to admire the genius and marvel at the lightning strike of talent it represents. However, in the case of Mozart, the story is totally false. A realistic examination of Mozart quickly dispels the myth of pure inspiration. Mozart's popular persona of inspired brilliance was the result of an overly ambitious publisher trying to sell magazines. Johann Rochlitz, a German magazine publisher, had a deep reverence for Mozart and published countless letters and anecdotes that were purportedly from or about Mozart. Biographers later discovered that many of his stories were exaggerated or pure fabrications.[6]

In reality, Mozart worked long hours in a highly iterative, rigorous process. He once described a set of string quartets he composed as the "fruit of long and laborious effort". Mozart would create numerous sketches, the music composer's equivalent of rough drafts, as he worked through the various parts of his musical compositions. He even improvised a type of compositional shorthand that made it easier to edit his work. Yes, there is creative genius but that genius is amplified through a rigorous discipline of composition as well as a spirit of curiosity and audacity. Therefore, we can also recast the story of Mozart's achievements as one of innovation: methodically discovering breakthrough ideas through trial and error, improvisation, and insight rather than a magical lightning strike of pure inspiration. Through his unique combination of inspiration and discipline, Mozart's ideas had the space and opportunity to reveal themselves, be refined, and ultimately brought to life in music. Interestingly, Mozart's approach can be found in the idea chases of very successful musicians of today. The innovative stories of Prince, Joni Mitchell, Michael Jackson, Carole King, Bruce Springsteen, Aretha Franklin, The Rolling Stones,

---

[6]Allen Gannett, *The Creative Curve: How to Develop the Right Idea, at the Right Time*, Currency, an imprint of the Crown Publishing Group, a division of Penguin Random House LLC, 2018, New York, NY.

and any others are similar in terms of grit, creativity, outside influences, and ultimately breakthrough success.

The Wright Brothers

If the story of innovation rather than inspiration prevails in art and music, is it also explanatory in other inventions or initiatives? The story of the Wright Brothers' invention of the powered flying machine offers some insight. Quite frankly, they should not have been able to do it; they were nobodies from nowhere. Their specialty was making bicycles. There were other inventors who were better funded, better educated, and had better access to the right circles of expertise and other critical resources. Yet, they somehow did it. Their starting line was certainly not one that would suggest a great predisposition for magical inspiration. It was not a "perfect moment" for beginning such a project. There was an established field of knowledge and many teams pursuing the idea. Many inventors perished in the pursuit of the flying machine. It was a dangerous endeavor. Yet, attributes that were important in making a great bicycle were also important in building a flying machine. Gears, balance, a method of propulsion, and a system of steering are common to riding a bicycle and flying a plane. So, they were more qualified than one might initially expect. Plus, the Wrights took a very scientific approach to the task and spent hours testing gliders and gathering data. Like Van Gogh and Mozart, they were immersed in the process, not waiting for perfect moments, and creating space for the big idea to emerge.

Somewhat ironically, the brothers themselves personified the dimensions of inspiration and discipline. Wilbur Wright, the elder brother, was a voracious reader and a master of the scientific method of invention. He was tedious, detailed, and very creative in the design of experiments to test theories about flight. Orville was the more mischievous of the brothers and not nearly as studious as Wilbur. He was a world champion bicyclist, which led to the establishment of their bicycle business. His adventurous nature and drive to succeed combined with Wilbur's skills in research created

the perfect context for perhaps the most influential accomplishment of the 20th century. It is perhaps the one story of breakthrough innovation where the inventors themselves clearly personify the critical elements that combine to form a successful chase for a very elusive idea. An idea that better funded and more accomplished teams (in the sense of formal education) failed to discover.

Martin Luther King Jr.

The story of Martin Luther King is another extraordinary instance of breakthrough innovation. As it should be, the story is often told in terms of his achievement: equal rights and equal opportunity for everyone. However, there is also a story of grit and hard work that describes how he reached the destination. Once again, it is not entirely inspiration. King suffered many setbacks in his quest. He was verbally and physically attacked. He was arrested several times by the police. Yet, he remained articulate, focused, humorous, and methodical. As King said, *If I cannot do great things, I can do small things in a great way.*[7] Rather than attempt to "cure" racism in people, King sought to change systems that produced racism. He saw a bigger picture and adopted a very calculated and persistent approach for achieving the breakthrough he sought. King plotted out a series of smaller objectives that involved local grassroots campaigns. He and fellow civil rights activists formed the Southern Christian Leadership Conference (SCLC), whose mission was to harness the moral authority and organizing power of black churches to conduct non-violent protests for civil rights reform. With King as its leader, the SCLC's initial focus was to lead localized campaigns to achieve specific goals: ending segregation in diners, buses, schools, or shops. With these early successes, the effort grew larger in scope and ambition. The full revelation of the breakthrough innovation was the March on Washington DC which led to the passage

---

[7]Martin Luther King, Jr., Clayborne Carson, Peter Holloran, Ralph Luker, and Penny A. Russell, *The Papers of Martin Luther King, Jr.*, University of California Press, 1992, Berkeley, CA.

of significant civil rights legislation. It also became a platform for King to advocate for other human rights causes such as poverty and workers' rights.

Like Mozart and Van Gogh, King drew heavily upon outside influences to guide his quest. The writings and actions of Gandhi were a source of inspiration and a blueprint for action. King felt such a strong connection to Gandhi that he visited India in 1959. That experience, according to King, deeply impacted his understanding of civil resistance. As he noted, *Since being in India, I am more convinced than ever before that the method of nonviolent resistance is the most potent weapon available to oppressed people in their struggle for justice and human dignity.* King was so dedicated to Gandhi's non-violent tactics that he surrounded himself with civil rights activists who had studied Gandhi's teachings. In turn, those activists incorporated Gandhi's blueprint into King's activism. Once again, this demonstrates that breakthrough innovation is not purely a "bolt out of the blue". In the instance of Martin Luther King, it is revealed or grown through a calculated, thoughtful, and organized effort that is persistent, patient, and perseveres. As importantly, the breakthrough is shaped and evolved by unconventional and unexpected influences. Knowledge and expertise "outside the normal boundary" create a leverage and space for the breakthrough innovation to be fully revealed and realized.

Sesame Street

If inventors, agents of change, and creative geniuses exhibit this combination of discipline and inspiration, is it possible that collections of individuals, a team, or an organization that achieved something extraordinary also followed this path of innovation? Alternatively stated, is this type of innovative behavior scalable? The answer is a resounding "YES". Let's take a look at Sesame Street. As an organization, Sesame Street (now Sesame Workshop) has achieved incredible innovation in Children's programming for over fifty years. Elmo, Cookie Monster,

Grover, and Oscar are renowned characters (Muppets) that are known around the world. Their programming addresses fun, educational, as well as difficult issues that confront children. It is done with a diverse set of actors, an urban context, catchy songs, animations, and celebrity guests that engage a wide audience. Yet, the idea was born out of rigorous science.

Against the backdrop of whimsical and loud programming that focused only on entertaining children, Joan Ganz Cooney and Lloyd Morrissette had a revolutionary idea. Could television be used to help disadvantaged children arrive for school more prepared to learn? The question is incredibly important, yet it was far from a perfect time to ask it. The Civil Rights movement was transforming the United States, the War on Poverty was raging, and there was not a lot of enthusiasm for the viability of children's television among network executives. The concept was seen as frivolous and uninteresting. Yet, at that time, many children were arriving at school unprepared to learn. Parents had no tools to help their children. Plus, differences in resources between families of "haves" and "have-nots" were creating nightmares for teachers. Through research, Cooney and Morrissette discovered that children learn and retain what they learn when the learning occurs with an adult. So, the most effective educational experience would be one that engages both a child and an adult. This revelation was the beginning of Muppets, celebrities, popular music, comedy, and other storylines that were intentionally designed to draw the entire family into the world of Sesame Street. Like Mozart and Van Gogh, Sesame Workshop draws inspiration from many sources, is inclusive, and continues to innovate to this day. It is an organization of people that achieves breakthrough innovation through curiosity, improvisation, and creativity that leverages a foundation of data collection, testing, experimentation, and refinement. Inspiration and discipline rolled into one. Leveraged and embraced by a diverse group of writers, actors, characters, and animators.

Street Artists (Banksy, Lady Pink, Crash, Vhils, Charmin 65, Above, and Roa)

Perhaps the most intriguing, inclusive, and impactful form of artistic expression is "street art". Street art began in the 1970s. It began with kids putting their names on public property (buildings, walls, train cars, subway cars, etc.). It then evolved into more elaborate works of artistic expression in the form of murals. Keep in mind, all of this activity is strictly illegal. Nonetheless, with the rise of hip-hop culture and the desire of underrepresented and less affluent populations to be seen and heard, graffiti and street art became a part of the experience in New York City. Lady Pink was one of the most prominent artists to emerge from this early scene. She gained enormous recognition through her pace of work and the ambitious expression of her artistic ideas.[8] Add to that the dominant impression that street art is the domain of males and her brand of breakthrough innovation is even more extraordinary. Soon, the illegal art of the street began addressing societal issues and sparking the emotions and imagination of those who saw it as expression and commentary rather than graffiti. Europeans flocked to New York and soon the practice spread overseas and around the world. Street art gave artists a new avenue of expression that was accessible, inclusive, and impactful.

In 2002, street artist Banksy created a series of stencils around London depicting a little girl with her hand extended toward a floating red heart balloon. Today, none of these stencils remain in their original locations. They have since been harvested by collectors and sold at auctions. Banksy's "Girl with Balloon" is consistently ranked as the UK's favorite piece of artwork. Framed prints authorized by Banksy routinely sell for millions of dollars. Very little is known about Banksy but his trail of artwork leaves lots of clues about this brand of breakthrough innovation. It is influenced by other artists and his keen perception about how his art reshapes the

---

[8]Henry Chalfant and Martha Cooper, *Subway Art*, Thames and Hudson, 1984, London, UK.

context within which it lives. In some respects, his art is the keystone of a chosen context, adding meaning, color, and perspective to a background that by itself is uninspiring. Along with his inspirational flair, it is clear to see the vision, planning, rigor, and experimentation that underlie Banksy's work.[9] This is true for all renowned street artists. There is a very observable process of cognition combined with exertion that guides and shapes their artistic endeavors. It is also a primary reason why this renegade form of expression has become one of today's most exciting avenues for idealism, commentary, and new forms of capturing big ideas in artwork.

Event Horizon Telescope

In French, the phrase *Esprit de Corps* describes a common spirit and discipline that binds a group of people together. This "something" is an important concept in explaining how fantastic accomplishments happen and what drives organizations and people to attempt what seems to be impossible. A great example of scientific *Esprit de Corps* is the EHT Project. The objective of this international consortium is to capture images of the very elusive black hole. This is a very ambitious and incredibly difficult task. A black hole is an incredibly dense and relatively small astronomical phenomenon that has such strong gravitational effects that not even light can escape from within it. It is only possible to see a black hole by observing the shadow it casts. This visible boundary is called an event horizon. The black hole that is the target of the EHT resides 55 million light years away from earth at the very heart of the Milky Way Galaxy. To acquire such a small object at such a great distance requires a very large telescope. In fact, to capture such the image, a telescope the size of the entire earth is required! Obviously, constructing such a device is impossible; however, this is where discovery steps into play.

As an organization, the EHT is an international collaboration of computer scientists, physicists, astronomers, mathematicians, and engineers who

---

[9]Carol Diehl, *Banksy: Completed*, The MIT Press, Boston, MA, 2021.

have created a computational telescope by uniting the technology of eight observatories around the world and integrating the expertise of well-focused research teams. The expertise and roles of the globally located teams consist of instrumentation, data processing, data analysis, simulation, multi-wave science, as well as engineering and computer programming. Each telescope within the network works in concert and is coordinated through extremely precise atomic clocks. Through the use of artificial intelligence and other computer algorithms, the images collected throughout the network are reconciled to create an image of the black hole at the center of our universe. In April of 2019, the lofty ambitions of the project were realized. The image that was captured provided physical evidence of Einstein's theories of relativity and also gave the world a glimpse of something that was once thought to be forever invisible.[10] It also represented the best aspects of breakthrough innovation. Focused groups working within themselves to practice and expand their science or art. These same groups also work vigorously between themselves to leverage their knowledge and achieve something beyond that which is achievable by any single group. It is an uncommon leverage of resources through deep collaboration. On top of this, there is "something" that drives members to focus harder, work ambitiously, collaborate freely, lift each other up, and endure hardship.

LEGO

It is not difficult to find commercial organizations that have captured the same sort of magic that is found in the EHT and Sesame Workshop. LEGO, the Danish toymaker, went from kingpin to near bankruptcy then back to industry titan by rigorously rethinking the activity of play. The Lego Group's namesake plastic construction bricks are among the world's most iconic toys; in many ways, they are a cultural phenomenon. The bricks that are manufactured today are still perfectly compatible with those produced 60 years ago. In its first incarnation, the company was

[10]Seth Fletcher, *Einstein's Shadow: A Black Hole, a Band of Astronomers, and the Quest to See the Unseeable*, HarperCollins, 2018, New York, NY.

heralded as one of the most inspirational and innovative toymakers of its generation. Yet, by 2004, LEGO posted a $292 million loss and was on the verge of bankruptcy. New technologies were reshaping the frontier of play. In response, the company leaned heavily on its inspirational underpinnings and created "gimmicky" product offerings designed to leverage digital and video platforms. The result was total disaster. In many respects, the company had over-innovated and lost its original identity. LEGO staged an amazing turnaround by balancing inspiration with a methodical approach based on careful collection of data, experimentation, and revised systems of project evaluation. Cross-functional teams, outside experts, and rigorous experimentation revealed new avenues of opportunity that leveraged the "core" of its identify. Artificial Intelligence, Robotics, and the Internet of Things (IoT) are all leveraged on the foundation of the original plastic brick. All of it designed to spur creativity in play rather than to pacify. In essence, the company rediscovered its identify and then reshaped it within the context of the new frontier. This effort drove customers back to the LEGO brand and returned the company to profitability.[11]

Further applying its skills in innovative discipline, LEGO has created a foundation that funds research into child development. The primary purpose of the foundation is to understand the interplay between toys and human development. Importantly, not just LEGO toys but any toy. Based on this science, design teams add new stories, games, and experiences that promote play, creativity, and problem-solving. If this sounds familiar, it is the same magic described earlier in the story of Sesame Workshop. Lego has now introduced its first sustainable pieces made from plant-based plastic, part of the company's commitment to use sustainable materials in core products and packaging. The unifying theme of the LEGO story is that these breakthrough innovations are "off radar" and somewhat counterintuitive if one leans entirely on inspiration or discipline. LEGO found a way to leverage both to reveal a frontier of possibility when the

---

[11]David Robertson, Bill Breen, and Thomas Vincent Kelly, *Brick by Brick: How LEGO Rewrote the Rules of Innovation and Conquered the Global Toy Industry*, Crown Business, 2013, New York, NY.

outlook was far from certain. It is a clear case of an organization that had achieved a breakthrough, then lost its ability to achieve the next breakthrough, but then gained it back. The avenue for the turnaround was developing innovative capability that may not have been necessary for the initial breakthrough (the plastic brick) but was essential for new breakthroughs.

Marvel

Another example of the LEGO experience is Marvel. By combining its core comic book with digital content and the power of gaming and movies, the company has continued to find novel ideas in characters, storylines, and content. However, the road has not been easy as the company deals with a very sophisticated and ever-changing customer base. Yet, Marvel combines elements of inspiration and discipline by building upon its recognizable core content while pioneering new space. Therefore, the content is uniquely Marvel, a consistent body of work, but also something new and engaging. Many of these new frontiers are revealed through *inexperienced experience*. For example, in Marvel Studios, directors who have had success in other genres but have no experience in the "superhero" genre are hired to expand the boundary of storylines and characters' personas.[12] The same is true for the actors they hire, the music they use, and the settings of their stories. All pay tribute to the foundational aspects of Marvel but also weave in new influences and perspectives. It takes hard work and a willingness to chase ideas that initially appear threatening. As experienced by Marvel, this is especially true if the organization has become too skilled at solving the same problem over and over again. Too often, employees are selected for experience that overlaps with that which already exists. Or, if the employee has a different experience, he or she is quickly socialized to the "norm" of the organization. In both of those instances, avenues for breakthrough ideas are lost. The less traveled paths to those bigger ideas are not visible or known to designers or leaders. In the

---

[12]Spencer Harrison, Arne Carlsen, and Miha Sherelavaj, Marvels Blockbuster Machine, *Harvard Business Review*, July–August 2019.

case of Sesame Workshop, LEGO, and Marvel, it is easy to see the value and impact of new inspiration, perspectives, and new methods for chasing ideas that might appear impossible. More importantly, these experiences further the notion that breakthrough innovation is a bit more intricate than that described by the various schools of thought. Maybe each school has something to contribute but none is the complete answer. It is almost impossible to fit any of the innovation stories perfectly into a matching school of thought. In addition, these stories remind us that innovation is like other capabilities such as running, weightlifting, playing a musical instrument, dancing, or art; hard work and practice must be maintained or the ability will fade.

Hopefully, you are now feeling comfortable with notion of breakthrough innovation as something that is within your grasp. Something that is not the playground of only the super-creative. Something that can arise from the actions and insightful interventions of someone in leadership or from someone on a team. Plus, you are now aware of the full innovation story of some very notable people and organizations. I hope you were surprised; I was. Yet, it made sense as I reconciled it with my firsthand experiences and numerous field interviews. Now, let's take a look at the main target of the chase — ideas. Note that the plural version of the word is intentional. It is critical to think of a big idea as more than one idea. Quite likely, it is many ideas that come together in a unique way to reveal a bigger possibility. The one big idea is the legend and myth of the rock star school. It is a fantastic story, but it is rarely fact. Collisions of events, technologies, inventions, and other innovations reveal new possibilities. Pursuing those frontiers requires more ideas, more inspiration, more discipline, stringing ideas together, and the ability to recognize that what lies ahead may require different ideas and different paths of success than what we left behind. Let's go there.

Idea Chase

Big ideas are hard to find, especially now. They hide from us like some elusive animal that blends in with its surroundings. They can do this effectively because ideas are typically many different animals hiding in many different places. They must be chased with the determination and stamina of an Olympic athlete. They masquerade as something untried, something risky, something out of the ordinary. Because of this, we tend to stick with the traditional, the tested, the safe. We leave the great idea to someone else. We become the follower. Ironically, that seems to be the very thing the great idea wants us to do — settle for something less and call it innovation. That way, the great idea can remain undiscovered until that unconventional eye recognizes it and turns it into the next great breakthrough. Then, it ridicules our lack of foresight. In contrast, average or below-average ideas are right there for us to see. They call us "friend" and remind us of the long history we have together. They play on our every bias and point to an easy and safer way to face a challenge. They help us chisel down big questions to smaller questions that are much easier to answer. Their home is in quick thinking, the things we did last time, and the solid belief that past solutions will work again; after all, what has changed? Now, before you think this writer has lost his mind by giving ideas (great, average, below average, and bad) the traits of a living being, consider their attributes and their power. Human communication and thought are inherently alive. They are shaped by cultural and societal interactions as well as new information and knowledge. They are manifest through a collision of thoughts, interactions, inspiration, and experiences. They might exist within a person or within a community. If not the full manifestation of something living, we can say that ideas are something more than non-living. And the great ones do not want to be found!

Breakthrough: An Idea of Ideas

So, if not something completely alive, *what are ideas?* And *how does one chase them?* To be honest, both ideas and the chase are elusive and somewhat difficult to frame with words or pictures. Yet, we all have likely experienced and benefited from both. In other words, we encountered them firsthand and felt the satisfaction of their revelation but also had difficulty explaining exactly what happened. Most likely this is because *a big idea is almost always an idea of ideas.*

Figure 2: Stars, Constellations, and Chasing Ideas

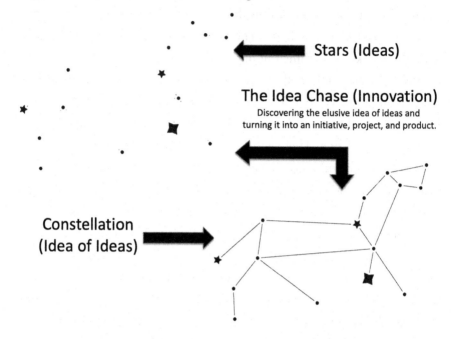

As illustrated in Figure 2, ideas are like stars. Stars are bits and pieces of light that illuminate the night sky. Each one is something beautiful, something wonderful. Yet, something even more fantastic is revealed in the constellations that stars form. Orion, Gemini, and the Dippers are the bigger ideas behind the nighttime stars. In a similar way, ideas are bits and pieces of something bigger scattered across our frontier of search. Each is a piece of a puzzle or each can be the puzzle itself. They are part of the answer or they can be the complete answer. If they are only part of the answer, they do not easily reveal how they can be combined to form the big idea or the breakthrough answer. This is where the idea chase enters the picture. The stars and constellations are part of the chase. In fact, there is a kaleidoscope effect in nighttime stars and constellations; they move and shift in the sky. The same is true for ideas. New technology, societal shifts, and numerous other things can cause ideas to shift, shine brighter, or burn out completely. To find the idea of ideas, we seek to find the pattern among bits and pieces of light in the night sky. We seek the bigger picture, the bigger answer, the order in the chaos. This is breakthrough innovation. The hunt for the elusive idea. If we are successful, then the constellation or the greater idea is revealed. So, the idea chase can be thought of as ideas, ideas of ideas, and the process we use for finding them. This is captured in Figure 2. At the top, chaos seems to prevail. The stars are wonderful but there seems to be no pattern. In the lower part of the illustration is Leo the Lion, the constellation hidden in the stars. This is the result of breakthrough innovation, our application of inspiration and discipline to the challenge. If we can see the constellation clearly before others, we win the idea chase. However, be warned; the stars are distracting, the process is demanding, and the constellation would rather not be discovered.

Now the key questions are as follows: *How do today's most innovative organizations and leaders approach the Idea Chase? What are the roles of Inspiration and Discipline in Breakthrough Innovation? How can I lead or help stage a successful Idea Chase?* These questions are the heart and soul of the remainder of our discussion. From Sesame Street to the EHT, to the amazing teams that brought us innovations such as the iPod, iPhone, nano-robots, gene editing, as well as a new frontier of vaccines, there is an approach that is definable and applicable. It can be used for any challenge an organization or team may face. It is the difference between discovering the great idea and just settling for the average idea. It is a leadership issue and it requires work, lots of it. However, the reward is great, and the journey can be unforgettable. There is a place for everyone in the story; all you have to do is believe it to see it. Yes, the world did change right before the pandemic of 2020; so did the art of chasing ideas.

Living on the Solution Side of the Equation

With that introduction, you might wonder how I fit into the picture. As a scientist and consultant, I have always worked on the solution side of the equation. My dream was and is to have a career of exploration and discovery. I think this path found its seeding in the Apollo space exploration program of the 1970s. This program and its ambitious goal of landing humans on the Moon found its way into my imagination and, for many elementary school kids growing up in the 1970s, became an embodiment of "magic" through creativity, engineering, science, and big ideas. For a moment in time, there were bigger ambitions, worlds to explore, and an army of wide-eyed dreamers ready to apply their talents to solving complex problems. Times like these come and go based on cycles of technological innovation, generational trends, and the "give and take" of societal needs. There are periods of technological revolution which usher in dynamic change as well as periods of "in between" where change is more incremental.

Through several research projects and consulting engagements, I have enjoyed firsthand access to labs, think-tanks, start-ups, as well as "skunk works" within established firms that are investigating, developing, and converting cutting-edge technologies into viable products and services.[13] I have already highlighted a few in this opening chapter. The ideas, discoveries, and breakthroughs observed from these organizations are incredible; in many respects, their efforts are the "tip of the spear" in terms of pioneering new frontiers. Most importantly, these organizations are doing things in a fundamentally different way than ever before. Therefore, understanding "why" they routinely discover big ideas and "how" they turn them into new avenues of value is to learn from the most "innovative of the innovative". It is also a chance to rediscover what works, what should be left behind, and what should be added.

In this book, I will describe the salient aspects of how today's most innovative organizations "work" in terms of ambition, values, beliefs, and drive as well as the associated tools and techniques that are used to uncover breakthrough ideas. Notice once again the important aspects

---

[13]Albert Segars, Seven Technologies That Are Remaking the World, Sloan Management Review, March 2018.

of this approach: There is an *inspirational* side as well as *disciplined* side. However, we will go one step further by combining the sides into a synergistic gestalt. We do this by surfacing seven key principles that underlie this important combination. These principles are the result of a multi-year research project, my firsthand experience, and years of field study. Framing innovation as a set of principles is something quite new. However, principle-based innovation represents the new form of discovery that is now guiding leading organizations in the post-pandemic world. As a leader, to know them is to open a path to greater frontiers in the search for ideas. Ignore them and the best you can hope for is an idea that is average and obvious. The principles are the "art" of leading the idea chase. They build a unique form of *Esprit de Corps*; a predisposition for accomplishing something great. This unique brand of chasing ideas is a leading indicator of tomorrow's workplace and has stark implications for how problems are framed, how people engage, how diversity is leveraged, and how solutions are identified. The approach is inclusive, diverse, equitable, and driven by community rather than messiah-like leaders.

Through the principles, you will see that ideas are born out of analysis, introspection, consensus, and inclusivity. It all starts with asking the big question. After all, the idea you get depends upon the question you ask. Ask a small question, get a small idea. Ask a big question, get a breakthrough idea. Once you ask the ambitious question, then techniques and tools ensure that all perspectives are identified, all voices are heard, and a collective mentality shapes the final choice of path. It is the ultimate team sport when done correctly. As part of the journey, I will demonstrate tools and techniques used for chasing ideas. You should view these as general tools for the idea chase and something that can be modified to suit your specific needs. The methods part of the puzzle is so important. Yet, it can be easily overlooked and, ironically, sometimes viewed as counter-creative. Don't believe the "arm-waving" motivational speakers that cry for more inspiration and less discipline. The most amazing organizations today have very structured ways of chasing ideas. You just need to dial in that process, place the burden of chasing ideas on a motivated team rather than yourself, and be prepared to be surprised. Rarely is the great idea the first idea or the one you carry with you into the process. It is more often where the "wild things are".

Today, this approach is being applied to discovering new modes of commerce, new forms of manufacturing, and new approaches to healthcare. Importantly, breakthrough innovation is a very broad frontier. It is not just developing new products, a new marketing campaign, or creating the new strategic strike. It is also developing programs of diversity and inclusiveness, creating better workplaces, partnering with the community, building benefits/compensation plans, and creating organizations that coexist with the earth's natural resources of land, air, and water. These and other important initiatives are sometimes framed as something different from innovation or an idea chase. It is a mistake. The most innovative organizations approach these challenges with the same vigor and same intensity as creating the next big product.

Importantly, this perspective also has deep historical roots and unlocks a cultural and methodical aspect of how something "more than ordinary" is accomplished. It speaks to the very heart of that "something" that separates an ordinary effort from an extraordinary accomplishment. It also reconciles how true innovation occurred in the past with how today's organizations are reshaping our lives. Most importantly, it takes the ideas of Diversity, Equity, and Inclusion and uses them as a framework through which we solve problems. For you and me, it is a way of thinking about the challenges we face and the frontiers we explore. It is also a way to instill a new form of leadership in the people we mentor, the teams we are on, or the teams we are trying to unite. This is more than a typical book about business or management; it is about a person, a group of people, a super project, or an organization that has struck a form of harmony or connectedness in chasing something bigger than itself. Such harmony can be found in a family, an athletics team, a social cause, a school, a church, a book club, a government agency, or a modern business. However, to find it, we must identify it. Accomplishing the extraordinary is likely something we have all experienced at some point in our lifetime; it is time to rediscover it, embrace it, and put it to work in the name of real progress. My hope is that these principles encourage you to chase those illusive ideas, shape them into an idea of ideas, and experience the thrill of the breakthrough innovation.

Seven Principles for Breakthrough Innovation

There should be a place where only the things you want to happen, happen.

— Maurice Sendak, Where the Wild Things Are

Perhaps all of us, at one time or another, have asked the question, "How did they do that?" It may have been at the end of a magician's "illusion", after a fantastic athletic feat, or at the conclusion of a perfect performance of a difficult song. We often experience the fantastic as an observer. In doing so, we marvel at the feat of an athlete, the skill of the performer, the genius of the artist, or the ideas of the inventor. However, there are also moments in our lives when we are part of the fantastic; we win the game when all odds were stacked against our team, we complete the impossible project on time and within budget, we survive a scare when we were sure that the worst would happen, or we walk through a crisis when all seemed lost. In some respects, these moments, good and bad, are the "times of our lives". It is also a time when you are connected to a group of people and a task in a way that is "beyond normal". There is a loyalty, a code of conduct, and sense of purpose that is beyond the normal rules of work or societal etiquette. It is a feeling of unique and important identity as you take on a quest. You are willing to give all you can to support those who are with you and to see the journey to its triumphant conclusion. It is also very likely that you leaned heavily on rationality, data, and careful analysis as you faced the challenge. There was more thought, more collection of data, and a sense that you had to address the right question. It was a time to be disciplined not careless. Whether you knew it or not, you experienced the duality of breakthrough innovation. A connectedness to your social community, a drive to deal in fact rather than speculation, and a purpose that was something more than yourself.

So, if we have all experienced or witnessed an extraordinary accomplishment at some point in our lifetime, perhaps now is the right time to understand it, harness it, and put it to work in our professional and personal lives. That is the purpose of this chapter. We will take the ideas we have developed so far and organize them into a bigger idea, hopefully a breakthrough idea. In doing so, I hope you will note that this book is itself a product of an idea chase. Let me explain. Inspiration, discipline, schools of thought, prior literature, the experiences of those who went before us, our experiences, as well as the examples described so far are all stars in the nighttime sky. In and of themselves, descriptions of these stars would make interesting reading. It might inspire you and create a sense of wonder. However, the breakthrough idea would be left undiscovered. What is missing is the uniting of these stars in the form of a constellation that is useful in guiding your next idea chase. This string of stars must be definable, actionable, and generalizable. After all, if our constellation only works for certain organizations or certain conditions, it is of limited use. In other words, it is not the big idea. So, let's get to work. The first stop on our journey is to describe the organizations, people, and methodology behind this research and book. With that, I will highlight some interesting insights about today's environment that are somewhat "off radar" compared to conventional studies and practitioner articles. We will then explore Seven Principles of Breakthrough Innovation that are critical for finding the elusive Idea of Ideas.

Looking to the Field for Answers

Armed with the concepts developed in Chapter 1, extensive interviews and surveys were administered to leaders, artists, and participants in organizations with track records of consistent breakthrough in finding unique and impactful ideas. These organizations, artists, and associated initiatives are the origins of product, artistic, and scientific discoveries that are consistently heralded as extraordinary by academics, journalists, and other innovators. This praise is corroborated by very prestigious awards and recognition. Grammys, Emmys, Academy Awards, Copyrights, Patents, Design Awards, Commissions, Community Awards, and Nobel Prizes are all represented in the initiatives, organizations, and breakthrough innovation described in this book. The frontier of our sample can be divided into four distinct areas: *technological, organizational, architectural*, and *artistic*. Examples of technological initiatives include the iPod, iPhone, Event Horizon Telescope, CRISPR/ Cas9, RNA-Based Vaccines, DNA Repair, Cloud Robotics, Micro Plasma Ions, 3D Projection Technology, Autonomous Vehicles, Classroom Technology, AI-Based Logistics, Data Visualization, Tele Medicine, and Digital Medicine. Examples of Organizational initiatives include Diversity, Equity, and Inclusion (DEI), Workplace Safety, Wellness, Compensation Systems, Training, Accessibility, Process Redesign, Hiring/Retention, and Employee Assistance Programs. Architectural initiatives include Green Building, Alternative Energy, City Planning, Airport Construction, Conservation, Residential Building, and School Construction. Initiatives in the arts include Hamilton (the musical), LEGO, The Emancipation of Mimi (Mariah Carey), Pixar's WALL-E, Black Mirror (BBC), HBO's Game of Thrones, ABBA's Voyage (Metaverse), Disney + (Mandalorian), Street Artists (Crash, C215, and others who wish to remain anonymous), and Sesame Street. Again, these are just some of the many big ideas that provided data and perspective for this research. There are many more that are equally or more impressive than those listed. Through careful examination of each initiative along with the host organization, artist, or team, the research objective is to determine how ideas, collections of ideas, and breakthrough innovation (the idea chase) are operationalized and applied to reveal the big idea. The details of the research methodology are included in Appendix. Rest assured this is a book that was reviewed by experts and academics in the field of innovation. It is also a book that is based on prior published research that was rigorously reviewed by academics. Most importantly, through the methodology, this is a book that captures firsthand accounts of how an idea chase occurs. It is *not* a set of opinions or war stories. With that in mind, let's get to the results. We will start with some discoveries that were "accidental", a bit off the path of the research objective. Yet, these findings provide critical perspective for fully understanding and applying the principles of innovation that are the "heart and soul" of the research project and this book.

A New Frontier of Innovation

In any ambitious endeavor, there are bound to be discoveries that are "accidental". For example, the discovery of penicillin, a group of antibiotics used to combat a variety of bacterial infections, was born out of a stack of dirty dishes. Scottish biologist Alexander Fleming took a vacation from his day-to-day work in the lab. He was investigating staphylococci, known commonly as staph. Upon his return, he found a strange fungus on a culture he had left in his lab. It was a fungus that had killed off all surrounding bacteria in the culture. This discovery on the way to discovering other things forever changed modern medicine. While not quite of the same magnitude, the research project underlying this book yielded some interesting insights about why breakthrough innovation is so important and why the chase for it is now different. It was a discovery on the way to other discoveries. The finding is this: An overwhelming number of scientists, innovators, entrepreneurs, and leaders believe we have encountered a new revolution. Something very different than that we have experienced and with new challenges as well as new opportunities. Like any revolution, it is not something that can be perfectly predicted, and it is something that is not recognized until you have been in it for

Figure 1: Revolutions and Their Impacts

Industrial Revolution

Technology Triggers: Textiles, Steam Power, Manufacturing
People: Work for Survival, Standardized Tasks, Stability
The Organization: Hierarchical, Command and Control, Exists to Find Efficiency
Innovation: In the Shop, Inventions, Inventors, Automation

Scientific Revolution

Technology Triggers: Railroads, Telegraph, Telephone, Radio, Utilities
People: Work for Salary, Advancement, Title, Incentives
Organization: Dual (Lab and Factory), Hierarchical, Exists to Find Discovery
Innovation: In the Lab, Experiments, Scientists, Science

Information Revolution

Technology Triggers: Internet, Digital Media, Broadband, Devices
People: Work for Standard of Living, Entrepreneurship, Empowerment
Organization: Matrix, Design Driven, Team-Based, Exists to Find Ideas
Innovation: In the Organization, Ideas, Creativity, Open Sourced, Latent Needs

Universal (Social) Revolution

Technology Triggers: Convergent Sciences, Blended Technology, Social Media, Society
People: Work for Quality of Life, Identity, Purpose
Organization: Virtual, Improvisational, Collaborative, Exists to Build Communities
Innovation: In the Network, Idea of Ideas, Crowd Sourced, The Greater Good

a while. These conversations, interviews, and data strongly suggest that the context (place, process, and people) and focus of our workplace have changed and are still changing. It also suggests that both societal and technological progression is reshaping the world around us in very different ways. Finally, it suggests that these changes are ushering in a new and challenging type of innovation, something that we have seen before. Clearly, things are different now. Things are so different that innovation itself is undergoing redefinition and reinvention. So, to develop this idea, let's place the new revolution within the context of past revolutions. This is illustrated in Figure 1.

A Universal Revolution

A very popular and useful way to describe time and its points of inflection is through revolutions. These revolutions usher in a new age that is fundamentally different from the age that preceded it. If you feel unsure, unfamiliar, out of touch, anxious, a little paranoid, and somewhat crazy, then it is likely that you have experienced a revolution and crossed from one age into another. Don't panic and do not surrender; even the most innovative people must adjust. Typically, these revolutions, ages, and associated impacts are initiated by and described in terms of technology. The *Industrial Revolution* (1760–1840) was defined by textiles, large-scale manufacturing of chemicals, steam power, and efficiencies in iron-making. The *Second Industrial Revolution* (1870–1940) was defined by railroads, telegraph, telephone, and electrical utilities. This was followed by the *Scientific Revolution* (1940–1970) that featured radio, aviation, and nuclear fission. More recently, the *Information Revolution* (1985–2007) was brought to life by digital media, mobile-multipurpose devices, the internet, and broadband technologies.

Interestingly, each of these revolutions created a pattern of innovation, a workplace, a motivation to work, and a guiding purpose. In the industrial and scientific revolutions, innovation was very scientific and very methodical. This is not surprising because so many of the innovative ideas (automation, aviation, railroads, radio, and telephone) were leaps in science, so the birthplace for many innovations was a laboratory or an inventor's shop, not the commercial world. The motivation for work was survival and work itself was a planned, repetitive, and predictable endeavor. The big organizations emerged and ruled the world. Legendary firms such as IBM, Xerox, and Dupont created a duality of laboratory-based discovery and automated factory floors. Scientific management was created and refined. Universities, trade schools, and high schools responded, and a workforce was created for the emerging reality and new age.

Just when it all seemed predictable, the information revolution radically changed nearly all these well-known relationships. The motivation for work became improved standard of living and empowerment. The commercial world was the birthplace of innovation, start-ups ruled the world, entrepreneurship curriculum found a place in the best universities, and workplaces were less hierarchical and built on teams. Innovation was often cast as business process redesign and design thinking. The experts called upon leaders of established organizations to "change on the fly". The idea was to mimic the start-ups and watch the innovative ideas flow. The focus shifted to design and novel products that met needs previously unknown started to appear. The matrix organization was created to preserve the hierarchy yet encourage lateral flows of knowledge and sharing of resources. In many respects, the information revolution ridiculed the industrial and scientific revolutions and buried them in the hoopla. It was a revolution like no other and it unwittingly planted the seeds for a new revolution.

Today, the world we now live in is quite different from the glitzy days of the information revolution. So much has changed. A pandemic, political unrest, changes in the cultural landscape, the gig economy, binge watching, climate change, ride sharing, online education, digital tokens, crowd sourcing, cybercurrency, along with the emergence of "postmillennials" or Zoomers have recreated the landscape. This new frontier which began around 2007 has its roots in digital technology, computational technology, life sciences, materials science, behavioral science, and sociology. For this reason, I call it the *Universal Revolution*.[1] It has also been called the "Social Revolution". In many ways, this new age is a more promising yet more challenging frontier. Let's start with technology. Convergence among technologies that were once distinct is now expanding the definitional frontier of science itself. Your mobile device is a great example of this phenomenon. It is part computer, part phone, part media device. These functions were once siloed but they converge in one device. It checks a lot of boxes and allows you to do more.

---

[1]Albert Segars, Seven Technologies Remaking the World, *Sloan Management Review*, October 2018.

Today, there is a whole new frontier of convergence. Digital technology is now converging with life sciences, chemical sciences, cognitive sciences, and material sciences to create possibilities that were once the playground of science fiction. We are not only leveraging nature but also creating it. Programmed enzymes, stem cells, collaborative robots, quantum computing, cybercurrency, blockchain, gene editing, virtual reality, ambient information, nanoparticles, and artificial intelligence are just a few of the new innovations that are creating radically different marketplaces. The birthplace of these new innovations is in the worldwide laboratory of freely available information, knowledge, and collaboration. In other words, within the network. This virtual laboratory is shaped, improved, and improvised through social media and other collaborative technologies. The role of the organization is to create and recreate these learning communities to meet its foreseen and unforeseen challenges. These new organizations are neither hierarchy nor matrix; they are networks. Collections of projects, opportunities, and initiatives that are driven by extreme collaboration, unique capabilities, empowered communities, and quick improvisation. In a sense, it is social networking used as a framework for acquiring, coordinating, and focusing the knowledge, skills, and capabilities of the organization.

A network-based organization fits the new reality and expectations of people and society. The important motivation for work is quality of life, identity, and purpose. If an organization is a candy store rather than candy, then finding a place that meets these needs is easier. Well-being has replaced wealth and its time is now, not down the road. The time devoted to work must "count" and it must make a difference. Purpose has replaced occupation and titles. What you have done is more important than the titles and degrees you hold. Collecting credentials and experiences rather than years of service is the basis for "identity". The workplace is no longer a fixed place at a fixed time. It can be anytime and anywhere there is a broadband connection. Air travel, lodging, and ground transportation form a seamless system with low transaction and coordinating costs. In many ways, it represents a new way to easily and quickly "carpool" to any job site. Digital nomads are supplementing or completely replacing consultants, contractors, and traditional employees. These nomads as well as residents are now more loyal to their teams rather than to the organization. There is a higher expectation for meritocracy and a realization that the prior revolutions included some communities and excluded others. Against this dynamic backdrop, there is also a new set of drivers that are changing what innovation is and what it should accomplish. Yes, even innovation itself is evolving to be more innovative! So, let's take a closer look at some of these "not-so-obvious" drivers.

There Are No More Easy Problems to Solve

The problems we now face and will face in the future are larger, more complex, and more difficult to solve. This is a resounding theme among almost everyone who contributed insights for this book. Information, technology, new discoveries, and the accelerated pace of change have created a mandate for innovation that has never been experienced before! The traditional ways of thinking about people, process, and place are no longer valid. Geography, workplaces, and time are now different concepts in terms of accomplishing work. That is frightening. Does it mean everything we know about innovation is wrong? No. Luckily, there are some salient aspects of the past that we can bring forward. However, it does mean that the way innovation is orchestrated in terms of people, process, and place is different. It must be to solve the difficult problems.

The key word here is *community*. The lone genius or the empowered team may not have the ability or social dynamic necessary to frame a complex problem. In contrast, they might have a superpower for framing smaller problems or turning big challenges into smaller ones. Teams are created by management and given the mandate of achieving a goal. Because they created the team, the responsibility for the outcome lies with management. There is nothing wrong with this; again, it was a hallmark of the information age and produced some good results. A community is more than a team. It is undertaken by a group of people to forge authentic, meaningful, and supportive connections. This in turn fosters camaraderie, communication, and empathy. It is action oriented; the group members build themselves into a community. They are also responsible for their actions and outcomes. There is a much more substantial "ownership" in the outcome, which creates a greater chance of success. So, in the context of solving complex problems and finding the idea of ideas, we must remember that opportunity may lie in enabling a community or social network. To enable the community, we must create convergent resources. Things that have been traditionally siloed (information, money, knowledge, expertise, people, process, and places) must be converged. This allows for greater leverage of talent and avenues for achieving bigger things. It is at the core of why diversity is so important. Consider this question: *Is a mural on a building vandalism or the inspired work of a street artist?* It depends upon your perspective. If we silo artists and artwork into galleries, museums, and studios, then we will miss some great creativity. If we converge the concept of art into any form of expression and enable a community (street artists), then we see a much bigger frontier. The world is more complex, it is more transparent, and what was once hidden is freely revealed. Maybe the routine of relying only on teams or traditional social structures is no longer the "sure thing" for the challenges that are faced. Bigger challenges require bigger perspectives; bigger perspectives are the playground of communities empowered by social networks rather than teams.

Sadly, communities, social networks, and resource convergence are the opposite of the beloved principles of scientific management. In a simpler world, scientific management rewarded the efficiencies of breaking down tasks, organizing by function, rewarding results rather than accomplishment, and managing it all through hierarchy. Today, these same principles are the hallmark of workplaces that are characterized as toxic. Plus, the scientific approach to management is not built for breakthrough innovation. It assumes that the velocity of change will be slow, that pay is more important than purpose, and the place of work is the center of the universe. Yet, some organizations hold on to these arrangements. They compete in today's world with the same assumptions of the industrial, scientific, or information ages. Many times, they do so in the belief that they will return when the pace of change slows, automation cools, and marketplaces become predictable. Good luck!

The key finding is that if your organization (people, process, and place) is only effective in solving simple problems, then there is danger ahead. Please do not interpret this finding as a threat. It is an opportunity. The way to approach the opportunity is to consider the types of challenges your organization is designed to handle. Ask yourself these questions: *What problems have we solved successfully? What problems present a challenge? What problems will confront us in the future?* Quite likely, you will conclude that without constant attention, the tougher problems ahead will overwhelm a complacent organization. This is the view of the most innovative organizations. Although they have achieved incredible breakthroughs, they continue to progress and build communities, social networks, and convergent resources to meet the challenges ahead; and, those challenges will likely be more difficult than those of the past.

Innovate "In" to Innovate "Out"

Let's face it, we can all remember the day when we or a friend, relative, or college roommate landed the big job at Dupont, IBM, Intel, Boeing, or Apple. It was something to celebrate, something that was impressive. Where you worked said something about your worth and your future. What you did for work and who you worked with was a secondary consideration. You landed the big job, the organization was your identity, and your first loyalty was to the organization. Such a "state of affairs" was wonderful for the marquee organizations, and they used it effectively to recruit, reward, and build their workforces. The message was "come to work for us and your worries will be over". It became a key underpinning of scientific management. MBA classrooms driven by Harvard Business School cases soon built iconic portraits of powerful organizations and their drive to maximize shareholder value. However, the wonderful mirage of the iconic corporation was first exposed when IBM, a company that boasted of lifetime employment, began downsizing. GE, Dupont, and other titans soon followed. Suddenly, cost cutting, total quality management, and business process redesign were the wave of leadership. It was the new way to increase shareholder value and the means to get there did not matter. All that mattered was the shareholder.

While this wave of process focus was raging, a counterrevolution was also gaining momentum. Issues of sustainability, poverty, values, and purpose began to define a growing population of future leaders. These "radicals" felt businesses should strive for more, "the greater good". The message was powerful, it made sense, it was inclusive, and it began spreading like wildfire. Teams replaced hierarchy and talent replaced job titles. Formal educational degrees were supplemented or replaced by certificates, know-how, or experience. The old guard was being questioned and openly challenged. Reconciling this generational shift has been difficult for many established organizations. The challenge is made even more difficult by technology, newly minted titans (Google, Apple, and Microsoft), and ever-increasing waves of entrepreneurship. In short, there is a new system of work and employee loyalty that is driving new forms of innovation. So, to innovate "out" into the marketplace, it is now critical to innovate "in" the organization. Allow me to explain further.

In a recent survey, it was discovered that executives and scientists between the ages of 25 and 40 identified more strongly with their work groups than the organizations they work for.[2] Such a finding challenges many traditional assumptions of how and why people perform within their jobs.

---

[2]Sydney Finkelstein, Why Companies Should Hire Teams Rather than Individuals, *Wall Street Journal*, October 29, 2017.

Among the millennial generation, social networking in and out of the digital realm is a readily identifiable trait. This phenomenon has rapidly spread to generations before and after the millennials. Perhaps the place where we work is not as important as the people we work with, the cause we work for, and the role we play. There is a blending of our social, ethical, and professional lives that is at the heart of our "identity". So, if the place we work at does not reflect the values we think are important, if there is no sense of camaraderie, and if the workplace does not provide a path of professional development that we find compelling, then we leave. It is critical that people find a place in the parade that is meaningful, valued, purpose driven, and enhances their identity. Recruitment, retention, and rewards should reflect the loyalty and value that workers have for their own identity as well as the importance workers have for their coworkers and the greater community. Without this context, staging an idea chase is more difficult and the bigger ideas are harder to find. The message is clear: Leaders have to apply the same amount of energy in building and maintaining an innovative workplace that they do in chasing the next big idea. This is true no matter how innovative you are or you once were; work, workers, and workplaces are changing fast. Plus, there does not seem to be a finishing line in sight.

The Day of the "Know-It-All Leader" Is Gone

Like workplaces, the art of leadership is changing fast. Traditionally, the role of leader was something close to the role of a superhero. The leader knows everything, is good at everything, and has time for everything. It was a very comfortable world. It is also a world that no longer exists. The sheer velocity of the world we live in coupled with mountains of information and uncertainty has created an environment where it is impossible to know it all. In fact, it may be impossible to know even half of what is out there. This creates enormous "learning fatigue" for leaders. Every day, there is more and more to learn and there is only so much that any one person can process! It is tempting for leaders to cope with this condition by isolating themselves, avoiding tricky decisions, or convincing themselves that everything is fine. Each is a recipe for disaster. Even the most innovative organizations and leaders have not experienced the pace of change that now defines the marketplace. Some have described it as living in "dog years" where everything is happening seven times as fast. Strategies that had a long shelf life must be improvised continuously to meet ever-changing conditions. Improvisation is not something easily accomplished in organizations with employees scattered throughout the world! Clearly, leadership is no longer something that can be bottled up in one or a few people. Now, it takes a more holistic view of what leadership is and a community to effectively apply it.

The key concept here is "unbundling". All of the traits, capabilities, and know-how that have been assigned to the "leader" must be unbundled and assigned to those that perform them the best. For example, the assumption is that the leader is the most articulate and is the best spokesperson for their employees. Statistically, this is not likely to be true. Someone else on the team is likely to be more talented than the leader in public speaking. Interestingly, this can also work in reverse. Someone who is articulate and pleasant looking may be deemed the "leader". After all, this is what we expect a leader to be. However, that person may not be the best leader. In fact, statistics tell us that there is no real association between presentation style and leadership. What contributes to these mistakes in perception is the unbridled tendency to bundle every superpower into one individual. In today's world, that is certainly a dangerous tactic. Instead, the most innovative organizations unbundle leadership and distribute it among team members. *Leadership Unbundling* is the best remedy for learning fatigue and it is an empowering gesture that engages more people and builds a better workplace.

Information Games and a New World of Information Symmetry

The impacts of the internet, World Wide Web, social media, metaverse, artificial intelligence, and technologies to come are still unfolding. Some of the impacts have been wonderful and others have been troubling.[3] Not only do good ideas spread faster but bad ideas also spread faster. There is noise, lots of it, and there is good knowledge. Yet, verification is difficult, and the packaging of information plays on every bias we possess. In a world of too much information, we are much more likely to gravitate toward the things that reinforce our view and justify our decisions. We also seek out information to support and reinforce our view. Sadly, there is plenty of information to support any view. False contradictions, incomplete information, polarizing narratives, speculation beyond the data, rules that do not exist, fabrication, and other information games create a complex environment for decision-making. So, we may choose not to participate. Our brain takes a shortcut and finds an easier solution; a heuristic, a simple rule, something done before. Many times, to apply the simpler solution, we simplify the problem. Information games will not go away; it is quite likely they will only intensify. So, to find the fast-traveling streams of good data, information, and knowledge, the process for innovation must account for the equally fast-traveling and damaging streams of bad data, information, and knowledge.

Along with information games is the phenomenon of information symmetry. Before the days of rampant technology, organizations enjoyed a world of asymmetric information. The organization was the holder of information and the rest of the world waited on the next big pronouncement. The information and knowledge flows were from one to many; from the organization to those who needed to know. Within this veil of information asymmetry, the organization could hide or distort information according to its best interests. There was no way for those impacted to question the information or easily discuss it with other interested parties. At least, there was no easy or non-costly way to do so. In such an environment, it was easier to guard company reputation,

---

[3]Scott Klososky, Did God Create the Internet? The Impact of Technology on Humanity, Future Point of View, LLC, 2016.

build brands, and create a compelling story about the organization and its mission. Then came the world of information symmetry. In this new world, information and knowledge flow freely at zero cost. The processes of investigation and discovery are easy, and much more about an organization can be freely discovered. Barriers that restricted information flows between people and organizations and among people are now set aside. Of course, this opens up opportunities to learn more about everyone but it also opens up opportunities for everyone to learn about you! The cost of coordination and the cost of search are zero. In fact, it is now less than zero; artificial intelligence allows products to find you! The shift in these costs is the driver behind every transaction you make on Amazon or eBay. So, there is now a significant percentage of every organization that is virtual, like it or not. And, that percentage of "virtual" is likely to grow.

One of the most interesting findings of this research is how information symmetry impacts recruiting. Many organizations have responded to the call for more diversity and better workplaces by altering their websites, media, and messaging. The idea is this: Look more diverse and progressive and then you will be able to attract an innovative workforce. As well-intended as it was, the idea was a complete failure for most organizations. Why? Because of information symmetry. Potential employees are able to freely communicate with former, current, and other potential employees. In many instances, the message of these communications was that nothing was different behind the website. While the organization signaled diversity, equity, inclusivity, and an engaging workplace, the reality was that processes, reward systems, and promotions still favored the most represented community. Plus, the same old boring organization lived behind the website. So, the underrepresented populations and most innovative talent found other places where the organization lived up to its media. The main lesson here is that communication, transactions, and information sharing are now networked. They flow from many sources to many sinks in nonlinear and unexpected ways. This presents challenges and it presents opportunities. The biggest danger is to ignore technological capability and the very quick adoption of those capabilities by employees, business partners, customers, and stakeholders. Technology has redefined and continues to redefine geography, time, place, and process. This new reality must be "baked" into the organization itself and the innovative endeavors that it chases.

Diversity As a Means of Building Resilience

A range of talent creates multiple perspectives which are critical for understanding the ever-changing world around us while staying true to purpose. Interestingly, the world around us, nature, is built on diversity. In fact, it is nature's core design principle. As ecosystems evolve from monocultures to diverse plant life, they become more resilient and are able to recover from "shocks" in their environment. A great example of this phenomenon is a prairie that produces food at multiple times in the summer. This ecosystem is more resilient to a hail storm than a neighboring corn or soybean field. The corn can be wiped out by hail and not recover because is a monocrop. A prairie can be damaged but the diverse plant life will still flourish and provide nutrients to the species that feed off it.[4] *So*, as a living and evolving system, nature adapts to complex environments through diversity. In the same manner, an organization must build resilience through diversity. Importantly, this type of diversity must be more than just an exercise in hiring people of different races, colors, and creeds. It is blending a diverse set of experiences, backgrounds, and talents into the very fabric of the organization. If the organization has a singular way of thinking, a limited perspective, and a narrow range of talent, you are not likely to see the constellation of stars that is the next big idea. If the organization has built resilience through diversity, then it has created a greater frontier for finding solutions while maintaining its focus.

---

[4]Kathleen E. Allen, *Leading by the Roots: Nature-Inspired Leadership Lessons for Today's World*, Morgan James Publishing, 2018, New York, NY.

The key driver for building resilience is to elevate DEI to a core value. It must become something that is important in defining the way a workplace is organized and managed. Values are the foundation of any organization. They define the philosophy for how challenges are faced, how people are managed, and how processes are formed. They create the sense of common direction and purpose that unite the members of the organization. If employees clearly know what the organization stands for and the standards they are expected to uphold, then their actions will support and reinforce those standards. As research tells us, it is possible to think you are diverse when really you have only hired people from underrepresented communities, while the old bias and reward systems of the old organization remain intact. To build resilience, four key values must take place: *representation*, *participation*, *application*, and *appreciation*.[5]

Representation is rooted in the idea that diversity is an asset: When we recognize the uniqueness of each individual and their diverse voices, our experiences become richer and more profoundly human. However, when organizations view representation primarily through a lens of socially meaningful categories such as race, gender, or sexual orientation, people can become identified with these categories and their uniqueness as individuals is overlooked.[6] Meaningful representation requires that marginalized people not be included merely for the optics or to fill a quota. Rather, organizations must remove barriers to demographic representation while also acknowledging and embracing the unique skills, backstories, and contributions of underrepresented individuals. When an organization pursues *participation* as a value, it will create an environment where everyone feels free to share their knowledge and free to contribute. This often requires a rethinking of the physical environment and how information is shared. Traditional meetings,

---

[5]Anselm Beach and Albert Segars, How a Values-Based Approach Advances DEI, *Sloan Management Review*, 63(4).

[6]Martin M. Chemers, Stuart Oskamp, and Mark Constanzo (Eds.), *Diversity in Organizations: New Perspectives for a Changing Workplace*, Claremont Symposium on Applied Social Psychology, 1st Edition, 1995, Claremont, CA.

conference rooms, and presentation technologies are actually exclusive rather than inclusive. Informal meetings, poster sessions, flip charts, and sticky notes invite even the shyest person to contribute their ideas. *Application* of DEI is the redesign of entrenched systems or processes that have led to exclusion. Creating a human-centered organization requires titles that reflect what a person does rather than their place in the hierarchy. Performance is based on what individuals and teams accomplish rather than how long someone has worked at the organization. Successful application should also be evident in an organization's products and services. If organizations are in the habit of designing for the average customer, they end up with products that do not match what a significant set of people need or want. When organizations apply DEI by adopting inclusive design, they learn to see that no customer that they serve is average[7] and they learn how to serve them better. Finally, *appreciation* is recognizing the value DEI brings, being grateful for it, and relying upon it to make your organization successful. Creating appreciation for DEI begins with how leaders communicate about it, especially when they recognize teams and individual employees for their accomplishments. When people are celebrated, it should be for what they contributed and the qualities that make them successful at their work — their skill at problem-solving or their way of dealing with difficult customers — and not their background or their sociocultural characteristics (which have nothing to do with why they excel at their jobs). Together, these values build resilience and a new form of meritocracy that is transparent, fair, and valued.

Innovation Must Be Innovative: Add, Subtract, and Modify

The final observation is the "elephant in the room". It is the obvious topic that everyone would prefer not to be mentioned. Some pieces of innovation (the schools or other techniques) that have provided the foundation for chasing ideas in the past are not well aligned for the

---

[7]T. Rose, *The End of Average: How We Succeed in a World That Values Uniqueness*, HarperOne, 2016, San Francisco, CA.

frontier ahead. In fact, most of the models are built on the assumption that problems that are now faced have been seen before, senior leaders are completely informed and in control, information flows are managed, and recruiting is simply finding people who "fit". It was a simpler world but, let's face it, it was also a boring world. There is a new frontier ahead with real possibilities that were just dreams a few years ago. So, new ideas cannot be built on the foundations of old ideas. This form of "additive innovation" is no longer enough to meet more difficult problems. Yet, this is the secret foundation for many schools of thought around innovation. It worked then, but it does not work now. There is a strong need to subtract old ideas to make way for the bold new idea. This presents a tough conundrum for organizations and leaders. The typical first response to a challenge is to "add". We create something more; we add more Legos to the structure. This can create tension in the organization when the addition seems in conflict with something that exists, or when the addition creates a level of confusion or complexity. For example, adding more rules or complexity to a simple game of "hopscotch" can create chaos among children on the playground.

To make way for the new ideas, it is now necessary to subtract, add, and modify. Adding, subtracting, and modifying seem like a contradiction. Typically, you do one of the three at the exclusion of the other two. However, upon reflection, this is a false contradiction. Doing all three is not only possible but also creates a critical path and space for breakthrough innovation. It's time to make innovation innovative again. In that spirit, it is time to add new principles, modify some old principles, and leave some old principles behind. We did some of this work when we discussed the schools of thought around innovation. When we transform the way we innovate, it then becomes possible to add new ideas, subtract harmful ideas, and modify other ideas. Importantly, this should be done with an eye toward reducing rather than increasing the tension within the organization. It is a delicate balance, it requires courage, it is bold, and it is necessary.

So, like all things, the way innovation is framed and executed must change to reveal the opportunities. Often, this is not the case. Committees, innovation czars, and innovation days are created to give the impression of innovation without really "owning" it. It is critical for an organization to "own" innovation. It is a core value, something woven into the fabric, a way of working, and something that is prized and rewarded. If this is not possible, then an organization is "taking its chances" as waves of technological and societal change reshape the landscape. The key is to take with us the pieces of innovation that still work, leave behind the pieces that do not, and invent new pieces that give us the energy, path, and momentum to find big ideas.

So, with these important drivers of breakthrough innovation explained, let's transition to the principles of the process itself. I call these principles the "Magnificent Seven". They represent an operationalization of "chasing breakthrough innovation" that is definable, measurable, and manageable. The principles explain why some innovative efforts succeed and why some fail. They also capture the critical aspects of inspiration and discipline that anchor the continuum of innovation. You will see pieces of each "innovation school" represented and, hopefully, it will help you reconcile and apply in today's context the breakthrough innovation of Van Gogh, Mozart, Prince, Sesame Street, LEGO, Disney, Banksy, Lady Pink, and Apple. That is the real value of the principles — they can be applied in many different contexts. This tells us that the story of breakthrough innovation is constant, not something that varies across contexts or businesses.

The Magnificent Seven

As listed in the following, seven key principles underlie the mutually reinforcing combination of *inspiration* and *discipline*. The *Principles* can be thought of as a deliberate and interrelated pattern of actions that are intuitive, improvisational, and responsive to the task at hand. They not only set the tone for the initiative in its beginning stages but also provide a gauge for bringing "lost" projects back into the fold. Most importantly, they operationalize the rather nebulous construct of innovation into something that can be described, measured, and managed. They are the backbone of the idea chase in some of today's most innovative organizations. These principles are as follows:

(1) **Be Ambitious** — Be determined to think bigger, ask bigger questions, and reach for something higher. Develop a compelling vision for the initiative.

(2) **Create Chemistry** — Create a set of shared beliefs, values, and codes of conduct that leverage the talent of the team or community. Working together should bring about better results than working alone.

(3) **Define Roles & Responsibilities** — Create defined roles and expectations based on the talents of members and the task at hand. Everyone should feel they have a place in the parade.

(4) **Build Trust** — Build a strong code of sharing resources, knowledge, and rewards. Open paths of communication, keep your word, and value honesty.

(5) **Lean on Data** — Chart a path and make decisions through extensive use of analytics, calculations, and experience. Focus on interpreting the data accurately.

(6) **Show Perseverance** — Demonstrate persistence, patience, and endurance in the face of calamity. Show grit and determination to follow through on difficult tasks.

(7) **Embrace Sacrifice** — Create and embrace a sense of selflessness, putting the interests of others ahead of sub-groups or individuals. You cannot do everything; choose the points of excellence that are worth the resources.

As noted earlier, the principles capture the symbiotic aspects of inspiration and discipline that have framed most innovation stories and formed the bedrock of well-known innovation schools. This is illustrated in Figure 2.

Figure 2: The Seven Principles of Breakthrough Innovation Across the Symbiotic Continuum of Inspiration and Discipline

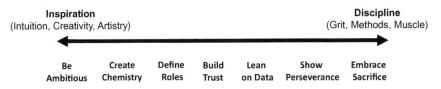

Ambition provides the lynchpin of inspiration. It sets the stage for looking at challenges from a bigger perspective. Chemistry addresses the "team" and "community" aspect of innovation: Putting the right people together so that their collective talent leverages and outshines their individual talent. Trust is based on sharing knowledge, communicating honestly, inclusion, equity, and reciprocal relationships. It provides the foundation for inspiration that is based on a community rather than an individual. Defining roles is at the intersection between inspiration and discipline. Critical roles and responsibilities are established and then they are assigned to those whose talents provide the best match. The goal is to make everyone feel that they have a place in the initiative that is important and made for them. Rather than being a "team member", you have a specific "role" to play. Through this process, we begin to operationalize and rationalize our talent.

The transition to discipline begins with leaning on data. This principle is one of the toughest to rationalize by itself. It seems too harsh when it is reconciled with inspiration. It also seems too mechanical or narrow when it is reconciled with discipline. Yet, when it is interlocked with the other principles, it takes on a very different life. It becomes something that brings focus to inspiration. It also brings more purpose to discipline. Risk management, project management, budgeting, and control are the hallmarks of perseverance. Yes, there is the coaching and leadership aspect of encouragement, but the heart of this principle is taking that tricky project or initiative and turning it into something of value. Big ideas frequently turn into projects that easily drift or run away. This is when discipline becomes important and when it is very tempting to melt the big idea into a smaller idea. Finally, sacrifice reminds us that it is impossible to do everything. At some point, it is necessary to sacrifice an initiative or long-standing idea to make room for the more promising idea. This takes grit, true grit. It is an investment question that requires data, analytics, interpretation, and ultimately a decision.

A Community of One

At this point, you might be asking the following: "How do these principles apply to me?" As we have established, the idea chase is rooted in a social and methodological dynamic between people and between groups of people. However, there is something a bit more to the approach observed in my research and described in this book. It is also a "way of thinking" that drives individual behavior and creates an ability to work seamlessly within groups, across groups, and by yourself. I call this "the community of one" and it is an important part of *esprit de corps* and something that each of us can apply to ourselves. This type of thinking integrates the principles in three key aspects of problem-solving: *vision, engagement,* and *approach.* It is a way of taking the principles of breakthrough innovation and integrating them into the way we as individuals approach challenges. Figure 3 illustrates the key aspects of blending principles into your organizational role.

Vision

Maybe one of the most talked about concepts of leadership is "critical thinking". It is a term that sounds important and, as it turns out, is really important, but it is also a term that is defined differently across contexts. From the observations of this research as well as my own experiences, I define critical thinking as the ability to correctly and consistently identify cause-and-effect relationships. It is also a part of a larger intuitive process called "vision". Vision is seeing a bigger picture and a bigger context in

Figure 3: Blending the Principles into Your Leadership Walk

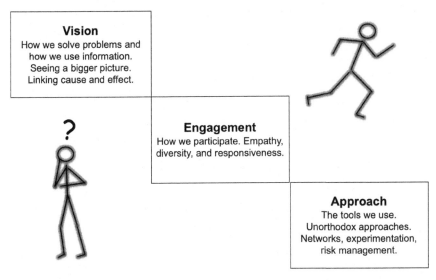

the challenges we face. I will provide a very simple story from the world of real estate to illustrate this point.

A large and modern residential neighborhood was built on land that was once farmland. The land rolls with swales and small hills and has at its center a very scenic farm pond. Given the encroachment of a nearby city, it was a perfect location for a modern neighborhood. As homes were built, roads constructed, and trees removed, the pond began to stagnate. Algae and other plant life were taking over the water. Soon, discoloration and bad odors prevailed. It was unsightly and also quickly became a public health concern. Responding to the crisis quickly, the neighborhood board and developer decided to "treat" the water with chemicals. A presentation by a local chemical company guaranteed that the problem would be solved. After a few treatments, the solution seemed to work. However, after another few months, the problem was back in a form that was now worse than its original presentation. The board convened, the developer met with the vendor and it was decided that more chemicals were needed. This new set of chemicals would mitigate the chemicals already added and treat the algae and other unwanted growth. I think you can see where this is going. The additional treatments did no better and other problems started to arise. After many treatments, a change of board membership, lower property values, and the helpful advice of an ecologist, it was eventually recognized that every body of water needs a source of water, typically a stream. It also needs a sink, typically another stream or pond. In other words, a pond is part of a living ecosystem. The building of houses and roads had taken away both the sink and the source. When this was reestablished with French drains and other natural structures, the pond became healthy again, no chemicals needed. Seeing the pond as something more than an isolated body of water is envisioning the issue within its proper context. We can then correctly identify cause-and-effect relationships and apply the right solution. It is something that the principles reinforce whether we are working in a team or working alone. Thinking bigger about the ecosystem, gathering data on how a pond thrives, and sacrificing some modern conveniences to reestablish the "sink" and "source" of the pond were all necessary to find the "breakthrough" solution. To reiterate the analogy of stars in relation to building big ideas, it is important to see the constellation in a field of stars. To do so is to create a greater vision for the challenge that is faced and the frontier of possible solutions.

Engagement

One of the most interesting aspects of leadership and everyday life is how we engage with others when there is a challenge ahead. In today's society, there is a strong tendency to "look after number one" and to evaluate everything from the standpoint of how it impacts "me". This is actually a very natural tendency that is based on our instinct for survival. Plus, it certainly does no harm to have fun and celebrate the unique things that make you the person you are. However, before we snap another selfie or walk past another piece of garbage on the ground that can easily be put in a receptacle, it is important to remember that all of us live in a highly connected and interdependent society, be it at work or at play. This is where an innovative mindset can assist. It may not be our responsibility in the form of a job to pick up a piece of trash that is blowing across the park, but it is our responsibility as a member of society to pick it up. In doing so, we help each other. Further, it is something we would expect others on the team to do for us. Innovative organizations have strong themes of selflessness and service. This is something that can be easily forgotten, yet it is something we can and should apply to our own walk of life. The principles reinforce this incredibly important value of community. Chemistry, sacrifice, and trust are all important aspects of creating engagement that is mutually beneficial, meaningful, and inclusive.

Innovative organizations also promote a strong culture of "identity" for their members. Everyone will have a well-defined role based on talent, capabilities, and accomplishments. When a member's role and responsibility are matched with his or her talents, then the member and the organization benefit. However, when this is not true, then feelings of displacement and discouragement are likely to follow. While this seems logical and obvious, it is actually quite at odds with recent trends in parenting and schooling. Overreliance on meaningless awards and promises that you can be anything that you desire has clouded our perception of where talents lie and how they can be used. We should encourage everyone, but we should do so in a way that recognizes their natural and acquired talents. To recognize talent that might exist or could exist when all evidence says it does not exist is to deceive. In addition, to recognize only a limited range of talent limits the range of organizational capabilities. Everyone has a talent and insight to contribute; it is very innovative to match that talent with a role that is needed for the challenge that is faced. Most importantly, organizations should expand their range of talent/roles and the reach from which that talent is identified and acquired. This is in the best interest of diversity and inclusion. Too often, "rules of thumb" rather than requirements drive our search for talent. It is important to assess the requirements of a project and creatively find the talent to meet those needs. This phenomenon is readily apparent in projects such as the Event Horizon Telescope, Sesame Street, and great inventions such as the flying machine. Unique talents that are leveraged and focused can create something that is magical. The lesson from the most innovative organizations is to develop talent, recognize the unique talents of others, build a meaningful range of talent, and engage in a way that leverages and celebrates all talents.

Approach

In the chapters to come, I will illustrate and discuss methods, tools, and techniques that leverage the discovery to chase ideas. This highlights the discipline part of the equation, yet there is also a distinct overtone of inspiration. To me, this is one of the most unique and interesting features of the principles. The key to success in the discipline-based methods is the art of creative improvisation. This is at odds with well-known frameworks in business that teach us to frame entire industries and disruptions with standard frameworks. It is also at odds with our natural tendency to use the same tools to fix every problem. In today's frontier, any innovative process must leave room for creative improvisation. We can think of a technique or method as a strong undercurrent that runs beneath a layer of creativity, improvisation, and inspiration. Again, framing breakthrough innovation as reinforcing principles places us in this context.

We live in a world of routine. A key unlocks a door; then we enter the house, office, or building. The bus or train stops a certain number of times between a primary point of departure and a destination, every day. Red means "stop", green means "go", and traffic conforms to government-designated lanes and speed limits. All of this is useful, and all of this is good. However, this world of routine can sometimes rub itself on us a bit too much when we approach a challenge. We look for the technique or approach that worked last time. We use the method of the company that leads the industry. We turn to the consultants to tell us about the current state of the art. We look to *Harvard Business Review* or a life coach for answers. Again, none of this is necessarily wrong, unless the challenge you face is unique and novel. At that point, it is likely that a method or technique that is unorthodox or "invented" might be necessary. Further, experimentation might be required and some method of taking a risk without being carelessly risky might be the difference between success and failure. The principles allow us to improvise when the challenge we face is bigger, unique, or more complex than the capacity or capability of conventional methods. A great example of this is Continental Army victory over the British Army in the American Revolutionary War. Instead of meeting the British on their terms, George Washington chose to use tactics and techniques he learned from Native Americans during the French and Indian wars. He relied heavily on the art of surprise, carefully chosen engagements, and ambush tactics that he had used during his earlier military engagements with the French.[8] Napoleon also revolutionized warfare by emphasizing movement of his army. By taking his troops back and forth across a theater of war, he was able to destroy enemy forces one by one rather than allowing them to combine.[9] Again, a mindset of innovation tells us that how we approach a challenge in terms of method or technique is critically important. Again, the symbiotic nature of inspiration and discipline applies to the challenge that is faced. Routine and a mischaracterization of the challenge are threats that can derail any of us whether we are the leader of a corporation, a minister, or just walking through everyday life. Sometimes, the unorthodox approach or the approach we invent is the key to discovering something more than ordinary. Improvisation is an art form and a way of thinking that can be critical in finding the method or approach that leads to success.

Together, envisioning a challenge, engaging with others, and approach provide a blueprint for how you and I, as a community of one, confront challenges. This is similar to classical models of decision-making such

---

[8]Thomas Fleming, *The Strategy of Victory: How George Washington Won the American Revolution*, Da Capo Press, 2017, Cambridge, MA.
[9]David Chandler, *The Campaigns of Napoleon*, Simon and Schuster, 1966, New York, NY.

as Simon's model of Intelligence, Design, and Choice.[10] However, a key difference is the dynamic that occurs when individual problem-solving combines with the collective efforts of a team. This is captured in the engagement stage. Ideally, we want everyone in the group to be thinking in a frame of breakthrough ideas and we want them all to leverage to the fullest their unique talents. We also want to make sure that the required talents for success are represented. That is no small task! However, when this occurs, the best of rational decision-making among individuals transfers to the efforts of the community. The community of one is a useful framework for applying the principles of innovation to our own walk through leadership or life. In the coming chapters, each of these principles will be developed further. I will also introduce tools and techniques that are used in innovative organizations to find breakthrough ideas, establish chains of cause/effect, manage risk, and develop strategies that address the real problem that is faced. Most of these techniques are unorthodox and improvised. However, they demonstrate the power of innovation as a duality of inspiration and discipline embodied by the seven key principles.

---

[10]L. Buchanan and A. O'Connell, A Brief History of Decision Making, *Harvard Business Review*, January 2006.

Be Ambitious

Win together today and we walk together forever.

— Fred Shero, Coach of the Philadelphia Flyers, 1974 Stanley Cup Playoffs

The principle of ambition is based on framing problems and challenges in terms bigger than their initial description or conception. It is very easy to frame problems in "small" terms. After all, it is a basic human tendency to structure uncertainty or challenges in a way that results in a rational, quick, and attainable solution. Given this tendency, a vicious cycle of "thinking small" can easily prevail as leaders frame problems narrowly and those charged with finding solutions continue to narrow the problem even further. Each party will continue this cycle until an answer is found; then, all parties will call it a "problem solved" and another example of innovation. It may be innovation but it is not breakthrough innovation. Ambition asks bigger questions, searches outside of conventional boundaries for solutions, and utilizes stories to build a shared context for possibilities that push the boundary of imagination. It is also something that is identifiable in leaders, followers, and throughout an organization. It can be embodied in a worthy cause, a new product, or an internal organizational initiative. It can give meaning and purpose to tedious tasks. It also provides the rationale and purpose for overcoming bumps that are encountered along the road.

Wear Ambition on Your Sleeve

As noted by many scientists and project leaders of breakthrough projects, ambition is something that is "worn on the sleeve". As humans, we can sense ambition. Further, ambitious people are naturally drawn to efforts that are challenging and meaningful. In contrast, a lack of ambition will most often result in a lack of effort or a sense that "the fix is in". Nothing kills energy more than an effort that is led by someone with small or no ambition; the immediate connotation is that the effort is not important or may go away. The American Civil Rights Movement is a great example of ambition "worn on the sleeve". Although equal rights for all citizens seem like an obvious and desired part of today's society, it was a very radical idea in the United States when this movement gained initial traction in the mid-1950s. Rather than seek selected rights for African Americans such as housing, bus transportation, or wages, the movement sought to secure the same rights for its people that were already given freely to Whites. Taking this ambitious mantle, Dr. Martin Luther King, along with Ralph Abernathy, Fred Shuttlesworth, Joseph Lowery, and many other activists, formed the Southern Christian Leadership Conference (SCLC). Leveraging the legal victories of the NAACP, this innovative organization offered training and leadership assistance for local groups seeking to fight segregation. Most importantly, the group made organized, non-violent protests its central method for confronting racism. King collaborated with friends and rivals, spoke up, and pursued something that, in its time, was deemed impossible. King was a master of connecting people, ideas, and opportunity that eluded other leaders. He was also one of history's best in terms of creating passion for and articulating an ambitious dream. It is important to remember the impression we first present and leave with those we interact with every day. To create zeal for an initiative, it is important to wear ambition on the sleeve. For leaders, this requires you to be visible, listen, ask questions, set goals, exhibit confidence, insist on inclusivity, and demonstrate a genuine work ethic that is inspiring to everyone around you. For organizations, it is a value that is recognized, appreciated, respected, and responded to by everyone.

Be Playful

Ambition is often cast as a serious, dark, and lonely construct. It is a drive or a quest with little room for comedy, casual conversation, or anything flippant. While determination is the backbone of ambition, a deeper look reveals that its reputation as a serious and rigid process is largely a myth. Humor, engagement, fun, anticipation, surprises, and even a little mayhem are typically part of breakthrough innovation. As it turns out, ambition does have a sense of humor and a very compassionate side that balances the drive. It is called playfulness. As research demonstrates, there are four key features of playfulness. The first is autonomy. The choice about what to do, say, or demonstrate should belong to the players. It should not be claimed by another person or a "boss" who is orchestrating the exercise. This creates an open invitation to play and a level playing field. The second step is absorbed interaction. If we add playfulness to the idea chase, people will lose themselves in what they are doing and become absorbed in the interaction. There is a blurring between them and the activity in which they are engaged. It is no longer clear how a result came into being. Who got that idea? Was it me, the other person, or the Lego bricks? It was all of us. Surprise is the third key feature of playfulness. Players should not be bound by a set plan or routine of what to say or do. Make room for surprises. If this happens, players engage in actions not previously thinkable, which can introduce surprises. Things happen that are unexpected and have not been designed deliberately. This improvised exploration and discovery of surprises lead to the fourth key feature of playfulness: a sense of increased competence. Surprising oneself is a big deal. People gain an unexpected boost about what they are able to do. In turn, this motivates them to see how much further they can go. Playfulness creates an important predisposition for ambition and bigger ideas. It also amplifies the signaling of a leader "wearing ambition on the sleeve", the culture of an organization that is idea focused, and a pathway that leads to bigger and more meaningful causes.

Create a Worthy Cause

In today's world, super projects have at their core goals and objectives that seem like magic. Exploring the center of our galaxy, engineering the DNA that is our basic building block, building robots that further extend our capabilities, and pioneering new forms of renewable energy are causes that push us past our current boundaries. Visionaries such as the late Steve Jobs were known for their ability to focus on initiatives and create a sense of urgency and excitement about their impact on the world. As noted by a former Apple executive interviewed for this book, "Steve Jobs believed that anything digital was Apple's business, other companies thought of themselves as makers of computers, there is a big difference between these two views". Likewise, biotech companies such as Genentech now view their business as "wellness". This means creating preventative therapies as well as traditional treatment-based therapies.[1] So, does this mean that we have to create this level of excitement and expectation about projects that may not be as revolutionary? The answer is Yes and No. As we will see in a later chapter, it is possible for an organization to invest in a big and risky project that has little return. It is very hard to build a theme of ambition around something that most know will not add much value. In contrast, it is also possible that an organization can take on a project that is small, less risky, and yet have substantial return. Therefore, the first step is to clearly frame where the value of the project lies. If there is no value relative to the effort required, particularly in large, risky projects, then some serious rethinking of the initiative should be undertaken. It is incredibly difficult to make a case for ambition in these instances. If there is underlying value but it is difficult to shape into a message, then it is likely the result of framing the value in terms smaller than it deserves. Dr. King could have focused only on improving the wages of African Americans. Instead, he saw the issue as one of equal rights for all. Therefore, it is critical to build a case for value that is more ambitious than how the challenge is initially presented. In other words, any challenge or

---

[1]Walter Isaacson, *The Code Breaker: Jennifer Doudna, Gene Editing, and the Future of the Human Race*, Simon & Schuster, 2022, New York, NY.

project definition is likely to be initially presented in smaller and simpler terms than the problem that needs to be solved. In fact, it often takes time, thought, and data to arrive at the right question. Yet, it is far better to spend time developing the right question in contrast to wasting time responding to a poorly developed question. Obviously, not every project needs to change the world, but if there is some clear sense of purpose or improvement that is logical, necessary, and requires the skills of those involved then the team will respond with the energy and enthusiasm needed to find and implement the bigger idea.

Make the Tedious Strategic

Even in the super projects that were researched for this book, it is possible to dive into the inner workings and find portions of the work that are not glamorous, are tedious, and could easily be disconnected from the great ambition of the overall project. This can happen in almost any organization. It is very noticeable that leaders and members of the more glamorous parts of these projects consistently reinforce the importance and contribution of everyone. They also keep everyone focused on the bigger ambition of the effort and the sense of accomplishment that awaits them upon completion of the journey. So, if the task at hand is implementation of software or rethinking a training program, it is important to tailor the ambition accordingly (you might not change the world), yet instill some sense of the bigger issue being addressed and the importance of efforts in reaching the goal. A "sense of pride" is essential for innovation and that "sense of pride" has its foundation in a purpose, a logical road ahead, and a significant role to play in success. Bill Belichick, who has won more Super Bowls than any other NFL football coach, captured this idea perfectly. His belief is that one of the most important players on a football team is the long snapper. This is the player who "snaps" the football over longer distances (15–20 yards) for field goals, extra points, and punts. If this player fails, then a football team will not be able to win the "game within the game", field position. So, after every game, Belichick finds the long snapper and thanks him for his contribution. He believes long snapping is a crucial task that will go unnoticed unless he takes the initiative to notice it. The game highlights will not feature the "snap of the day", reporters will not interview the long snapper, and no long snapper has ever been named most valuable player. Yet, the task is critical. Following the coach's example, fellow players quickly began to congratulate the long snapper after a team win. Big ambition is full of glitz and glamour and also full of detail. Make sure to acknowledge those who carry the responsibility of less glamorous, but critical details.

Explore the Possibilities

An unfortunate artifact of most formal educational experiences is the quick hunt for "the" answer. In our math classes, we are given equations and the task is to find the answer. We hunt for the answer in multiple choice questions, true/false, and short answers. There is nothing wrong with this approach, until we enter the world of complexity and uncertainty. In this context, answers may be elusive, information may be incomplete, and there is no clear recipe. Unfortunately, when this occurs, there is a strong tendency to reframe the challenge so that it looks like a structured problem — something that is familiar and has a clear solution. The psychologists call this "convergent thinking" or thinking "fast". The basic idea is that we strongly favor gathering familiar information, relying heavily on past successes, framing a small problem, and then falling on a solution fast.[2] An everyday example is purchasing a new vehicle. If you have driven a certain make and model for a long time, you will tend to stick with that vehicle, even if your situation in terms of transportation needs has radically changed. In today's world of social media, influencers, political journalism, and expert panels, it is easy to fall into a trap of convergent thinking on almost any issue. Perhaps the most dangerous aspect of convergent thinking is that it works just often enough for us. Therefore, it becomes the first thing we lean on when uncertainty strikes.

---

[2]Daniel Kahneman, *Thinking, Fast and Slow*, Farrar, Straus and Giroux, 1st Edition, 2011, New York, NY.

An alternative and more innovative way of facing a challenge is to ask a simple question: "What Is Possible?" Doing so moves us to a broader frontier of possible solutions and pauses our inborn desire to fall on a solution fast. This is a very noticeable trait of initiatives that follow the principle of ambition. It is also something that resounds throughout history. Let's look at a modern-day super project first. Photographing the black hole at the center of our galaxy is an impossible task for any single observatory on Earth. No single facility has the equipment that is needed for such a feat. A convergent approach might be to simply build a bigger and more powerful telescope. This might be particularly true if you are the chief scientist at one of these observatories and you have always wanted to expand your facility. In contrast, the approach used by EVH is to combine the capabilities of several telescopes and, using sophisticated computer technology, make them operate as one. This is a novel approach that is borne out of thinking more broadly. Psychologists call this *Divergent Thinking* or thinking *slow*. This type of approach considers and evaluates possibilities before falling on a solution. Importantly, these possibilities are purposefully drawn from very different perspectives than normally considered. At first, these possibilities may seem more like fantasy than a real solution. However, upon further investigation, many of these possibilities are not only feasible but are also well-hidden breakthrough ideas. History is full of the accomplishments of divergent thinkers. The Wright Brothers' design of the flying machine was radically different from other designers of the day. The leading expert of aeronautics at the time, Octave Chanute, told the brothers their machine would not fly. Many lives were saved when Chesley Sullenberger and Jeffrey Skiles landed a damaged passenger jet safely on the Hudson River. Their solution was so unorthodox that the pilots were initially investigated and then heralded by the Federal Aviation Administration. Many journeys into the fantastic begin with that simple question: *What Is Possible?* Now, let's take a look at this principle of ambition in the form of a technique. It is called Frontier Building. I will first describe the mechanics of technique and then I will illustrate its use within the world of cinema and animation.

Frontier Building

The primary objective of Frontier Building is to create visual frontiers of possibility. We challenge ourselves to think bigger about the problem and the range of solutions. The development of frontiers answers the question of *What Is Possible?* by framing a set of possibilities, building a creative context for describing possibilities, and setting the stage for objectively assessing a course or courses of action. The magic of the approach is its symbiotic combination of discipline and inspiration. The method is applied to guide and structure the effort but there is also plenty of room within the technique for inspiration and creativity. It takes the principle of ambition and operationalizes it into an approach that is structured, revealing, and yet fun. Yes, as discussed earlier, playfulness is an important part of innovation and, as we will discuss in the next chapter, a huge part of building team chemistry is storytelling, humor, and creative conversation. So, along with the mechanics of the technique that is illustrated in Figure 1, it is important to keep the exercise playful. This will unlock the full potential of the participants and take away a bit of the edge as difficult conversations unfold.

Figure 1: Thinking Bigger: Frontier Building

- Gather data to develop a question of interest. Create clarity, challenge assumptions, see things in a new way, encourage critical thinking.

  Data ➡ Question? ➡ Data ➡ Alternatives

- Choose two broad dimensions (D1 and D2) that frame possible solution space.

- Make sure the dimensions are not too closely related.

- Frame the dimensions as extremes (e.g., Traditional, Non-Traditional)

- Develop frontiers and narratives (stories)

- Develop trajectories, solutions, and impacts

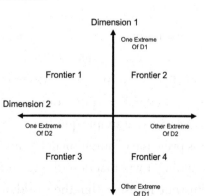

Ask a Bigger Question

The first stage of frontier building is to develop a question of interest. An easy way to chisel down an ambitious effort into something less is to fall on a question too quickly. In most instances, it takes data, information, and analysis to arrive at the right question. Plus, that "right" question is almost always a bigger question than the one we first ask. In other words, there is an inherent risk of "overfitting" the question. Overfitting is asking a very specific or localized question to solve a more general or unknown problem. A bigger question of interest will frame the issue in clear and challenging terms. It will challenge assumptions, frame things in a different way, and will be something that might apply to several contexts, businesses, or situations. Too many times, we frame questions in very small terms. We tend to focus on the symptoms of a problem rather than step back and see a larger system of relationships or a larger context of cause and effect. Most likely, this is our default setting, and some effort is required to think a bit bigger than the problem as it is presented to us.

A great example of this thinking is the thought process of the Wright Brothers. They asked the question *How do birds fly and how do they sustain flight?* rather than *How do you build a flying machine?*. This avoids overfitting the question to a limited and localized set of data points. Sustained flight became their question and their quest. Following this thinking, they discovered the three key aspects of flight, roll, yaw, and pitch. Other inventors failed miserably because they overfitted the question to their experiments and sets of collected data. Their view of flight was that of a glider powered by a sling shot. In contrast, the Wright Flyer demonstrated controlled and sustained flight, and history was made. Too often, the question is *How do we build something?* rather than *What are we building something for?*. Although it seems like a "play" of words, there is a big difference between the questions. The lesson is clear: Take some time and collect the necessary data to arrive at the right question.

Frame the Solution Space

Once a bigger question of interest has been developed, the next step is to frame frontiers of possibility. Again, the key thought is to reveal *What Is Possible?*. We do this by choosing two very broad dimensions that reveal frontiers of solution space. Broad dimensions help us build a bigger fishing net to capture ideas. Again, the tendency will be to frame these dimensions in a small manner and localize them to your immediate context. RESIST THIS AT ALL COSTS! If these dimensions are too small or overfitted, then we will exclude a lot of prior art and a lot of untried possibility. Prior art are solutions that have been attempted and untried possibility are solutions we have not tried before. We want a canvas of everything that has been done and everything that could be done. The most helpful allies in developing these dimensions are small words. The words *Why*, *How*, *When*, *Where*, *What*, and *Who* are not big or complex words but they ask big questions. For example, if the question is, *How might a company expand its market share?*, the *Who?* may be customers. The *What?* may be products and/or services. These broad dimensions are the essential elements for any company seeking to expand its market share. Notice how we stay away from localizing the question. The question is *How might a company gain market share?*. It is not *How might our company gain market share?*. Next, we take the dimensions and frame them as extremes. Again, we do this to build a bigger fishing net for catching ideas. For this question, it seems useful to anchor each of the dimensions using the labels *traditional* and *non-traditional*.

As illustrated in Figure 2, this gives us a robust set of frontiers that reveal how market share might be expanded. In the Northwest grid, a firm sells more of its traditional products to traditional customers (Market Penetration). In the Southwest grid, the firm expands its market by selling traditional products to non-traditional customers (Market Expansion). In the Northeast grid, the firm expands by selling non-traditional products to traditional customers (Cross Selling). In the Southeast grid, the firm pioneers new markets by selling non-traditional products to non-traditional

Figure 2: Using Frontiers to Frame Strategies for Growth

Each quadrant is a frontier (and a story)…..

Describe the assumptions, opportunities, and risks of each frontier.

Each frontier needs an identity……

Choose a "playful" descriptor for each frontier.
Something that captures the context of that space.

Use frontiers to map industry dynamics…..

How are we positioned? How are competitors positioned? What does the future hold?

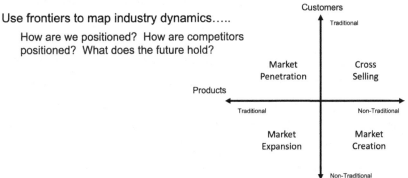

customers (New Market Expansion). With this context, it is now possible to develop stories about how firms in and out of the industry have accomplished success or met failure within each of these frontiers.

Throughout my research, I have seen several variations of this technique. I have also built upon this approach to incorporate storytelling as well as identification of prior art in solution building. To bring this together in an example, let's look at the process of a very innovative media enterprise. The task before them is to create a new series of science fiction movies that build upon and expand on a prior well-known series. As expected, the problem is initially framed in a very rational way: *How do we create a science fiction series that will meet or exceed the return objectives of our parent organization?* While certainly a question that seems right out of the MBA classroom, it is inherently small and it is localized. The initial sample of "prior art" that will be heavily considered and that will dominate discussion will be the prior series of films as well as other science fiction movies that have been successful on those terms. Therefore, the initial and strong tendency will be to write, direct, and distribute a similar series of films. However, in doing so, a vast collection of films, stories, and approaches that are not classified as successful science fiction will go unnoticed and undiscussed. In other words, a lot of prior art is ignored, the problem is localized to the science fiction genre, and the frontier of search is very limited.

True to the attribute of ambition, the small question was quickly elevated to a bigger question when an innovative group within the organization took over. Rather than focus the question only on science fiction or even films, the question was elevated to *How do you tell an amazing story?* This is a much more ambitious question and now the frontier of prior art is everything from Shakespeare to Broadway plays. The trap of localizing the problem is now avoided. Using small words, the team framed the critical two dimensions of any "story" as *How?* and *What?* The *How* aspect of a story was defined as storytelling. This dimension frames a frontier of how a story might be told. On one extreme, storytelling can be traditional. It is one to many, builds on the storyteller's description of main characters, and is primarily a single story. On the other extreme, storytelling may be non-traditional. In this instance, there may be many storytellers, many perspectives of main characters, and several stories rather than one main story. Importantly, as this dimension was developed, many examples of prior art were easily revealed. Also, the exercise became engaging and fun as prior art was classified in terms of its storytelling. The important point is that a larger canvas of ideas began to take shape around how a story might be told. Again, this is done without localizing it to the company, a genre, or even the industry.

The "What" dimension is the story that is told or the plot. A traditional plot is like a fairy tale with "good characters" that win and "bad characters" that lose. The flow of the story is very linear. In addition, there is typically a moral in the story and everyone lives happily ever after. A non-traditional plot might have twists and turns where "good" characters lose and "bad" characters win. The story may have no real moral, be nonlinear, and may have some surprise that is unexpected and unseen. Again, the ideas started to flow very freely when the dimension of "story" or "plot" was stretched to extremes. It became very easy to identify and discuss literature, plays, television shows, and films that fell at various points along this continuum. When the dimensions are placed together in the form of a grid, then it is very easy to visualize and discuss a frontier of how you might tell an amazing story.

As shown in Figure 3, a final, and very important, part of the frontier build is to give "fun" names to each grid. This aids in identifying forms of prior art, builds a common lexicon, and keeps the conversation playful. The names should be indicative of the grid's content, provide a useful context for conversation, yet keep the tenor light and fun. In my own consulting work, I have used songs from Aerosmith, R.E.M., and the Rolling Stones; television shows; and movies. Basically, any scheme of

Figure 3: Telling an Amazing Story in Cinema

labeling that is representative of each grid and yet creates a simple and fun mental picture. As illustrated below, for this particular task, the group chose movies. Traditional storytelling with traditional stories is labeled "LA LA Land". This is the feel-good frontier with lovable characters and fairy-tale endings. There is nothing wrong or right with this frontier and it is important to make that clear as the exercise progresses; it just exists. That is what is important for now. Traditional storytelling with a non-traditional story is labeled "Sixth Sense". Here, there is a strange twist. Something unexpected is revealed in the plot that surprises the viewer yet provides an alternative rationale for the story's chain of events. A traditional story with non-traditional story telling is "Blade Runner". In this frontier, much of the story is filled in by images, music, non-verbal expression. A great example is Cirque Du Solei where images, music, and sparse dialog create a story that is typically told by people in words and dialog. "Pulp Fiction" represents non-traditional storytelling and a non-traditional story. True to the film, this space captures more complex stories and more complex modes of storytelling. Again, these movies give a visual and descriptive context to each frontier.

Interestingly, the "bread and butter" of this particular company is LA LA Land. Therefore, every instinct will pull them in that direction. In fact, most science fiction movies fall in the LA LA Land grid. Notice, however, and this is extremely important, that the space represents only 25% of available frontier. If a decision-maker or decision-making group frames a problem too small or localizes it to their context, then it is likely that a huge amount of prior art and untried possibility will go undiscovered and undiscussed. In this instance, the search begins and ends in LA LA Land. Yet, there are compelling cinematic stories being told in the other grids. In fact, these types of stories have given rise to the streaming media industry. To ignore this frontier is dangerous. Luckily, it was not and the final strategy for the science fiction series was to start it in LA LA Land but then quickly evolve it to Sixth Sense. The result was fantastic. In many respects, the company broke the mold of how this series was cast by using multiple frontiers and doing so strategically. To round out this discussion, let's look at one more example from the world of animation. Again, we will see the clever use of Frontier Building to identify possibilities. This is followed by stringing together ideas in a very creative way to create something non-obvious and purely breakthrough.

Creating a Picture for Words (or Vice Versa)

A magical aspect of art is the interplay of an idea described in words and that same idea presented in a physical form such as a sculpture, painting, animation, or illustration. The words can trigger this transformational process or the image can trigger the process. Sometimes, it is the interplay between the two that triggers the process. From street artists, to master painters, to animators at Disney and Pixar, capturing ideas in artwork is an intricate process that requires planning, thought, and more planning. The street artist Banksy plans for months and sometimes years before the final artwork is created and seen. Because of the nature of Banksy's presentation, the artwork must be executed quickly and there is very little room for error. This requires careful selection of the site, preparation of stencils, paint, and coordination of helpers. All of this is carefully rehearsed before the actual art is created. While you may suspect that this is a routine applicable to only street artists, this process and attention to detail is similar for major animation studios such as Disney, DreamWorks, and Pixar. There is a lot that can be learned from this approach as well as the innovative frontier it reveals. Like the prior example, much of the value is based on initially building out the elusive frontier of possibility. In other words, thinking slow before thinking fast. It's the magic behind street art as well as incredible presentations of stories through animation. So, let's once again use Frontier Building to find the bigger idea.

Typically, for professional animators, the creative process begins with words, a script. For street artists, it may begin with an idea or a statement. In either instance, there is no visual concept of the characters or context beyond that of the imagination. So, it is important to search the frontier for how an idea or story *might* be presented in pictures or art. Let's take a look behind the scenes of this process with a real-world example. An animation studio begins work on a script that features a lone robotic character that spends his days tidying up the planet. The robot eventually encounters another robot and together they encounter wonders and adventure in the greater universe. Initially, this seems like a very straightforward innovation. Just animate a robot that looks like a trash can and move on to the next project. While very tempting, taking that path is thinking small. The first question that must be asked is as follows: "How might we animate a robot?" In framing this question across two definitional axes, we must then ask the following: "What two dimensions define all robots?" We want to build a frontier of possibility that is not only useful and robust but also focused on the task at hand. Again, small words that ask big questions are very useful here. *What* describes the physical characteristics of a robot. It is the arms, legs, eyes, antennae, and other form factors. *Who* describes the persona of a robot. It is the personality, character, and other attributes that define it from the perspective of engagement. So, we can label our axis as "Form" and "Persona" and we have a very robust yet focused set of definitional dimensions. However, that is not the magical part. If we anchor the dimensions as "Robotic" and "Human", we now have a frontier of possibility that is recognizable, robust, and accessible for everyone on the idea chase. This set of frontiers is illustrated in Figure 4.

As illustrated, four frontiers of search are now revealed. Each grid has an "identity", and it is now easy to fill each grid with prior art. *Rosie the Robot* from the animated series *The Jetsons* is indicative of a robotic form and robotic personality. Again, this is the traditional frontier but it is only 25% of possibility. *Pinocchio* is a puppet with a very human personality — a very clever example of robotic form and human persona. Granted, he is not exactly what we envision as a robot, but on further review, he is a form and persona combination that should be considered. Another great example of this combination is the Tin Man from the Wizard of Oz. This is a key piece of the idea chase: don't get too caught up in titles or labels.

Figure 4: How Might a Robot Be Animated?

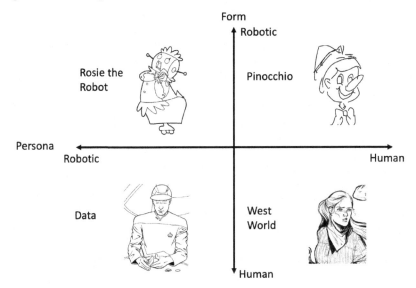

We want to consider all interesting and compelling form and persona combinations. *Data* from the *Star Trek: Next Generation* television series is a very interesting combination of human form and robotic personality. Another example, though not quite as whimsical, is the Terminator. The final grid, *West World*, is the complex combination of human form and human persona. In this space, the human-like character lives in the fuzzy boundary between human consciousness and robotic logic. So, once we have populated the frontiers and discussed their positives and negatives, how is a decision made? The answer is to lean on data. In this project, two examples from each grid were created and placed within selected parts of the script. These eight representations were then tested on a primary audience as well as a secondary audience. In both the primary and secondary audiences, the grids below the horizon scored terribly. However, the grids above the horizon scored very positively with Rosie the Robot out scoring Pinocchio by a thin margin in the primary audience. Interestingly, Pinocchio scored higher in the secondary audience with Rosie the Robot trailing by substantial margin. This is a bit of a conundrum; however, there

is more innovative muscle to apply. Why choose one frontier if it possible to gain the benefits of both? Let's explore the magic.

Animation Magic: The Moon Illusion

As you guessed, developing the frontier of possibility is not the end of the innovation in this story. There is still plenty of room for "breakthrough" ideas within and between the grids. A very innovative trick of animators, street artists, and filmmakers is the "Moon Illusion". In this instance, there is an incredible opportunity for its application. First, let me explain the Moon Illusion. An incredible sight in the nighttime is the rising and setting of the moon. Quite likely, we have all experienced this incredible phenomenon at some point in our lives. The moon looks incredibly large! As we gaze upon it, we can't help but believe that the moon is closer to the Earth. It is a fantastic sensation. However, it is also an illusion. Photographs prove that the moon is the same width near the horizon as when it's high in the sky; however, that's not what we perceive with our eyes. It is a trick our brains play on us as we reconcile the shape and size of the moon with the mountains, sea, trees, buildings, or anything else that provides perspective. The same trick is often used by artists and animators. The street artist, Banksy is a master of the craft as are animators at Disney, Pixar, and DreamWorks.

In the instance of our robot story, there is an obvious opportunity to animate primarily in the "Rosie the Robot" grid. As noted earlier, this is where the data say the sweet spot lies with the primary audience. However, the Pinocchio frontier scores very high with the secondary audience. So, there is an opportunity to reach a wider audience if we can capture some aspect of this interesting space. Enter the Moon Illusion. To achieve this "two for one", the robot is primarily animated in the *Rosie* space; however, the script, sounds, and movements of the robot invite you, the audience, to imprint upon him characteristics that are human. It is your imagination that moves the robot to a more "humanistic" personality. You want to believe it, you want to see it, you will personalize it, and you do just that. However, it is an illusion. Stage magicians, Broadway plays, Cirque Du Solei, and other entertainment extravaganzas rely on some form of the Moon Illusion to engage their audience. That's the salient point of the technique and the moment an idea becomes breakthrough. The animation is delivered incomplete. Your imagination and your preferences help to complete the design. It is an old trick refined and made very effective by Apple. You receive from Apple all the necessary building blocks needed for computing, entertainment, or communication. However, you complete the design by adding cover photographs, your fingerprint, playlists, apps, and other features that are unique to you. It is a masterstroke of breakthrough innovation and a hallmark of the principle of ambition. All of it built on the very same illusion you see when the harvest moon rises above the cityscape. Although we have described it within the context of art and animation, the Moon Illusion and concept of incomplete design are ideas that have application in many contexts. It is the important yet elusive interplay between the perception, engagement, and value that can only be found by revealing possibilities and innovating within and between them.

In this chapter, ambition is presented as both a characteristic of leadership as well as a method for framing challenges and solutions within a broader context. While the examples used were from the modern-day world of media and animation, the same process has been used throughout history to tackle tough challenges. The Vikings' discovery and use of the compass for navigation as well as the irrigation techniques discovered by Navajo people are incredible examples of framing questions in a bigger context and seeking the idea of ideas that is beyond the ordinary. In both instances, the results were life changing. The implication is that breakthrough ideas not only solve immediate problems but also open up frontiers of new possibilities. The challenge is to overcome currents of organizational process and structure that are formed to address small problems and reward small ideas. Interestingly, even the most innovative organizations can migrate toward less ambitious modes of innovation. We saw this in the discussion of LEGO. To keep ambition alive, it is important not to wait for a "perfect moment" to be ambitious. Always strive for the most out of any innovative endeavor. Also, don't wait on the organization to sanction or endorse a breakthrough idea chase. Ambition, if we cast it as a living thing, seems more comfortable and more impactful in a focused community of people that are motivated by a cause. These communities can exist within a larger organizational structure that is designed for rationalizing work rather than spurring innovation. In some sense, it is a radical community living within the more non-radical frame of the larger organization. For life sciences and biotech organizations, this combination is critical in developing ideas that are innovative yet safe for the marketplace. Genentech has mastered this approach and continues to refine it. So, do not be quick to declare your cautious, rational organization an obstacle. Think of it as something leverageable. Quite likely, the rationality has a place; it just needs the counterbalance of inspiration that ambition can provide. The main point for all of us is to think beyond the noise that typically accompanies a challenge. New ideas and an idea of ideas are often not pretty in their first incarnation. They are also not easily recognizable. Add to that the tendency of organizations and people to fall fast on familiar solutions and achieving ambition becomes an even more elusive task. So, many times, to think ambitiously is to work against the grain. Yet, that is an important aspect of the magic. Part of the thrill in chasing breakthrough ideas is knowing you have overcome an obstacle or a current that is running against you. Conditions will never be perfect to unleash ambition but the time is always right for asking bigger questions, exploring different spaces, and asking "What Is Possible?".

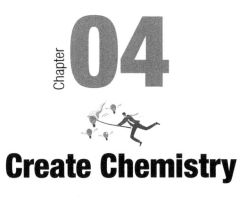

Chapter 04

Create Chemistry

If you want to lift yourself up, lift up someone else.
— **Booker T. Washington**

We live in world of human interconnectedness. These interconnections are governed by many things, including experiences, expectations, relationships, codes of conduct, values, beliefs, and history. As complex as these interactions can be between one person and another, the complexity skyrockets when applied to groups of people. Most interestingly, these social structures are not always formally defined or formally applied with rules and regulations; they emerge over time. In addition, the manifestation of these structures can lead to fantastic outcomes or outright war. The difference in how a group performs can be that drastic! Often, this phenomenon is called "team chemistry". It is often measured quantitatively by psychologists as a combination of work styles, personalities, or skills. In my research and experiences, it seems to be this and something a little more. It is a set of values, codes of conduct, expectations, and way of working that emerge, are adopted, and form a noticeable and valued "identity" for the group. Through chemistry, a set of individuals accomplish more together through their shared talent than they could accomplish individually through their own talents. The whole is greater than the sum of its parts. It explains why a less talented set of people working collectively accomplish more than a group that is more talented but working individually. The thing

to remember is that collective talent will outshine individual talent. The bigger the challenge, the more drastic the effect. Being a part of such a group and chasing something together that we could not achieve on our own is likely something that each of us has experienced at some point in our lives. Letting go and putting our faith in the abilities of others is a challenge. Yet, as discussed earlier, it is the way to navigate a more complex world and build an empowering place of work. There are key pieces of chemistry that can be defined, measured, and managed. Achieving it does not require luck. However, if luck grants it, then try not to ruin it!

Chemistry and Breakthrough Innovation: A Novel Partnership

It is very tempting to think of codes of conduct, expectations, and rules as something that might impede chemistry. After all, a work environment of "free-wheeling", "be yourself", "entrepreneurial" individuals who defy corporate tradition is a very appealing and entertaining notion. Plus, as we saw in the "mosh pit" school of innovation, the logic holds that such "uncontrolled chaos" results in better ideas, happier employees, and a threat to firms that have been around too long. While a great story, the opposite seems true, and the connectedness of people through informal and formal rules is a key principle in the search for extraordinary ideas. However, chemistry is not formality in the traditional sense (organizational design, processes, decision rights); it is structure that forms organically and is rooted heavily in the values, beliefs, and work ethic of the group. These values and beliefs coalesce into a set of unwritten but highly recognizable codes that guide members and are enforced through outcomes and peer pressure. As illustrated in Figure 1, some very important aspects of chemistry are as follows: *Consensus, Human Touch, Frugality, Ceremony, Storytelling,* and *Loyalty*. Together, these emergent codes of conduct create a high level of self-determination among group members. They feel necessary, they feel competent, and they feel connected. Most of all, there is a connectedness beyond formal rules, which creates a sense of novelty, commitment, and identity to their community. In a sense, it

Figure 1: Chemistry: Unwritten Rules and Codes of Conduct

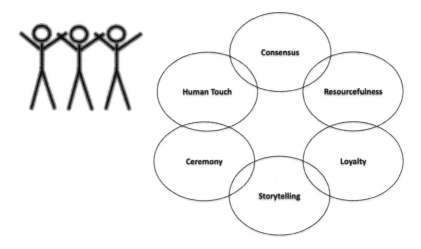

is a bond and a system of loyalty manifested as a set of expectations that are recognizable, demonstrated, and revered. As we discussed earlier, research demonstrates that people are more loyal to a community built on chemistry than they are to the overall organization. So, let's take a closer look at the following six key pieces of chemistry.

Consensus

Chemistry begins with establishing authoritative boundaries. This makes it a bit different from a mosh pit. Plus, as always, we want to do this with an eye toward balancing inspiration and discipline. In an ambitious Idea Chase, authority is something earned and not bestowed. Plus, authority is not command and control; it is coordination, communication, and coaching. Consensus is the driving force of authority and the leader is tasked with creating the means and methods to reach it efficiently and effectively. Perhaps the toughest aspect of this characteristic is determining when a consensus emerges and dealing with the potential fallout if all members are not in complete agreement. However, knowing that consensus rather than an executive decision will guide the effort is a powerful stimulus for robust discussion, expansion of boundaries, and

collection of data. The space is not only open for inspiration but also shaped by discipline.

Sometimes, it is necessary to reframe how consensus is measured in order to achieve it. In keeping with the principle of ambition, we must elevate achieving consensus to something beyond taking a poll or a vote. Consensus is accurately capturing the temperament of the group on an issue of interest, not counting the votes of individual members. There are many problems with taking votes. First, we may frame the question incorrectly. Second, we reduce the response to "yay" or "nay". This will likely simplify the problem. True consensus takes conversation, it takes illustration, and it takes time. Much of this is not written about in management or decision-making literature because it is not glamorous or easy. Let me give you an example in my primary line of work, academics.

In academics, there are levels of achievement that must be reached before a promotion is granted. Academics start as an Assistant Professor. With the right amount of publications, quality performance in the classroom, and the endorsement of leading academics from other universities, an Assistant is promoted to Associate Professor and given tenure. Later on, with more publications, excellent teaching, and positive endorsement from outside academics, the Associate Professor may be promoted to a Full Professor. If the Full Professor achieves national recognition for his or her research, is a leader in their field, and is recognized by esteemed outside influencers as a leader in the field, then a Chaired Professorship is granted. All along the way, the hurdle is more rigorous as is the scrutiny by faculty both inside and outside the Academic's university.

For many long years, I served as the chairperson of the committee that evaluated and made recommendations for promotion. Part of this process was taking a "vote" among the nine committee members about the merits of the case. By policy, this had to be a vote of "up" or "down". Surprising to me, in some instances, the votes of the committee did not reflect the verbal consensus I heard in deliberations. For example, the discussions about a candidate might be lukewarm, yet the vote would be 9-0 "up". The only time I saw the votes match consensus was in the extreme cases. A candidate that was discussed as "extraordinary" would be 9-0 "up". A candidate that was discussed as terrible and unworthy was voted 9-0 "down". In cases that were in between, there was always a unanimous positive vote. This was compounded by the problem that in-between cases were the most populous and the ones that required careful consideration. Clearly, our leaders, who counted on our assessment, were not getting the consensus of these difficult cases.

The problem is that the simple system of voting is not likely to capture the discussion or the "difficult-to-measure" in between. Although we were expected to deliver a vote, we were not bound to a system of voting that says one person gets one vote. We needed a system that would represent the conversation but still deliver a vote. My guess, at the time, was that people, even hard-core academics, had a hard time voting "down" even if they believed that was the correct vote. I tested this assumption by bringing two dishes and nine marbles to the next meeting. I told the group that they no longer had to vote "up" or "down". Instead, I wanted them to each think about the right amount of marbles that should go in the "up" dish and the right amount that should go in the "down" dish. I detached the act of voting "up" or "down" from the individual and assigned it back to the group. To be completely honest, I thought my scheme could be loved or hated. After all, these are academics we are talking about. To my relief, the technique was embraced and is still in use by the promotion and tenure committee. The votes finally began to reflect the conversation and, most importantly, those making these final decisions had a better source of information. To me, the lesson was clear; you have to make sure the technique from which you measure consensus truly measures consensus. Often, it does not.

In organizations rooted in true innovation, I saw many instances of "creative consensus". There is copious use of "yellow sticky notes" to register comments, kudos, or questions about different designs or different alternatives. The beauty of the "stickie" is that it does not represent permanence. You can move your "vote" if other information causes you to rethink your first response. They can be color coded to represent varying forms of expression. You can "vote" multiple sticky notes. In no instance did I observe the one vote "up" or "down" form of determining consensus. I did observe some isolated instances of formal techniques such as Delphi or the RAND-UCLA Appropriateness Method. However, most of the activity I observed was very similar to my "marble" exercise or the Deep Dive technique of IDEO. The main observation is that organizations that are routinely successful in the idea chase drive decision-making through some form of creative group consensus. This type of consensus making takes time, face-to-face conversation, and a creative approach. It is not likely to emerge in a large gathering of people watching a PowerPoint presentation. Ironically, this is very reminiscent of ancient communities that relied on councils, passing the talking stick, and kinship (status based on relationship, experiences, and achievement). Past and present, creative consensus is an aspect of building chemistry that is inclusive, engaging, and impactful. The reward is better information, transparency, elevated empathy for your team members, and better decisions. It is quite likely that the best idea lies within the experiences and insights of the group rather than the exalted leader and a PowerPoint deck. The leadership task is to build a space of discovery and decision-making that is inclusive in its range of voices and inclusive in its reach of exploration.

Human Touch

Human Touch is also a very key aspect of chemistry. Of course, this is a sensitive and important issue in today's society, and boundaries must be respected. That said, it is very noticeable that a handshake, a respectful embrace, a high five, a fist bump, eye contact, or even a nod does wonders to connect members of a group. In one of my earliest projects for the

Defense Research Projects Agency (DARPA), members of our group developed a "handshake". In fact, this handshake was more of a gesture. Similar to the characters played by Paul Newman and Robert Redford in the movie "The Sting", we touched the side of our noses with our right index finger to acknowledge each other, acknowledge our connection, and honor our work together. We did this when we saw each other on or off the job. To this day, when I run into an old colleague from that project, we share the "handshake". It bonds us and helps us to remember a very special time and place. Such gestures are nothing new. Secret societies have had "secret handshakes" for hundreds of years. In the military, a salute is a signal of respect and connectedness. The origin of the salute is to demonstrate recognition, friendliness, and honor for the person you approach. I found the protocol so powerful that I developed "handshakes" with my own children when they were preschoolers. When I returned home from a business trip or from a day at work, it was the first thing we did when we saw each other. Now, it is the first thing we do when one of them returns home from a trip. I am amazed at how meaningful it became to them and me and how it reinforced their place and my place within our family.

In this same spirit, Texas kindergarten teacher Ashley Taylor assigns a student each day to be the "greeter" for her class. Each child is greeted by name, given a handshake or a hug, and welcomed to the room. As noted by the teacher, this quickly became a favorite ritual of the class and created a connectedness among the students.[1] Throughout the day, the activities of the class require the kids to be both speakers and listeners. This requires eye contact, clear speaking, and respect. The simple activity of greeting and being greeted in the morning has improved these skills, which improve their interaction with each other and with other kids and adults. Barry White Jr., a fifth-grade teacher in Charlotte, NC, has even developed a unique handshake with each of his students. Every morning, he greets

---

[1] ABC News, Kindergarten Handshake Ritual Is Kids Favorite Part of the Day, May 30, 2018.

them with their unique handshake. Given the tumultuous environment of today's schools, it is easy to see how important human touch can be in making students feel connected, safe, and interactive. If this approach works for children, then why not in the workplace or in other situations?

Interestingly, corporations and other institutions are learning to appreciate the benefits of human touch. Prior to the COVID-19 pandemic, companies such as Google and Apple completely passed on telework. IBM, which had 40% of its employees working remotely pulled thousands of its workers back into the workplace.[2] These same organizations continued the trend as soon as breakthroughs in COVID-19 vaccines were developed and returning to work was deemed safe. While telecommuting allowed some companies to save millions on buildings and facilities, it also cost them meaningful and impactful collaboration among their employees. In many instances, the pandemic amplified many negative effects of isolation. Yes, it was possible to communicate and coordinate with teleconferences, webinars, and similar technologies, but it may not equate to true collaboration. A serious collaborative effort requires well-developed relationships among people. Face-to-face interaction is rich in vocal cues, facial expressions, movements, and non-verbal feedback. In fact, through "emotional contagion", we subconsciously match body positions, movements, and breathing rhythms to others when we are engaged in genuine rapport.[3] Informal conversations are also the genesis of the most creative ideas. Without spaces and opportunities to stage these conversations, we are limited to the outcomes available through formal meetings, text, webinars, and conference calls. As discovered by many organizations, these outcomes are small and not very compelling. This is not to say that many of today's technologies are useless or damaging. It is to say that they do not fully replace the richness of human touch

---

[2]Carol Kinsey Goman, Why IBM Brought Remote Workers Back to the Office — And Why Your Company Might Be Next, *Forbes*, October 12, 2017.
[3]S.G. Barsade, The Ripple Effect: Emotional Contagion and Its Influence on Group Behavior, *Administrative Science Quarterly*, 47, 644–675, 2002.

and they must be carefully supplemented with opportunities and spaces where richer forms of collaboration can take place. So, do not be too quick to hire communities of "digital nomads" and place your faith entirely in emerging technology. The most innovative organizations are not taking this route. Instead, they are rethinking and redesigning physical workplaces to leverage new technology. Automation, data visualization, simulation, and other tools are now part of interactive workspaces that are open, inviting, and built upon wellness and collaboration.

On a personal level, human touch is a very basic instinct, and it is something that is increasingly hard to experience in the workplace or even in everyday life. It is possible to be surrounded by people and still feel alone. Taking meals together, a fist bump, walking the trail around the company pond, tossing a ball to each other, or simply knowing something about the members of your community is to bring human touch back into the dynamics of "getting things done". These gestures and forms of person-to-person interaction are readily apparent among members of today's most innovative projects. They are evident in the way workspaces are constructed, in the way conversations occur, and in the way responsibilities are owned and quickly shifted if needed. Many times, I have seen this spirit carefully preserved through photographs of members and the entire team prominently displayed on desks, walls, and even mobile devices. As discovered by many organizations, it is easy to drive out human touch. To do so is to drive out needed mechanisms for true collaboration. It also runs against the grain of the human need for interaction, conversation, and basic engagement. We are programmed to expect, respond to, and initiate verbal and non-verbal information. When these channels are shut down, we struggle and only the basic forms of communication and coordination are present. The art of true collaboration remains beyond grasp and our place in the initiative becomes uncertain. New technology will be an important partner with human touch in collaboration. However, breakthrough idea generation seems more organic and spontaneous than that provided through exclusive use of technology-enhanced communication. The key is to find the right mix of high-tech and high-touch. Perhaps the continuum of breakthrough innovation is a useful tool in this regard. If we think of innovation as a life cycle, we can place the inspirational pieces in high-touch environments and the disciplined pieces in high-tech environments. Of course, the pieces may not separate themselves out in such a distinct manner. However, there is now a great opportunity to apply technology to the innovation life cycle to build efficiency, visualize data, enhance inclusivity, and examine more possibilities. The best organizations have struck the right balance between high-tech and high-touch as they combine the capabilities of new technology with facilities and meetings that leverage social engagement.

Resourcefulness

Another key element of chemistry is *resourcefulness*. At its most general level, resourcefulness consists of two important notions: (1) identifying the resources you need and (2) creatively making the most of the resources you have. In other words, it is important to *take only what you need* and *get the most out of what you take*. Rather than automatically adding resources, it is important to also think about subtraction.[4] Being resourceful brings focus to the task, eliminates distractions, and integrates the notion of efficiency with innovation. This is an incredibly important combination in creating a sense of momentum and agility within a highly ambitious effort.[5] Knowing what you need in terms of resource (time, talent, money, materials, and management) to accomplish a task can be thought of as *resource focus*. In some sense, we bring focus to and shape a project through resources. Getting the most of the resources you have is *resource leverage*. Too many times, seemingly creative efforts turn into ordinary efforts because of the wrong resource focus. Maybe there are too many resources, not enough resources, or the wrong resources.

---

[4]Leidy Klotz, *Subtraction: The Untapped Science of Less*, Flatiron Books, 2021, New York, NY.
[5]Bill Murphy Jr., 7 Things Really Resourceful People Do, Inc., March 28, 2014.

Relatedly, efforts can stall or fail if we do not leverage or apply resources to maximum effect. Maybe we underutilized the money or talent available to us and, as a result, the outcome was less than what we hoped. Both of these are important and noticeable traits of resourcefulness. Let's explore these notions just a bit deeper.

Resource focus addresses "how" a project is shaped by budget, workspace, assets, data, metrics, talent, management, and organizational rules. It is the knack for knowing what is needed in terms of resource to accomplish a task. More broadly, it can be thought of as the collective resource response to the challenge at hand. Most often, wayward organizational focus is framed as a lack of resources. Great ideas and more creative paths are made inaccessible by a lack of budget or organizational importance. However, I respectfully suggest that it is more often too much resource that sinks the great ideas. This excess includes too many (or the wrong) analytics, cumbersome methods of reporting, too much management, too much organizational publicity, and too many rules. In addition, there may be too much budget, too much technology, and/or too many people. As aptly stated by a Methodist Pastor I heard one Sunday, *committees have killed more churches than the devil himself.* Maybe having too much resource is worse than having too little. This suggests that the most likely but least obvious pitfall for an organization that is rich in resources is a tendency to spend its way out of the very best ideas! In all of the successful projects I researched or participated in firsthand, there is a strong sense of "knowing what you need" to accomplish the extraordinary. There is also a strong tendency to be frugal and rational in shaping the resource focus. Excess in terms of PowerPoints, data, personnel, reports, consultants, and other corporate baggage is something that is avoided. In fact, this frugality seems to be a source of pride. Office space is designed for accomplishing work, not for establishing status or brand. Open designs, tables, chairs, and lots of sunlight are shared by all members. There are no signs of conference room tables, tiered classrooms, or extravagant and fixed LCD projection systems. Instead, carts on wheels move equipment from place to place as needed. If projection is needed, a blank wall will do and the presentation is brought to those interested not vice versa. Most importantly, the money that is typically spent on facilities and offices is saved or invested into talent, travel, or employee development. This concept of "open spaces" in work is not new; however, it exists within the other aspects of chemistry such as human touch, consensus, storytelling, and the larger principles of ambition and roles/responsibilities (to be discussed later) to the task at hand: no more or no less.

Resource focus is perhaps an overlooked characteristic of accomplishing something special. Yet, its influence can be found throughout history and in the modern world. In describing the defeat of the British Army at the hands of the Continental Army during the American Revolution, it is often noted by historians that the British had too many ships, too big of an army, and too many generals. Their resource focus was not aligned with the task at hand. The same might also be said for the United States' experience in Vietnam. The resource focus of the American military was shaped for large theaters and world wars, not the jungle. In modern business, the rebirth of Apple is often attributed to Steve Jobs refocusing the resources of the company on the projects that mattered most. The lesson for us is that it is important to know exactly what resources you need to bring to the task at hand: no more or no less.

Along with resource focus, it is important to leverage the resources we possess. This is particularly true when the resource focus, in terms of amount, is less than we desire. In the most innovative organizations, talents and time are carefully cultivated in the name of leverage. The ability of team members to fill in for others when needed is prized and is paid forward. It is an identifiable part of Chemistry and creates a sense of comradery and a code of conduct that "the show must go on". In some instances, this may place a hardship on a member, but it is gladly tolerated because help is always on the way. Therefore, it is important to have not only a primary talent but also a set of secondary talents that can be a bridge when a fellow member is unable to perform; it is a very powerful context for breakthrough innovation.

While it is easy to think about resource leverage in terms of getting the most for the money, repurposing materials, building common computer systems, or sharing office space, the real benefit is leveraging organizational talent, skills, and thinking. True leverage across these dimensions involves combining skills and talents such that they leverage each other and can be recombined for different forms of leverage when needed. Therefore, the goal is not to find a "perfect" or fixed leverage for talent, it is to find combinations or a portfolio of talent that allows the organization to create needed forms of leverage on demand. A great example of this is found in patterns of human thinking. As described by physicist Leonard Mlodinow, humans think in rational, logical thought when we follow rules. We plot the drive to a destination, calculate how much gas it will take, and determine when we should depart. This line of thinking works well in structured environments. There is nothing wrong with this pattern of thinking; however, I would also argue that it works well when the task is to accomplish the ordinary, not the extraordinary. If it is the overly dominant or the only pattern of thinking within an organization, then we should expect ordinary outcomes. That said, this type of thinking is critical once a new idea is identified. There must be order and process to get work done. There is also elastic thinking. This is the type of thinking we do when we figure out what rules should exist or bend existing rules. It is the thinking that happens when old rules no longer seem valid or simply don't work.[6] I would argue that this is the type of thinking that is required to find breakthrough ideas. If it is present enough within the organization, then extraordinary things are more likely.

---

[6]Leonard Mlodinow, *Elastic: Flexible Thinking in a Constantly Changing World*, Penguin Group, 2019, London, UK.

Both of these archetypes were on display during the flight of Apollo 13. This third mission to the moon in 1970 was considered to be somewhat "routine". However, two days into the mission, an oxygen tank on the spacecraft exploded severely crippling critical systems. Loss of power, loss of cabin heat, loss of potable water, and, most importantly, loss of oxygen placed the three astronauts in a very grave situation. There was a very real possibility of marooning the men in space. Very quickly, logical and rule-based thought gave way to more elastic thinking. Importantly, it is useful to think of this as a shift in dominance rather than one pattern of thinking replacing another. Many rules, policies, roles, and standard operating procedures that had guided past Apollo missions were no longer useful. The task was not to land the astronauts on the moon, it was to rescue them from space. New structures were quickly adopted, old structures modified, and useful old structures were kept to match the new task. Through incredible ingenuity and resourcefulness, parts of the spacecraft were repurposed to extend power and breathable air. New tests and resulting analytics were developed on the spot to test possibilities and arrive at solutions. A new course was plotted and the moon's gravity was used to propel the craft back to earth.[7] Similar to the mission control of Apollo 13, being resourceful is the ability to adopt the right balance of thinking such that rules can be invented, followed, bent, and broken when necessary. This is counterbalanced by the rational process of encoding and institutionalizing the new rules along with the old rules that remain. If this kaleidoscope of thinking, talent, and skills turns so that it meets new challenges, then the high-water mark of resource leverage is achieved.

As made famous by the Beatles (a group that had and then lost the principles of breakthrough innovation), "we get by with a little help from our friends". Knowing when to call on a friend is a very identifiable part of resource focus and resource leverage. There is power in leveraging the resources of friends or allies but there is also an innate pull to go it alone.

---

[7]Jim Lovell and Jeffrey Kluger, *Lost Moon: The Perilous Voyage of Apollo 13*, Houghton Mifflin Company, Boston, MA, pp. 349–350, 1994.

Somehow, reaching for help is a sign of weakness or a sign of uncertainty. Collaboration was a major way of "doing" very innovative tasks among communities of old. Tribal nations were based on shared interest and the synergies made possible through cooperative efforts. In 1876, the Arapaho, Cheyenne, and Lakota tribes engineered one of the most stunning military victories of all time on U.S. soil. Sitting Bull and Crazy Horse led as many as 3,000 Native Americans against General George Armstrong Custer. Within an hour, Custer and all of his soldiers were dead. Although Custer was told that he faced a large number of warriors, he wanted to believe that his force was adequate for the task. Some historians believe that Custer was more concerned about the warriors escaping rather than defeating them. Although not the same context, it is easy to see cooperative resourcefulness in today's most breakthrough projects. The Event Horizon Telescope is a testament to cooperation across observatories and their various working groups. It is the only way to build a telescope the size of the planet Earth, the very thing that is required to look into the center of our galaxy. The Korean government along with business partners and Chonnam National University are pioneering the field of micro robotics using collaborative arrangements in research and development that bridge the boundaries of business, academics, and government. The research center OpenAI is a collaborative effort of Silicon Valley investors and technology companies to promote and develop Artificial Intelligence so that it benefits humanity.[8] Certainly, there is ample ambition in the cause of OpenAI. In addition, there is a deep sense that resourcefulness in the form of collaboration will be critical in achieving the aim. The outputs of the effort are impressive. The institute has produced bots that can defeat humans in video games as well as language processing software that can create fluid text from the prompt of a few sentences, phrases, or key words. Throughout history and in today's world, effective collaboration within and between organizations is a hallmark of resource focus, resource leverage, and resourcefulness.

---

[8]John Markoff, Artificial-Intelligence Research Center Is Founded by Silicon Valley Investors, *The New York Times*, December 11, 2015. Retrieved December 12, 2015.

Ceremony

Ceremony and rituals mark important events and key moments in life. Weddings, birthdays, funerals, national holidays, and graduations are some very prominent forms of celebration and ceremony. Rituals are also forms of ceremony, but they can also be something a little more personal such as kissing a baseball bat before heading to the plate or taking a deep breath before you speak in public. Together, ceremony and rituals provide a unique sense of identity and shared meaning within a community. Throughout history, aboriginal tribes celebrated the new year, the harvest, victories over enemies, as well as death (celebrated as new life). They also practiced healing rituals that brought tribal members into harmony with themselves, the tribe, and the environment. Ceremony and ritual were so powerful within the Native American Tribes that they were banned by the United States government in the late 1800s as a means of subjugation. At that time, U.S. Interior Secretary Henry M. Teller ordered an end to all *"heathenish dances and ceremonies" on reservations due to their "great hindrance to civilization"*. The impetus for this action was the practice of the "Ghost Dance". This dance was a spiritual movement that came about because conditions were so bad on Indian reservations that they needed something to give them hope. It prophesied a peaceful end to white American expansion and preached goals of clean living, an honest life, and cross-cultural cooperation by Native Americans. The attempts to suppress the traditions of Native Americans eventually led to the Massacre at Wounded Knee on December 29, 1890. When the Seventh U.S. Calvary was sent into the Lakota Sioux's Pine Ridge and Rosebud Reservations to stop the dance and arrest the participants, approximately 150 Native American men, women, and children were killed. Such a tragic event highlights the power of ceremony and the lengths communities will take to protect it. So, what is it about ceremony that makes it so important? As illustrated in Figure 2, there are seven elements that underlie its power: *priority, memory, purpose, gateway, externality, confidence,* and *gratitude.*

Ceremony provides a visible exhibit of what is important within an organization. Awards that recognize adherence or reflection of an

Figure 2: Elements of Ceremony

Priority – Emphasize What is Important

Memory – Frame Past and Present Achievements

Purpose – Know Who We Are, What We Stand For

Gateway – Passage From One Place to Another

Externality – Invite the Outside In

Confidence – Zeal to Take on Challenges

Gratitude – Thankfulness and Humility

organization's core values tell everyone what is valued and what is rewarded. In my institution, the University of North Carolina, these values include excellence, teamwork, integrity, leadership, inclusion, and community. Scholarships, awards, and other events are built around these values to empathize their priority above all else. Ancient communities celebrated agriculture and the environment as a means of acknowledging their importance for survival. Ceremony also provides a scrapbook of memories. Achievements of the past and those who achieved them can be remembered as new heroes are enshrined. Hall of Fame ceremonies in professional sports are great examples of this ceremonial construct. These ceremonies honor the history of the game by remembering past hall of famers, great moments, and the new class of inductees. The past, present, and future are captured in a single ceremony. Purpose and gratitude are also on display in such a ceremony. Through awards, thanks, recognition, and recollection, members gain a greater understanding of why the organization is important, its role models, and how it all contributes to a greater purpose. This is particularly true if the organization, individual, or group is recognized by outside organizations. Together, knowing what is important, celebrating how it was achieved, showing gratitude, and underscoring purpose are a huge catalyst for understanding the values, vision, and contribution of an organization.[9]

---

[9]Patti Sanchez, Why Your Company Needs More Ceremonies, *Harvard Business Review*, July 27, 2016.

Another very important aspect of ceremony is its role as a *gateway* from one stage to another. Graduation ceremonies represent an important achievement of an individual but, as importantly, they also signal the beginning of a new stage of life. Most often, we attach ceremonial passage with something positive. The promotion, the playoff win, entering a new market, and earning the degree are all great examples. For sure, these passages are important. However, ceremonies can also be powerful in marking difficulties, setbacks, as well as an urgent need to move on. To mark the passing of Apple's OS 9 operating system, Steve Jobs presided over a mock funeral for the technology. A coffin appeared on stage and Bach's Toccata and Fugue in D Minor echoed through the crowded exhibit hall. The ceremony drove home Apple's message to the Mac software developers in attendance — drop whatever work you're doing on the old Mac OS and shift all your efforts to the operating system of the future.[10]

An often overlooked but important role of ceremony is to draw those from outside the community into the community. Again, this is done at graduation ceremonies when parents, relatives, and friends are brought to the university to celebrate with graduates. In the workplace, it is typically believed that family and work should be separate. Therefore, workplace events should not be open to family. Yet, as discovered by an NHL hockey coach I interviewed, negative impressions of the organization among players often have their genesis in the opinions and observations of girlfriends, spouses, moms, and/or dads. To mitigate this, the organization actively included parents, siblings, girlfriends, and spouses of the players in events that celebrated their role in the player's success. There is an important lesson here; ceremony can build key externalities to those that influence community members. Although it is most likely good policy to separate work from family in everyday tasks, sincerely reaching out to acknowledge those standing with members in their walk of life is important. One of my mother's most cherished possessions was her "Mistress of Engineering Degree" given to her by Georgia Tech. It recognized her contributions

---

[10]Phillip Michaels, Jobs: OS 9 Is Dead, Long Live OS X, *MacWorld*, May 1, 2002.

as a working professional and partner while my father obtained his Undergraduate Electrical Engineering Degree. Throughout her life, she was a bigger fan of the school than my dad! Later on, my dad received a similar commendation from the University of South Carolina in recognition of his support for my mother as she achieved her Master's degree.

Finally, rituals and ceremony provide needed confidence to take on tough challenges. The pep talk before a big game, touching a cherished icon before taking the field, locking arms and counting down, and the Icelandic Skol Chant are all strong rituals that reduce stress, focus energy, and create zeal. Importantly, these are also rituals and celebrations that draw attention to and celebrate the collective not the individual.[11] Clearly, ceremony engages people around the things that matter most. We experience a sense of comfort and belonging. We are also reminded of values, responsibilities, experiences, and role models that define who we are and why we are on the journey. Although rituals require time, they are incredibly efficient in transforming self-doubt into a driving will to succeed. They can also be transformative as organizations pass from one stage to the next. While it is not efficient to celebrate everything, it is important to celebrate the important things. It is also important to celebrate real milestones and realization of ambitious goals. The organizations I observed and have been a part of struck the right balance — highlighting the best aspects of the organization and its members without incurring celebration fatigue.

Storytelling

Closely tied to ceremony, Storytelling is a primary means of creating common vision, common dialogue, and common knowledge within a community. Beyond data, information, charts, and facts, stories provide context, meaning, and application. From the beginning of time, stories have been the primary vehicle for capturing events and experiences that are then passed forward. Stories provide a greater boundary of

---

[11]Paolo Guenzi, How Rituals Effects Performance, *Harvard Business Review*, February 25, 2013.

Figure 3: Stories and Storytellers

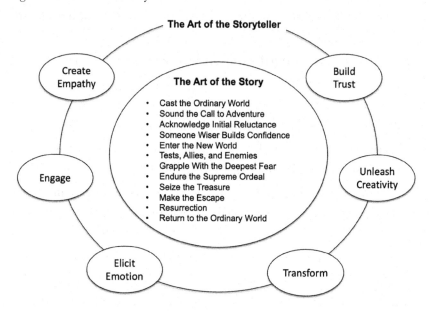

understanding about what has happened, what is happening, and what might happen. These stories can be recollections of events or they can be myths and legends. In both instances, there is typically a hero, a journey, and a lesson learned. This progression is shaped by the storyteller and our own imagination. This is what makes them so compelling and useful. As illustrated in Figure 3, we can understand storytelling by examining the art of the story and the art of the storyteller.

There is no shortage of books, TED talks, and consulting reports about the characteristics of a good story. Among these works, one of the most popular themes is the approach of Disney and Pixar.[12] There are many good points and lessons in this approach but they tend to co-mingle storytelling with the story itself. Of course, the two are intertwined in the context of a movie but it is useful to untangle them to understand how

---

[12]Dean Movshovitz, *Pixar Storytelling: Rules for Effective Storytelling Based on Pixar's Greatest Films*, 2nd Edition, Bloop Animation Studios, 2017, New York, NY.

Figure 4: Frontiers in Religious Worship

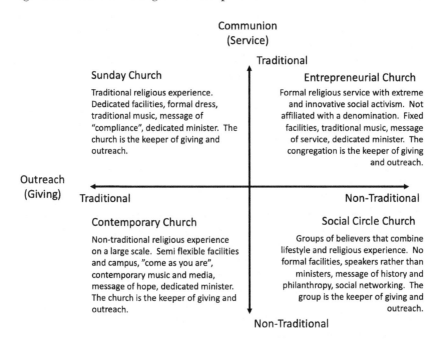

storytelling is accomplished as mechanism to transform and influence within an organization. Plus, much of the approach popularized by Pixar has its roots in myths, tales, and legends that were created by ancient communities. The heart of these stories is captured in an incredible work by John Campbell, *The Hero with a Thousand Faces*. In this work, Campbell uncovers the central theme that underlies almost all tales of old.[13] This progression is also found in modern stories such as *Star Wars*, *Stranger Things*, and *Harry Potter*. It is a recipe that is compelling and can be applied to almost any context. I call this "the art of the story".

To illustrate the typical progression of myths and legends, I will use a story about one of my consulting/research projects. The goal is to illustrate the frontier-building technique I discussed earlier in a fun and engaging way (Figure 4).

---

[13]Joseph Campbell, *The Hero with a Thousand Faces* (*The Collected Works of Joseph Campbell*), 3rd Edition, New World Library, 2008, San Francisco, CA.

On a typical Sunday, I was attending church with my wife. I was looking forward to having a scrumptious lunch after the service and then taking a hike around the lake. "The hero (me) is cast in his ordinary world".

As I was leaving the service, the pastor pulled me aside and asked a favor. He wanted to know if I would be willing to consult with leaders of the denomination. The church was in trouble and needed my help. "The call to adventure is sounded".

I had never consulted with a church. I knew very little about the industry of religion and declined. "The hero is reluctant and sees the challenge as troublesome".

My wife, learning that I had declined, tells me that it would be a good and noble act of service to help the church. Perhaps it would atone for some of my sins! "A wiser presence encourages and builds confidence".

I meet with a council of Bishops but charge them nothing for my time or expenses. They describe a crisis: declining attendance, the closing of churches, and dwindling financial support. They attribute this to changing society, lack of morals, media, and affluence — anything except the church itself. They are planning to launch an advertising campaign to bring the lost back to the church. The cost is millions of dollars. "The hero enters the new world".

I ask them if I can test the assumption they are making and elevate the question. We need to determine if spirituality is really on the decline. The issue is bigger than the denomination and we are making assumptions without data. They politely fire me. "The hero is tested".

After a few weeks, as they are getting ready to write the check for the advertising campaign, they call me back and allow me to test the assumptions. After several rounds of survey, I discover that spirituality is on the rise! There are more people of faith now than in the past. Therefore, if there are more people of faith and traditional church attendance is falling, the question is, how are people exercising their faith? I am fired again. "The hero grapples with his deepest fear".

Once again, I am called back. They are reluctant to purchase the advertising now that some doubt has been cast on their line of thinking. I am given a chance to investigate further. I use frontier building to frame the bigger question of how someone of faith might worship. I use the dimensions of communion (what a person of faith seeks) and *outreach (how a church gives to its community) to build frontiers. Further research strongly supports these frontiers. There is a broader landscape of spirituality beyond the practices in traditional churches. I am fired again. "The hero endures the supreme ordeal".*

After some additional contemplation and some testimonies from leaders who are convinced by the analysis, the denomination accepts the frontier as true. They begin to see a larger world of faith around them and accept its legitimacy. I am asked to help them navigate this new frontier. "The hero seizes the treasure".

After several meetings, the denomination is on a productive path. My time with them ends. I decide that research and consulting within the context of religion is very difficult and, in the future, I will find other ways to atone for sin. "The hero escapes".

I am changed by the experience. I learn that change happens over time and outside of formal meetings. I also learn it is possible to win a war even if you are losing all the battles. "The hero experiences resurrection".

I go back to my church and listen to the sermon. I wonder how my church might change. I think about the lunch after the service and the walk around the lake. "The hero returns to the ordinary world".

The power in this story form is its use of struggle and breakthrough to solve an extraordinary challenge. This is the heart of true innovation. Although I did not pre-plan my story to follow the hero progression, its adherence to the form makes it a powerful mechanism for illustrating the technique of frontier building. It is one of my most popular stories and I get requests for it at many of my presentations. It is amazing to see how members of a successful idea chase use the same types of stories to bring life to complex datasets, pictures, images, and numerous complex problems. The myth can be used to tell the simplest comic book story, the most sophisticated drama, or to explain how something as sophisticated as gene editing occurs. When told with humor, twists, and insights, stories create lasting meaning, context, and a means of connecting. The myth is infinitely flexible and capable of endless variations without sacrificing any of its magic. Ironically, it outlives us all.

Great storytelling is at least as important as a great story. As illustrated, the storyteller must create empathy. The listener must be given a reason to "care" about the story and its characters. A good technique is to make the characters as much like the audience as possible. After all, we enjoy seeing ourselves in the story and relating to their plight. The storyteller must connect or engage the listener. This is done by making the story relevant and of value. Linking the story with a pressing issue or a needed lesson reminds the audience of the value to be gained. The storyteller must also elicit emotion. Through emphatic tone, humor, and other non-verbal cues, the audience can be drawn closer to the characters and story's progression. Leaving a cliffhanger moment or building a "twist" in the tale draws out curiosity and an emotional stake in the characters. In a related manner, the listener should be transformed. A view might be changed, an assumption challenged, or a different perspective born. If the storyteller is really successful, then the listeners' imagination becomes part of process which can unleash an important avenue of creativity. This is part of the magic of a Cirque Du Solei performance. The audience's imagination becomes part of the storytelling. Finally, the storyteller should create a bond of trust between themselves and the listener. The best mechanism for this is "believability" through the passion of performance. Because of the storyteller's zeal for telling the story, the audience begins to trust and bond with them; it seems like the story is only told to them because of the occasion or because they might be particularly receptive. Making the audience feel that they are the only ones hearing the tale is a hallmark of great storytelling and performance. It is the same magic that performers such as Joni Mitchell, Bruce Springsteen, Mariah Carey, U2, and The Rolling Stones have maintained for so long.

Loyalty

In today's world, loyalty may be the most elusive aspect of Chemistry to achieve; yet it is critically important. In the context of breakthrough innovation, members are loyal to their community and the good of the community supersedes the good of an individual member. Loyalty brings out the very best in people's talents and skills. It also creates resolve and tenacity when times are the darkest. In fact, when recounting experiences and the times most cherished, many of my interviewees talked about the hardest times and the part of the journey when they were most sure that failure was at hand. To them, this was when loyalty was most important; it was also part of the legend of their work and experiences. Loyalty is also a key component of the idea chase. When we know that others "have our back", we are more likely to take chances, generate novel ideas, and communicate more honestly. In contrast, a lack of loyalty is a harbinger of suspicion, misinformation, and selfishness. The concept of loyalty is so powerful that "whistle blowers" are typically not held in high esteem, even if they are right. If they are wrong, then the ostracism is even more intense, even if they had good intentions. In a similar vein, betrayal is typically viewed as one of the most unforgivable transgressions in society. All this is to say that loyalty is powerful and must be managed carefully. The key is to create loyalty to the objective, to the values that guide behavior, to the integrity of the tools that accomplish work, and to each other. However, we do not want to create "blind loyalty" such that rogue actors emerge and an "echo chamber" is created that silences any contrary opinion. A community that creates this balance should not experience the "whistle blower" or instances of dramatic betrayal. Again, it is difficult to achieve. Even the twelve disciples of Christ had trouble with loyalty. Yet, it is something very noticeable in the extraordinary efforts of today's best idea chasers.

Again, there are many books, articles, TED talks, and motivational speeches about the topic of loyalty. They all have something to offer and some of these notions will appear in the descriptions to come. However, I witnessed and experienced a brand of loyalty that was bit different and perhaps more modern in the projects I observed. This perspective was also evident in the people I interviewed. The four key aspects of loyalty that were voiced consistently are as follows: (1) *The right people*, (2) *Collective individualism*, (3) *Transparent communication*, and (4) *Equity*.

This is a very "hard" fact of life: Some people can only be truly loyal to their interests. There is a tendency by them to be selfish in framing the world around them with a blatant lack of concern for the interests of the organization or other members. As famously said by the character Annie Savoy in the movie Bull Durham, *The world is made for people who aren't cursed with self-awareness.*[14] I will leave it to the psychologists to frame this personality type and its root causes. I will say that the most noticeable characteristic seems to be extreme zeal for their self-interest and extreme apathy for almost anything else. Yet, to those who frame the world this way, their self-interest is the best interest of the organization. Therefore, in their mind, they are the ultimate team players! Now, this is not to say that a person with extreme self-interest is not talented or needed. In contrast, they may be the most talented; after all, they have spent a lifetime honing their skills and persona. It is to say that, in the long run, a collection of talents that work together as a group will typically outperform the super-talented, self-interested one. Fans of professional sports have seen this phenomenon for a long time. Yet, business professionals of sports teams cannot resist betting the franchise on the super-talented, super-self-absorbed star. In achieving the extraordinary, the right people are empathetic, comfortable with the capabilities (and limitations) of their skills, polite, considerate, thoughtful, curious, and out to achieve something meaningful. They are also tolerant and very clever in effectively managing those who may not exhibit these characteristics. The main lesson is that a collection of the right talents and right set of personality traits is the key to sustained success and bigger ideas. It is critical to achieving the right kind of loyalty.

So, with all the discussion about organizations, communities, and selflessness, does this imply that individuality and a "place in the sun" for individuals and their achievements are bad? NO! A big part of existence is the embrace and recognition that one is given by peers for a job well

---

[14]David Rettwe, The Wisdom of Bull Durham, *Psychology Today*, April 18, 2016.

done. Even better is the recognition of a member from those that are external to the community. Collective individualism is a structure that encourages individuality within the context of the collective. It is that moment when the Most Valuable Player of a team recognizes that his/her achievements are the result of teammates and the encouragement of the fans. In contrast, it is not a tweet, action, or news conference that puts the focus on the individual and takes it away from the team and the task at hand. It is allowing a member to fully utilize their talents and enjoy some autonomy while working toward the goal of the collective. Again, this can be hard to manage. The line between individual behavior that boosts the collective and an act of rogue behavior is very thin. However, in the very best organizations, there is a strong sense of cultivating the creative aspect of entrepreneurial activity and the rational responsibility of working within the collective.

Transparent communication forms a strong foundation for loyalty. In my own experiences in academe, I have received an email explaining that a senior administrative person has resigned to devote time to their first love, research. It is a great story, but I know that the person was asked to step down and that there is now some chaos in the senior ranks. I also have a little less loyalty to the institution and those that lead it. Maybe it was better to communicate nothing at all, communicate in person, or just say there has been a change in leadership. Oddly enough, there seems to be an inverse correlation between transparent communication and adverse events. Not so in very innovative organizations: communication lanes are open and only facts are allowed to ride in both sunshine and rain. In addition, those communicating are accessible and visible. This is a phenomenon that is tough to initiate but equally tough to abandon once it is started. Honest communication is an acquired skill; it allows the group to correct the course, avoid surprises, and creatively seek solutions. This flow must be multi-way. From top to bottom, side to side, and bottom to top. Interestingly, many generals, CEOs, and other leaders never knew their organizations were in trouble until it was too late. They were told exactly what they wanted to hear rather than what was actually happening. Aesop's fable about the emperor and his clothes is more than a story — it is a critical lesson in transparent communication.

Equity is critical to building loyalty. The literature in human resource management and organizational behavior is replete with first-class research on the importance of equity. Yet, it still seems difficult to define and even more difficult to achieve in practice. This is attributable to the complexity of equity as a construct. So, let's break it down just a bit. The first critical aspect of equity is accessibility. An organization should be accessible to people from a wide range of backgrounds. If everyone in the organization looks the same, thinks the same, and acts the same, then you are not likely to solve complex problems or uncover novel solutions. The second critical aspect of equity is opportunity. Everyone should have an equal opportunity for success. This means multiple paths to success. Furthermore, the organization must recognize that some of those paths to success should be paved with additional support and resources to leverage the talents and level the playing field for some of its members. Think of this as providing a "left-handed" baseball glove to those who are left handed rather than asking them to play right handed. Finally, consistency must prevail in rewards, recognition, and promotion. Systems of reward that are not understood or ever-changing create suspicion and invite counterproductive gamesmanship. Empathy is critical in understanding how a reward system inspires or deflates members of a community. Many systems of recognition and reward have not aged well. Yet, they are treated as the foundational bedrock of an organization's identity. Building equity requires the hard task of "innovating in" before "innovating out". It is tempting to overlook it, yet it is critical for building the preconditions necessary to reveal bigger ideas.

As evidenced by the amount of discussion, Chemistry is a very important aspect of building a community that will successfully chase the extraordinary. Chemistry exists between people, within groups of people, and between groups of people. It is an elusive concept because it is not something that is mandated or structured by organizational policy and procedure. It emerges over time and it is shaped by the experiences, beliefs, and expectations of members. Viewing Chemistry from this lens is a way to assess its state and, if necessary, make needed repairs. Its absence can make the most talented individuals seem ordinary and underachieving. Its presence can leverage the talents of ordinary people resulting in overachievement and incredible feats. A case in point is the journey of the Wright Brothers. Two ordinary bicycle makers achieve the feat of building the world's first flying machine. Competing teams, with greater talent and resources, failed at the same task. A huge part of the success was the Chemistry between the brothers, their helpers, and the people they met along the way. They leveraged their resources, moved forward through consensus, described the flight of birds through stories, celebrated victories, and exhibited loyalty to each other and those who helped them. The brothers demonstrated that ordinary people could accomplish the extraordinary when the principles of breakthrough innovation are in full force.

05

Define Roles and Responsibilities

Everybody is a genius. But if you judge a fish
by its ability to climb a tree, it will live its whole life
believing that it is stupid.

— Albert Einstein

A few years ago, I was conducting some research on unusual businesses. We called it the "businesses gone wild" project. I was in South Africa visiting and experiencing cage diving tours with great white sharks. Basically, these tours take adventurers to where great whites swim, chum the water with blood, and then lower people (in steel cages) into the water for an up-close look. I was amazed as the Captain reminded tourists to keep their hands in the cage. I asked him if any had lost limbs on the adventure. He quickly replied, *Yes! Sharks do not like to be petted.* Evidently, there is a strong urge to reach out and pet the sharks once you are among them. The Captain then asked if I was ready to go on a cage dive. I immediately declined; I was there to observe. I was also there to explore the link between cage diving operations and the increase in shark attacks on local beaches. I was no fan of the operation or of the fact that the South African government sanctioned the tours. The reaction bought me a lot of good-natured ridicule from the Captain and some of the mates. *Mr. College Professor, Mr. Brave American! Are you afraid of sharks!* I looked at the Captain and replied, *Not if they are on land. If they are on land and I have a baseball bat then they had better be afraid of me!* As observed by Einstein, everybody is a genius in their proper context. It is a source of pride, a crucial aspect of building belonging in the workplace, and an important form of identity.

Within the context of breakthrough innovation, the principle of *Roles* and *Responsibility* is rooted in the role that members play in the journey and the ability to adapt swiftly to new roles when needed. I think I can speak for many people when I recall the times that I have been part of a project team and was not sure why I was there or what I was expected to do. This is especially true in academia or in a church. In fact, I have been on some academic committees where consultants were hired to do the work we were tasked to do. I guess our collective role was to find someone else to solve the problem. Typically, when you are a part of meetings without focus or clear lines of responsibility, a leader will eventually emerge, make the problem small, and arrive at a quick solution (recall the chapter on being ambitious). No to worry, as this unfolds, you can spend the time drifting into a world or random thoughts. *I wonder if vegetarians eat animal cookies? Isn't it cruel that packages which say "easy opening top" are the toughest to open? If you are scared half to death twice, do you die? How much time did that guy spend learning that pencil trick? If you cut a hole in a net then are there fewer holes?* You get the idea. For all of us, being part of a project without a clearly defined role and responsibility is an invitation to drift into the world of stranger things. In organizations with a strong sense of roles, everyone has an identity that is important and synergistic with their talents. There is no time for random thoughts because during the time spent in a meeting or out of the meeting, the group is counting on you to fulfill a responsibility.

There are three important aspects associated with the assignment of roles and responsibilities: (1) defining the critical roles needed for the group to succeed; (2) matching the talent, capabilities, and interests of members to roles; and (3) coordinating sets of activities across roles. It is also important for the group to take on an identity. Similar to a professional sports team, all members play a primary role, can take on another role if needed, and are all bonded by the logo, colors, and mascot that seal the identity. When all this happens successfully, you belong, you contribute, you coordinate, and you are quite likely to achieve. You have a key element necessary for the Idea Chase. Let's take a look at each of these dimensions.

Critical Roles

Roles within communities are legendary. In Native American Nations, some of these roles include Chief (Leadership), Elders (Wisdom), Hunters (Sustenance), Skinners (Materials), and Shaman (Medicine). These roles have been compared to the social tasks that are needed and frequently occur within start-ups.[1] However they are defined, roles describe the way a group works together and how each individual behaves, contributes, and relates to others. Knowing the various roles and who holds them is key in managing expectations, building trust, and creating critical channels of communication. In some group contexts, these roles may be combined into a single role and attributed to the leader. This "messiah" model is found throughout military, autocratic business organizations, religion, and some governmental organizations. It is an attractive model. Nothing inspires us more than the thought of a magnanimous leader who seems to know the future and can navigate us to the promised land. This is true within a project team or in a major business organization. However, it is highly unlikely that anyone can be good at every critical role and also manage them all simultaneously. Therefore, it is important to "unpack" the roles that are typically bundled in leadership and distribute them to the people most able to perform them effectively. While doing this, it is important to redefine the role of leadership.

---

[1] J. Greathouse, Are You a Business Shaman, Skinner or Hunter?, *Forbes*, June 4, 2016.

So, what are the roles that are critical within a project? A starting point on this quest is to determine what behaviors are critical for group success. In the 1970s, Dr. Meredith Belbin and his research team at Henley Management College began observing teams to discover factors that distinguish high performance from low performance.[2] The research revealed that the difference between success and failure for a team was not dependent on factors such as the intellect of individual team members, but more on the behavior of those individuals. Belbin and his team began to identify separate clusters of behavior, each of which formed distinct team contributions or "Team Roles". They defined a team role as "a tendency to behave, contribute and interrelate with others in a particular way". Belbin's work uncovered nine archetypal team roles, all of which have essential parts to play in successful team work over time. These roles are as follows:

Cerebral Roles

Plant: *Creative, imaginative, unorthodox. Solves difficult problems. Excusable Weaknesses: Ignores incidentals. Too preoccupied to communicate effectively.*

Monitor Evaluator: *Sober, strategic, and discerning. Sees all options. Judges accurately. Excusable Weaknesses: Lacks drive and ability to inspire others.*

Specialist: *Single-minded, self-starting, dedicated. Provides knowledge and skills in rare supply. Excusable weaknesses: Contributes on only a narrow front. Dwells on technicalities.*

Action Roles

Shaper: *Challenging, dynamic, thrives on pressure. The drive and courage to overcome obstacles. Excusable Weaknesses: Prone to provocation. Offends people's feelings.*

---

[2]Meredith R. Belbin, *Management Teams: Why They Succeed or Fail*, Butterworth-Heinemann, Oxford, 2003.

Implementer: *Disciplined, reliable, conservative, and efficient. Turns ideas into practical actions. Excusable Weaknesses: Can be inflexible. Slow to respond to new possibilities.*

Completer Finisher: *Painstaking, conscientious, anxious. Searches out errors and omissions. Delivers on time. Excusable Weaknesses: Inclined to worry unduly. Reluctant to delegate.*

People Roles

Coordinator: *Mature, confident, a good chairperson. Clarifies goals, promotes decision-making, delegates well. Excusable Weaknesses: Can be seen as manipulative. Offloads personal work.*

Team Worker: *Cooperative, mild, perceptive, and diplomatic. Listens, builds, averts friction. Excusable Weaknesses: Indecisive in crunch situations.*

Resource Investigator: *Extrovert, enthusiastic, communicative. Explores opportunities. Develops contacts. Excusable Weaknesses: Overoptimistic. Loses interest once initial enthusiasm has passed.*

Belbin's framework provides a nice context for understanding roles as behaviors that lead to extraordinary performance. It also aligns well with the roles of ancient communities. The Elder matches Belbin's role of the Plant. The Shaman is the Specialist. The Primary Warrior is the Shaper. The Chief is the Coordinator. A Tribal Judge is the Monitor Evaluator. The Spiritual Guide is the Team Worker. The Tribal Skinner is the Completer Finisher. While these matches are my own observation and there is room for refinement, the point is that these behaviors are shaped as formal roles that are identifiable and distributed in such a way that the community is predisposed to function at its most effective level.

Within the projects examined in my research, roles are very prominent and, while matching the general framework of Belbin, they are a bit more defined and a lot more creative. Themes that give definition to the roles are based on everything from science fiction movies (The Matrix,

Star Wars, Star Trek), fantasy novels (Harry Potter, Lord of the Rings, Story of Fire and Ice), comic book heroes (Watchmen, Avengers, Justice League) to characters found in video gaming (League of Legends, World of Warcraft). No matter how they are identified, the roles are those deemed essential by members in coordinating and moving the group toward its destination. There are a few other distinguishing features of the roles. First, the role a member adopts is a *primary* role. It is possible to adopt a secondary role. This is actually encouraged to build "reserve" talent in case of unexpected changes within the group. Second, a member can participate in the execution of all roles. One is never fully restricted to a particular playground; if someone has a contribution beyond their role, it is encouraged. However, the member is responsible for the execution of their primary role. Third, a member can switch roles if there are problems or an unexpected lack of fit. It is not encouraged but it is better than rigidly adhering to role dysfunction. Finally, an observation: If an important responsibility is not assigned as a role, it will typically not get done. Therefore, it is critically important to establish roles and responsibilities before you launch the project. Imagine a sports team that defines and assigns responsibilities as the game is being played. Only extreme luck, or an opponent that assigns no roles, would allow the team to prevail. In Figure 1 are some of the most colorful, impactful, and common roles I have observed in research and in experience. They are mapped to Belbin's behavioral archetypes.

The cerebral roles and responsibilities address the activity of critical thinking. *Are we addressing the right question? Have we localized the problem? Have we identified the right sequence of cause and effect? Have we drifted away from the problem? What is fact? What is conjecture?* To me, this is the hallmark of modern leadership. Yet, it can be found in the activities of ancient communities. The architect is responsible for providing the vision, coaching, and direction needed to achieve the goal. It is a role that demands a lot of presence, ambition, experience, listening, and patience. The architect accomplishes the role by "walking around"

Figure 1: A Sample of Key Roles and Responsibilities

Cerebral
_____

Architect: Provides leadership, vision, coaching, and direction.

Wizard: Provides research, data, scientific experiments.

Oracle: Provides expertise in critical subject matter.

Action
_____

Flamekeeper: Keeps track of time, finds resources, schedules

Rainmaker: Boundary Spanner, finds unconventional paths, networks.

Author/Historian: Transfers ideas to words and words into stories and documents.

Artist: Transfers ideas to art. Creates visuals, charts, illustrations.

People
_____

Facilitator: Stages formats of discussion, referees, negotiates, reasons.

Seeker: Roams among other teams. Gives and receives information & knowledge.

The Voice: Transfers ideas through the spoken word. Speaks on behalf of the group.

and asking questions. This is not a new idea, but it has been lost with the emergence of email, PowerPoints, and telework.[3] To be present and to be engaged as an architect is to signal importance and concern. It also builds a strong disposition for positive chemistry. It is not enough to have an open-door policy. You must ask members of the community to open their doors to you.

The Wizard is typically the role I have played on projects. I love the role, I am qualified for the role, and I have done very well in the role. However, I have a strong sense of curiosity and I love to be around people. The Wizard's life can be very solitary from time to time. Therefore, I have sometimes asked to be a seeker (discussed in a little while) where I can

_____

[3]Henry Mintzberg, *Simply Managing: What Managers Do — and Can Do Better*, 1st Edition, Berrett-Koehler Publishers, 2013, Oakland, CA.

roam among other teams and learn what they are doing. I have always been denied the request. I was told that I like to talk too much and would have trouble returning to my team with the knowledge I have collected; probably true. The Wizard is responsible for science. Data, experiments, surveys, the latest articles, seminars, and conferences are the playing field. Data and research are authenticated, filtered, and organized so that the team has the best set of facts and the best science available for consideration. It requires a heart for science, a curious mind, and a deep knowledge of the tools of statistics. However, this does not necessarily imply that a Ph.D. is required. Wilbur Wright played the role of wizard in the invention of the flying machine. He had a knack for experimentation and a devotion to the scientific method as a means of discovery. Wilbur was self-educated in science and sharpened his engineering skills building bicycles in the family business. His highest educational credential was a high school diploma. The main lesson is not to "guess" about science, data, and information. Make it a role and responsibility and assign it to someone who is science minded and on a quest for the truth.

An Oracle is a person who can give wise and authoritative knowledge. This role has also been called "the genius". In many contexts, this role is given to someone who is not a member of the team. It may be an outside expert or a consultant who has subject matter knowledge of some aspect of the project. The role may also be assigned to someone within the organization but who is working on a different project with a different team. I have played this role a few times for research teams seeking grants from the National Science Foundation or the Defense Research Projects Agency. Typically, a research team will be told by a reviewer that they need additional subject matter expertise to win a grant. I will be called upon to play that role and be a permanent part of the research project or just a temporary resource. It is a fun role to play and the major requirement is to provide focused expertise while helping to shape the bigger picture. This is similar to Belbin's "Specialist" role and it is critical to know when the limits of a team's knowledge have been reached and an

Oracle is required. The motion picture "The Matrix" demonstrates these important aspects of the role. The name, as used by some of the projects researched, is a nod to the movie's character.

Acton-oriented roles are the "icebreakers" of getting things done. They remove obstacles, find paths, document findings, and keep the work on track. The Flamekeeper is tasked with managing the time and resources of the project. Scheduling, tracking time, tracking resources, and finding resources are the responsibilities of this role. The Flamekeeper can be thought of as the source of rationality and accountability within the team. They also take on the responsibility of a quartermaster. Finding and allocating resources as needed. Again, there are people who are incredible in this role. Attention to detail, a process mindset, a sense of time, a knack for provisioning, and the ability to administer a gentle "nudge" are the requirements.

The Rainmaker is an interesting role and responsibility. This person is responsible for boundary spanning, finding unconventional paths, and networking within the organization. A Rainmaker knows everyone and knows where to seek the unconventional. They have a passion for building and growing relationships. In some sense, it is similar to the "fixer" that is popularized in mobster movies. Someone who can clean up a mess or find avenues to do what seems to be impossible. I once worked in a fascinating project for the J4 staff of the Department of Defense. The goal was to identify supply routes for U.S. forces that were deep in the country of Iran. We came up with some very innovative ideas. However, they were rejected by leadership as "unlawful" and costly even if they were possible. Immediately, our team called upon the Rainmaker to investigate the claims. This person knew lawyers, legislators, flag officers, and almost everyone in the pentagon. The Rainmaker quickly determined that the concerns were not valid. The supply routes were not forbidden by law and not very costly. Plus, they could be established very quickly. He also discovered other supply routes that were unconventional and effective. None of this would have been possible without this role. A typical group would have stopped at the first push back and an opportunity for breakthrough discovery would have been lost.

The Artist and Author/Historian can be discussed together. They perform essentially the same responsibility, just in a different medium. The Author transfers ideas to words while the Artist transfers ideas to art. First, let's say that they are among the most important roles. An idea is only actionable if it can be communicated from one person or group to another. The process of idea capture, whether in word or in art, helps to refine the idea. It also subjects the notion to its first proof of concept. Second, the skill set and disposition for these roles typically require something beyond formal training and education. It seems to be an innate skill. A level of creativity is required in this role that is difficult to describe but obvious when it is in action. Simplicity seems to be part of this skill. An artist or author should be able to capture ideas in a form that is not tedious or distracting. Engagement is another aspect of the transfer. Artwork and written words should engage the audience and elicit discussion, debate, and ideas for further steps. Playfulness is also part of the mix. Humor, color, pictures, analogies, twists, and interactivity all help create an experience that captures the work while keeping the gates of imagination and creativity open.

The final set of roles is rooted in the interactions of people. The Facilitator is the peacemaking role of the team. This person stages formats of discussion, referees, and makes sure that every voice is heard and counted. The best-known incarnation of this task is the "talking stick". Also known as a "speaker's staff", this carved wooden staff was an instrument of aboriginal democracy used by many tribes, especially those located along the Northeast Coast of North America. The talking stick may be passed around a group, as multiple people speak in turn, or used only by leaders as a symbol of their authority and right to speak in public.[4] The facilitator

---

[4]Edwin L. Wade, *The Arts of the North American Indian: Native Traditions in Evolution*, Hudson Hills, 1995, Manchester, VT.

is responsible for being the living, breathing talking stick of the group. This can be a tough task, but there are people who have enormous talent in this regard. They tend to be the observers, note takers, acute listeners, and masters of equity within the organization. Those trained in Human Resource Management tend to excel in this role. Notice also that this role is separated from the cerebral roles. As noted earlier, it is important to unbundle roles that are typically bundled into the leader's role. This is the most important role to unbundle. Leaders, typically found in one or more of the cerebral roles, love the talking stick. It is important that they not get too much time in its company.

The Seeker is the knowledge gateway from one team to another. The responsibility of this person is to visit other teams. Bringing knowledge to their discussions and bringing back knowledge to their "home" team. There are two significant contributions of the Seeker. First, there is a leveraging effect. The Seeker can leverage knowledge created by one group to help the efforts of another group. This is true even if there is no knowledge to report. While working on a cybersecurity project for DARPA, our Seeker visited other groups that were working on similar projects throughout the Department of Defense. When she returned to our group for a report-out, only one PowerPoint slide was presented. It read, "They are as lost as we are!". We eventually found our way as did other teams but it was good to know that we were not the only one struggling in the beginning. The second effect is efficiency. In large organizations, it is likely that efforts, experiments, and information are duplicated. The Seeker can identify existing and potential redundancies, saving the organization time and money. Seekers tend to be curious, extroverted, loaded with initiative, and able to communicate. They also know that it is important to not get distracted and report back to their home team. For this reason, I will likely not be a Seeker although I would love to give it a try.

The Voice is the role and responsibility of presenting the findings, conclusions, and recommendations of the team to outsiders. They also capture and interpret the feedback they receive. Again, notice this is not automatically tied the leadership role. It can be part of the leadership role but it is not required to be so. In some sense, this can be thought of as the ambassador or diplomat of the team. Professionalism, knowledge, empathy, presence, improvisation, humor, the ability to gather feedback, and stellar communication skills are the main requirements. The main goal is to ensure that the teams' voice is heard accurately and effectively in a presentation setting. In the best cases, the Voice knows when and where other members should carry part of the presentation, when no presentation is needed, and how to integrate the team's presentation with the presentations of other teams. Of course, the Voice works closely with the holders of other roles, particularly the Artist, in shaping the message and presentation for external audiences.

Matching Talent with Roles

A very important yet tricky aspect of this task is matching the role with the prevailing talent of the member. In some instances, a member may view themselves as perfect for a particular role when, in reality, another role is best suited for their talents. I remember auditioning for my elementary school's production of *The Frog Princess*. I wanted to be the Prince. The Prince would accompany the Princess, wear a sword, and wear a cool cape. The Princess would undoubtedly be played by "the girl" that I and every boy had the biggest crush on. I tried very hard to get the part. I sang, I danced, I left it all on the stage. However, I did not sound like a Prince, I was not as tall as a Prince, and let's face it, there were other guys who looked more like a Prince than me. I saw the final roster and did not see my name listed as Prince. Worse than that, I was not a fan of the guy who got the part. I walked home terribly disappointed but quickly moved on to reading comic books and doing homework. Later that afternoon, I heard the phone ring and heard my mom talking in an animated fashion. She bolted into the den where I was reading the latest Spiderman comic and told me that I was expected at the rehearsal for The Frog Prince. I had been cast in the role of the Frog! Well, if you know the story, the Frog plays a major part and gets a kiss from the Princess. Turns out the Prince does not get a kiss. Not what I had initially hoped for in a role but it was very cool; I was the best Frog I could be. I still get compliments on the performance. The moral is that every role is important and that there is glory in playing the Frog as well as the Prince. Sometimes, there is more glory in being the Frog. In one of the projects I observed, there was a group of computer programmers called the "blue-collar immortals". They took turns bringing an old steel lunch pail to the lab. The pail represented their "blue-collar" contribution to the project and their devotion to taking care of the tedious coding details that would make others cringe. They were a proud bunch and very happy to be Frogs. It was a badge of honor.

It is also possible that once a role is assigned, it becomes obvious that the desired match does not exist. If you have been in academe long enough you will experience this phenomenon a few times. It is typically found in the appointment of a stellar academic to a Deanship. In the corporate world, the same thing happens when a person is promoted to a level of incompetence; it is known as the Peter Principle. In contrast, when a person holding a role seems to accomplish his/her responsibilities effortlessly, then there is evidence of desired fit. If there is an obvious lack of fit, it is a mistake to think the person will grow into the role or that things will magically get better over time. This only frustrates the person in the ill-fitting role as well as those people in roles that are aligned with their skills. This rapid response was observed in most of the teams studied. It was amazing how quickly these mismatches were resolved without conflict or disruption. Most often, the mismatch is noted by the member themselves, and roles are recast accordingly. These were rare cases as careful thought and attention was given to assignment of roles. Finally, to reiterate, it is very desirable for members to play a few roles when needed. It is also possible that a role is only needed for certain parts of the project and will come and go as needed. This aspect of role adaptability among members as well as recurring and non-recurring roles allows the team to adapt.

There are wonderful tools and techniques for matching talent with roles. Belbin's framework provides a behavioral basis for creating this alignment. The Margerison-McCann Team Management Profile is a tool that can help match skills with potential roles. Using a set of 60 questions, this profile establishes baseline information about each member's traits and work preferences. These work preferences provide insight into an individual's interpersonal and team-building skills, their organizing and decision-making abilities, and their leadership strengths. Their archetypes are as follows:

- **Reporter-Adviser:** Supporter, helper, tolerant, a collector of information, knowledgeable, flexible, dislikes being rushed.
- **Creator-Innovator:** Imaginative, future-oriented, enjoys complexity, creative, likes research work.
- **Explorer-Promoter:** Persuader, "seller", easily bored, influential, outgoing, likes varied, exciting, stimulating work.
- **Assessor-Developer:** Analytical and objective, developer of ideas, experimenter, enjoys prototype or project work.
- **Thruster-Organizer:** Organizes and implements, quick to decide, results-oriented, sets up systems, analytical.
- **Concluder-Producer:** Practical, production-oriented, likes schedules and plans, takes pride in reproducing goods and services, values effectiveness and efficiency.
- **Controller-Inspector:** Strong on control, detail-oriented, low need for people contact, an inspector of standards and procedures.
- **Upholder-Maintainer:** Conservative, loyal, supportive, personal values important, strong sense of right and wrong, work motivation based on purpose.

Along with work preferences, behaviors, and traits, roles can be based on personality profiles, past experiences, preferences, and peer suggestion. However, based on my observations, these forms of assessment may miss some key aspects of skill and disposition needed to effectively perform a role, especially if the goal is ambitious, the team is eclectic, and the context is driven by discovery, invention, and problem-solving. There is a lack of playfulness in these approaches and a potential for politics to outweigh collective interests. As implemented by a few teams, a great first step might be to have members take a few tests that match them to movie stars, a member of the Beatles, or other aspects of "pop culture". There are several of these non-scientific tests that can begin a basis of discussion about role fit and "break the ice" in terms of placing member in roles. Importantly, precision is not the goal; it is assigning primary responsibility for fulfillment of the role to an able member. In a few teams, members were first sorted into the "Hogwarts Houses" of Gryffindor, Hufflepuff, Ravenclaw, and Slytherin as featured in the Harry Potter fantasy novels.[5] This provided an initial, and incredibly accurate, read of personality characteristics that might lead to greater success in a role. The houses are illustrated in Figure 2.

Gryffindors were noted to be very strong in the role of Wizard, Genius, and Seeker. Slytherins seem suited for Architects and Seekers. Hufflepuffs tend to be strong as Flamekeepers, Authors, and Facilitators. Ravenclaws show strength as Artists, Authors, and Genius. I suggested using the Pottermore test to a Two-Star General in the U.S. Army as a way to align skills and behaviors with roles. I told him that I had taken the test (Gryffindor) and been assigned a role in project based on the result. I also told him that I used the test in consulting projects to establish teams and that the results were fantastic. It really works! His enthusiasm was quite a bit less than mine; something like a blank stare. However, he returned to his command, read the first Harry Potter book (he had no clue who Harry Potter was), and then gave it a try. Not only did he become a fan of Harry Potter, but he was also completely amazed by the improvement in his team's performance. They became more innovative and took on greater challenges with ease. I asked him if he had taken the test, he had, and was classified as Slytherin. I suggested he visit Harry Potter World

---

[5]The Sorting Hat — Pottermore, https://www.pottermore.com/writing-by-jk-rowling/the-sorting-hat.

Figure 2: Harry Potter: The Houses of Hogwarts for Assigning Roles

The Houses of Hogwarts

Hogwarts is a fictional British school of magic for students aged eleven to eighteen and is the primary setting for J. K. Rowling's *Harry Potter* series. Hogwarts is divided into four houses, each bearing the last name of its founder. Students are assigned to their house by the Sorting Hat.

Gryffindor:
Values courage, bravery, nerve and chivalry.

Slytherin:
Values ambition, cunning, leadership, and resourcefulness

Ravenclaw:
Values intelligence, creativity, learning, and wit.

Hufflepuff:
Values hard work, patience, justice, and loyalty.

and get a Slytherin Wizard's Cloak and a wand. The cloak looks much cooler than Army dress uniforms. Again, I got the blank stare; I don't think it will happen. Anyway, this is a creative way to develop roles that keep the task fun but also enlighten members about their predispositions for success. Together, formal behavioral frameworks and creative techniques can provide a broader perspective of a person's work preference and a more engaging process. The end result should be a "seating" of roles and responsibilities such that they are understood, valued, and managed effortlessly by their owners.

Find Your Identity

A final aspect of roles and responsibilities that must be acknowledged is role *cohesion* and *identity*. If there is harmony between people and their roles, then there must also be harmony across the roles. The first bridge to cross in that quest is the correct identification of needed roles. It is likely unwise to place a banjo player in a jazz band. Likewise, a saxophone player probably has nothing to add to a folk band. When you have the right combination of roles, then the team takes on cohesion and an identity. That is the final piece of the roles and responsibility quest. Within the context of music, the band takes on a sound and vibe that is identifiable. Within a Broadway play, the story takes on a context and progression that is driven by the interplay of roles. Within a sports team, there is a way of playing and sometimes a swagger that reflects the assigned roles and the shared record of success. The key question to ask is as follows: *What must happen for us to achieve success?* The next step is to determine what underlying roles are needed to support that sequence and where role "breakdowns" might damage the overall progress.

The second bridge to cross is giving the group a visible *identity*. I have worked with project teams in the Department of Defense for many years. These teams are assigned problems or challenges to solve with a big emphasis on thinking innovatively. It is a part of my career that I enjoy. However, when I first started this work, teams were numbered (team 1, team 2, etc.) and there were no roles. They basically took the problem statement and went into a workspace to begin solving the challenge. They immediately began looking for the quickest way out of the assignment. The most innovative thing they did was list ideas on a chart in hopes of finding something to call the task complete. I was amazed by this given that my experiences with projects and problem-solving were quite different. It was also ironic because these very smart men and women had strong connectivity and strong identity within their respective services. However, all of that was lost when the task was set up in this manner. The first thing I did was give each group a name. I am a big fan of NHL Hockey (go Carolina Hurricanes!), so I assigned each group a team that was near their home base. Now, team 1 was the Boston Bruins, team 2 was the Chicago Blackhawks, etc. Doing this gave them a different context of who they were and who other teams were. In other words, we have added *identity* to the mix. There are team colors, there are team mascots, and there is a feeling of belonging. A few members told me that their favorite hockey team was assigned to another group; yet, they became a fan of their assigned hockey team because it bonded the members in that context. There is a lot of power in giving a group a sense of identity through adoption of a team name, team colors, and a team logo. I am still amazed at the difference a dose of identity makes in connecting members and instilling a sense of collective pride.

In sum, it is important for organizations to establish well-defined roles that are derived from assessment of behaviors, work preferences, and trails. It is also important to add a touch of creativity and fun in identifying these roles. There should be harmony between the owner of a role and his/her responsibilities. Force fitting a person to a role or hoping for some miracle adaptation is not encouraged. Allowing someone to grow into a role is encouraged; there is a difference. There should be cohesion across roles. The interplay between roles is critical and points of potential breakdown must be identified. These points of breakdown may not be in the glamorous or high-profile roles (e.g. the Quarterback); they may arise in the less glamorous roles and responsibilities (e.g. the Long Snapper). Finally, a sense of identity adds a level of connectedness or esprit de corps that reinforces role ownership and pride of craftsmanship. Taken together, these elements set the stage for greater coordination and greater accomplishment. Your place in the idea chase is known and embraced. This principle rests on the inspirational side of the innovation continuum. However, the perspective of discipline can certainly be felt as a defined place for participants who organize and rationalize the critical tasks and create a community that can acquire and share knowledge.

Build Trust

*Courage is what it takes to stand up and speak;
courage is also what it takes to sit down and listen.*

— Winston Churchill

Trust may be the most difficult principle to tangibly capture in description but it is also a unique bond that holds a community together, particularly in the very toughest times. As noted in Churchill's quote, it is the courage to speak and the courage to listen. This is most likely to occur in a context where one feels safe and supported in both rain and shine. That context has to be predictable, reliable, and reciprocal for all members of the community. When there is a strong presence of trust, then an organization will almost never lapse into chaos or disarray. Instead, when times are toughest, tightly connected groups tend to become more resilient, more egalitarian, and develop a greater bond that is built on mutual trust.

In World War II, England braced for aerial bombardments intended to cause mass hysteria and break the spirits of its citizens. The Churchill government was worried that people would move into bomb shelters and never move out. These shelters might also become a breeding ground for discontent, criminal activity, and espionage. To the surprise of the British government, the complete opposite occurred; throughout the Blitz, the people of London went to work, returned to shelters in an orderly manner, and adopted codes for conduct (chemistry) to deal with the chaos. Sharing resources, caring for others, and credibly communicating amongst each other created the principle of trust that allowed Londoners to endure a campaign of bombing that was more intense than that found on the battlefield.[1] In today's world of public health crisis, shifting marketplaces, and revolutionized workplaces, building this same type of trust is critically important.

We learn trust at an early age, often from experience. As a young boy, I would often accompany my uncles and grandfather on hunting trips in Montana. Sometimes, we would go hunting for raccoons. While cute, a raccoon will destroy a field of corn. So, it is sometimes necessary to decrease the population. These hunts occur in early winter, late at night, in muddy fields and woods that are in the middle of nowhere. You release the dogs; they chase the raccoon up the tree and you "take care" of the raccoon with a shotgun. One very cold night, we were hunting in a field that was very unfamiliar to us. The land had lots of old barbed wire fences, streams, and other obstacles. However, we had a guide, Mr. Kelly. He was an older gentleman, chewed tobacco, used filthy language, and was not exactly fit. My grandfather told us to take him along and trust him; he knew the land very well. All during the hunt, my uncles and I talked about how we wanted to ditch old man Kelly. He was slow, talked all the time, and made fun of us. Suddenly, we heard a screech at the edge of the woods that was horrifying. We aimed a light toward the noise; it was a very angry mountain lion. These are animals that are mean and do not like to be disturbed. Once the lion saw the light, he charged. Mr. Kelly yelled to us, *FOLLOW ME!* Instead, we dropped our flash lights and ran like hell. We ran through a few streams, tracked through mud, jumped, and fell across fences. We seemed to be running in circles. We finally found our way back to the main road. We were out of breath, covered in mud, wet, and bleeding from the barbed wire and thorns of the bushes

---

[1]Tom Harrison, *Living Through The Blitz*, Faber & Faber, London, 2010.

we had run through. We looked back toward the fields and woods we had just crossed. My Uncle Randy asked, *I wonder what happened to old man Kelly?* I said, *The lion probably got him, poor soul, he deserved better.* Suddenly, we hear a voice ring out from the darkness, *What took you boys so long?* It was Mr. Kelly, not a drop of mud on him, no sign of exhaustion, standing there with a cold can of beer. He knew the shortcut, he knew mountain lions will not chase you for long, he knew being calm was better than acting like prey, and he knew where the truck was parked. It was a lesson in trust. Sometimes, the most trustworthy person may be a troll, not a movie star, star athlete, or yourself.

So, how can trust be framed so that it is something we can diagnose and perhaps treat within an organization? There are two interconnected aspects that seem very important. First, there is the overall context or "standard" of trust. This is the landscape or culture of trust within an organization and how it manifests itself in principles or standards. It is based on behavior, ethics, expectations, and codes of conduct that may not be formalized in words but are well known in action. It is similar to the principle of chemistry discussed before but different because it involves deeper aspects of a relationship between members as well as the relationship between the organization and its members. These relationships are built over time through experiences. The second aspect is the manifestation of trust. That is very simply the exchange of knowledge. Organizations with high thresholds of trust will create and share knowledge seamlessly. This flow is a manifestation of the standard of trust and provides the fuel necessary for the best ideas and the best innovative outcomes.

The Standard of Trust

An effective standard of trust among a group of people is built through actions, experiences, the test of trying times, as well as the test of the best of times. It is part of the fabric that connects people and it is something that, when maliciously broken, is almost impossible to completely repair. Of course, there are many academic studies and consulting frameworks that

Figure 1: Standards of Trust

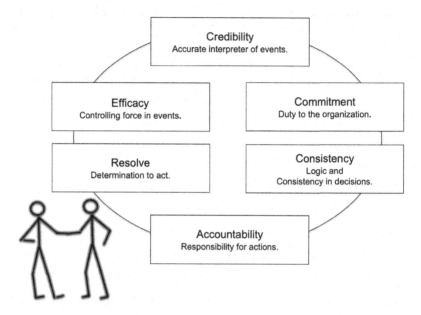

capture this concept in many different ways. In a prior piece of research, I used many of these ideas to build a definition of trust between an organization and its shareholders.[2] The context I examined was the digital communication of corporate crisis to shareholders (employees, customers, and shareholders). It was interesting to find that the standard of trust within the organization was a very accurate predictor of the effectiveness of communication.[3] In other words, receivers of the communication were able to sense the trustworthiness of organization through their digital communications. This trustworthiness was not "baked" into the communication. Instead, effective organizations had strong standards of trust that were reflected out through their communications. These standards of trust are found in organizations rooted in discovery as well as the amazing communities of old. As illustrated in Figure 1, these

[2]Albert H. Segars, Effective Communication of Corporate Crises through the Internet, *Business Strategy Review*, 14(3), Autumn 2003.

[3]Albert H. Segars and Gary F. Kohut, Strategic Communication through the World Wide Web: An Empirical Model of Effectiveness in CEO's Letter to Shareholders, *Journal of Management Studies*, 38(4), 2001.

dimensions are as follows: *Credibility, Efficacy, Resolve, Consistency, Commitment*, and *Accountability*. This framework embodies aspects of *strategic trust* (trust in leadership), *personal trust* (trust in each other), and *organizational trust* (trust in the organization).[4] It should also be viewed as a chronology of trust; actions of the past, present, and future. This provides a perspective that is grounded in both experiences and expectations.

Credibility

Within the context of discovery, organizational credibility is the accurate interpretation and communication of data, information, and knowledge. Concepts such as honesty, genuineness, and integrity are a part of this construct. A lack of credibility is one of the hardest obstacles for an organization to overcome. An organization can be forgiven for many things, but a lack of honesty is a stigma that is hard to shed. Honest workers will select themselves out of organizations lacking credibility to find refuge in firms with values more consistent with their own. It will also be hard to recruit the best thinkers and innovators. Research has shown that these people are most motivated by an organization's values and purpose.[5] Within breakthrough organizations, three main themes capture the notion of credibility: (1) *Knowing things as they really are,* (2) *Quickly communicating what we know honestly,* and (3) *Communicating the important things we know to those who need to know.* In a sense, it is a collective understanding and "way" of working in which value is placed on facts, established cause and effect, and honest observation. Conjecture, partial information, inference, and wishful thinking are very hesitantly invented or communicated. If they are part of a discussion, great effort is made to note that the conversation has progressed beyond the boundary of fact and data. Rapid, fluid, and accurate communication of facts and

---

[4]Robert M. Galford and Anne Seibold Drapeau, The Enemies of Trust, *Harvard Business Review*, February 2003.

[5]Robert B. Cialdini, Petia K. Petrova, and Noah Goldstein, The Hidden Costs of Organizational Dishonesty, *Sloan Management Review*, Spring 2004.

events is practiced throughout the organization to fight off speculation and rumor. This extends to personnel announcements, budget information, parking, and even the menu at the cafeteria. However, this does not imply that there is a flood of unbridled information flowing in the organization. Too much information, without a method to organize and prioritize it, harms credibility. Important information can easily hide in the tsunami of everyday communication. Members can also feel overwhelmed or fatigued by constant communication. The magic is creating flows of data, information, and knowledge that are accurate, prioritized, and readily accessible to those who need it most.

Efficacy

The University of North Carolina at Chapel Hill (UNC) is a fairly innovative organization. There is a "Carolina Way" of ethics, community, and values that seems to distinguish it as an organization. UNC has a long history and a tradition of excellence. However, the University also had an artifact of history that became very divisive and tested its sense of connectedness. The object was a statue of a confederate soldier that stood at the main lawn of the campus. Erected in the early 1900s, the monument became more divisive as the years rolled by. Protests emerged and calls for action became louder, from those who supported and those who opposed the monument. The Chancellor of the University made it clear that she opposed symbols that might cause division. She also noted that she was not able to do anything about the statue. State law as well as rules and procedures made it impossible to act. A clear misapplication of adding rather than subtracting! Of course, this only enraged those on both sides of the issue.[6] This is an example of very poor organizational efficacy. If an organization is not a controlling force in events, then trust is broken within the organization and between the organization and other constituencies. Yet, saying "it is out of our control" is a very tempting tact for leaders and organizational members to take when times get tough.

---

[6]Valerie Bauerlein, UNC Chancellor to Step Down Amid Silent Sam Rift, *Wall Street Journal*, July 15, 2019.

Organizations can lose control of their destiny due to budget constraints, competitors, regulatory penalties, shifting winds of management, or the inability to understand their environment. If this happens, it is critically important to quickly regain a sense of organizational efficacy and establish a new direction and new sense of control. The message must be as follows: *We control our destiny; it is in our hands.* Anything else is an acknowledgment that chance or the will of others will determine who we are. Operationally, this may require modifying goals, visibly engaging the challenge, or competing in a totally different manner. Imagine a coach telling players at halftime, *there is nothing we can do, we are beaten.* Even if it is true, there are other games that will be tainted by that reaction. It is much better to reframe the challenge and say *let's win the second half.* Many comebacks have been built on that idea. To continue the story of UNC, a group of angry protestors illegally toppled part of the statue on a summer night. This compounded the impression that UNC had lost control and eventually the Chancellor was forced out. Before she left, she did have the remaining part of the stature removed, ironically a hint that she did have authority after all! Organizations can function without control of their destiny, but they are not likely to accomplish very much. Innovative groups have a strong sense of determination even when the darkest clouds gather. Elections have been won, laws changed, and nations born because determined people believed in their ability to control their destiny.

Commitment

Organizational commitment is the bond or duty a member feels toward their organization. In some sense, it is putting the organizational interests above one's own self-interest. In an ideal situation, self-interest and organizational interest will be the same. A great insight into commitment is offered in the "three-component model" developed by John Meyer and Natalie Allen.[7] Affective commitment describes the desire of a member to

---

[7]John P. Meyer and Natalie Allen, A Three Component Conceptualization of Organizational Commitment, *Human Resource Management Review*, 1(1), Spring 1991.

stay at the organization. If there is positive affective commitment, then a member desires to stay with the organization. They feel valued, satisfied, and are cheerleaders for the organization. Continuance Commitment is the need to stay at an organization. If this is positive, then other alternatives are not attractive. The member will not be better off or perhaps they might be worse off if they leave for a different organization. Normative Commitment describes the obligation a member feels for remaining with the organization. It is the dissonance one might feel for considering a departure. Perhaps they would disappoint other members by leaving. Or, leaving might adversely increase the workload of fellow members. If normative commitment is high, then there is a strong feeling by members that separation from the organization would create disappointment or hardship. Therefore, there is a strong tendency to remain. Commitment manifests itself in the completion of tasks. A committed group of people will do all that is necessary to see a task through to completion. In other words, they do what they say they will do. If for some reason they cannot complete a task or fulfill the obligation, then they will say so. Perhaps the most iconic example of this is the children's story of "The Little Engine That Could".[8] In the story, a long train must be pulled over a high mountain after its engine breaks down. Larger engines are asked to pull the train and for various reasons they refuse. The request is sent to a small engine, which agrees to try. Through determination, optimism, dedication, and commitment, the engine succeeds in pulling the train over the mountain. A modern version of this is captured between Yoda and Luke Skywalker in the Star Wars movie *The Empire Strikes Back*. Yoda asks Luke to use his new-found Jedi skills to raise his star fighter from the swamp. Luke bemoans the task and says "Alright, I'll give it a try." Yoda responds, "No! Try Not! Do or Do Not! There is no Try!". Both of these examples are endearing testimonies to the power of commitment. It is a bond that seals the efforts of a group to a task and assures members that each is there for the other. Without it, organizations may experience a lot of activity but very little to show for the effort.

---

[8]Rev. Charles S. Wing, Story of the Engine That Thought It Could, *New York Tribune*, April 8, 1906.

Resolve

Resolve is the determination to act. An organization decides what it should do and then it embarks on the course of action. This should be thought of as a verb rather than a noun. It is action oriented, purposeful, and synonymous with "strength of will". Trust is built on seeing strategy, promises, and plans become actionable marching orders and outcomes. For this to occur, it is sometimes necessary to ignore obstacles and prepare to endure for the long haul. It is the drive that allowed a troubled and nearly deaf musician named Beethoven to compose some of the world's most memorable music. It is the determination that drove a woman named Helen Keller to learn to communicate and also become the first blind person to earn a Bachelor of Arts degree, to read Braille (in English, French, German, Greek, and Latin), and to write and publish numerous books. It is the audacity of Pixar in challenging the assumption that toys could not talk or have feelings that created "Toy Story".[9] It is also the ingenuity demonstrated by mission control in the rescue of Apollo 13. In the immortal words of Gene Krantz, the flight control director, "Failure is not an option." Trust is built on the promise and delivery of determined action. Excessive wish making and empty promises create an environment that is anything but innovative. In fact, it is likely to create an environment that is combative and devoid of hope. Yet, in government and in some business organizations, we see copious amounts of hype and less delivery. Not so in super projects or in very innovative organizations. The difference seems to be how organizations frame the target of their efforts. Innovative entities follow more of a scientific approach in guiding their efforts. They ask questions that can be investigated, they link data to theory, and they develop empirical methods to investigate the question. This reveals a clear path of action that can then be pursued vigorously. In contrast, less innovative entities spend endless amounts of time half-heatedly chasing multiple paths.[10] Even worse, they stall at the point of

---

[9]Walter Isaacson, The Real Leadership Lessons of Steve Jobs, *Harvard Business Review*, April 2012.
[10]Jack Zenger and Joseph Folkman, The 3 Elements of Trust, *Harvard Business Review*, February 2019.

action through excessive investigation and debate. As mentioned earlier, this can be a symptom of a built-in tendency to add rather than to subtract, or an inability to prioritize and develop a clear focus. Either of these conditions will undermine resolve and create doubt and tension within the organization. For real discovery to occur, resolve must arrive in a timely fashion and must be a visible, recognizable, and definitive call to action.

Consistency

Logic, accuracy, and fairness are the defining traits of organizational consistency. Ideally, an organization reflects its values and beliefs through decisions, rewards, and actions. Consistency removes tension which leads to increased levels of trust. We can count on people to show up, we can see that decisions are made to further objectives, the objectives are aligned with righteous goals, we benefit fairly from our efforts, and all of these things are true day after day. In the realm of commerce, Amazon has built a new empire of business by building predictably and reliability into shipping. Uber and Lyft have risen and fallen based on the levels of consistency in their transportation services.[11] In both instances, customers seek consistency in the services offered and develop a level or trust and loyalty when those expectations are realized. Within an organization, members seek the same signals and signs of logic from leadership, stakeholders, and each other. A lack of consistency creates an environment in which performance measurement is difficult. It is simply not possible to measure the progress on a journey if the destination is constantly shifting. Messaging (*What* is to be accomplished), structuring activity to take on the task (*How* we will accomplish it), and equity in rewarding the activity (*Why* we accomplish it) must be fair and logical to meet the standard of consistency. This leads to trust and efficiency of effort. There is a shared understanding among members, greater coordination, and a better predisposition for something beyond the ordinary. It is very interesting to note that a perceived lack of consistency in organizations

---

[11]Greg Benslinger, Uber Posts Slower Sales Gains, Widening Loss as It Prepares for 2019 IPO, *Wall Street Journal,* July 16, 2019.

by employees is the foundation of a "toxic" workplace and a major driver in "quiet quitting" or dramatic departure.[12] Consistency takes work. It is quite likely that leaders believe that consistency exists when it does not. This is because consistency lives within as well as at the junction of strategies, policies, values, and beliefs.

Accountability

The final standard of trust is accountability. This can be thought of as the organization's responsibility to its members, the members' responsibility to the organization, and the overall responsibility to the "greater good". Let's start with the greater good. This is rooted in the core belief that an organization should commit itself to humanitarian and social issues and minimize its impact on the environment. While this is commonly thought of as a new and modern principle, it has its genesis in Native American Tribes.[13] These tribes believed that there was a reciprocal relationship between the earth and people. Myths, gods, and ceremonies honored and memorialized aspects of nature and its role in life and living. In today's world, a central theme of accountability is positive coexistence between the planet and the organization. The minimal threshold is to do no harm while the ambitious threshold is to improve the world. This is a powerful stimulus and is not necessarily generational. Purpose and legacy are key incentives for motivation and effort for almost everyone.[14] It is part of our DNA. Within the organization, it is important to have systems of accountability that are based on driving improvement, have two-way avenues of feedback, and have established lines of ownership between responsibilities and those expected to accomplish them. There is a great story in baseball that highlights accountability and how easy it is to misattribute and misshape it. The great baseball manager and Hall

---

[12]Jack Zenger and Joseph Folkman, Quiet Quitting Is About Bad Bosses, Not Bad Employees, *Harvard Business Review*, August 31, 2022.

[13]Annie L. Booth, We Are the Land: Native American Views of Nature, *Nature Across Cultures*, Kluwer Academic Publishers, pp. 329–349, 2003, Amsterdam, NL.

[14]Daniel H. Pink, *Drive: The Surprising Truth About What Motivates Us*, Riverhead Books, 2009, New York, NY.

of Famer Frankie Frisch sent a rookie out to play center field. The rookie promptly dropped the first fly ball that was hit to him. On the next play, he let a grounder go between his feet and then threw the ball to the wrong base. Frankie stormed out of the dugout, took the glove away from the rookie and said, "I'll show you how to play this position." The next batter slammed a line drive right over second base. Frankie came in on it, missed it completely, fell down on the ground when he tried to chase it, threw down his glove, and yelled at the rookie, "You've got center field so screwed up nobody can play it." The moral of the story is that sometimes the most difficult aspect of accountability is holding ourselves accountable. Because of information symmetry, the growing realization is that not all profit is honorable, and a sense of greater good and accountability as an organizational trait has also changed. There is a higher bar, a need for greater explanation, and an expectation that anything gained (or lost) was done so in the right way.

The Manifestation of Trust: Knowledge and Knowledge Flows

Another important aspect of trust is its manifestation in the creation and flow of knowledge throughout the organization. The standards speak to the cultural aspect of trust. Knowledge and knowledge flows are trust captured in action. The two go hand in hand and together provide a means to assess how well an organization is positioned to capture, convert, and apply what it knows and what it learns. It is useful to look at this from two perspectives: first, the capability of an organization to create knowledge and, second, the flows of knowledge throughout the organization.

Knowledge Capability

A key to understanding the success and failure of knowledge management within organizations is identification and assessment of preconditions that are necessary for the effort to flourish. Of course, strong standards of trust must be in place to set a cultural context. However, other

Figure 2: Trust and Knowledge Capability

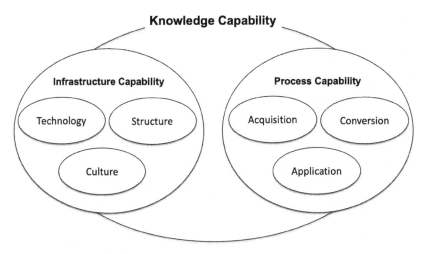

preconditions that address knowledge capability must also be in place. Organizations must develop an "absorptive capacity" — the ability to use prior knowledge to recognize the value of new information, assimilate it, and apply it to create new knowledge.[15] Therefore, beyond the standards of trust, organizations must develop the capability to learn, archive what is learned, and combine what is learned with what is archived to create new knowledge. Then, there must be an efficient marketplace of knowledge within the organization. As illustrated in Figure 2, a useful way to frame knowledge capability is to separate it into two components[16]:

(1) *Infrastructure Capabilities*: The basic foundational characteristics of an organization needed for creating and exchanging knowledge.
(2) *Process Capabilities*: The combination of methods and people used in creating and exchanging knowledge.

---

[15]W. Cohen and D. Levinthal, Absorptive Capacity: A New Perspective on Learning and Innovation, *Administrative Science Quarterly*, 35, 128–152, 1990.

[16]A. Gold, A. Malhotra, and A. Segars, Knowledge Management: An Organizational Capabilities Perspective, *Journal of Management Information Systems*, 18, 185–214, 2001.

Infrastructure Capabilities

Technology comprises a crucial element of capability needed to capture, archive, and create new knowledge. Through the linkage of information and communication systems in an organization, previously fragmented flows of information and knowledge can be integrated. These linkages can also eliminate barriers to communication that naturally occur between different parts of the organization. Since technology is multi-faceted, the organization must invest in a comprehensive infrastructure that supports the various types of knowledge and communication that are critical. It is very tempting to think of this capability as something new and modern. Far from the truth! Drawings in caves, on parchment, and on animal pelts were technologies used by ancient tribes to capture and share knowledge. Dance, song, stories, and ceremonies were also used for the same purpose. Signal stations, lighthouses, and Morse code are also clever ways to transfer knowledge. The point is that it is important to think broadly about technology. It is a means of capture and a means of flow. This can be through a conversation or a sophisticated system of digital technology. Applying the right amount and combination of high-tech and high-touch is the magic in establishing the technological capability. The answers to key questions should not live in email, texts, complex digital archives, or tweets. There needs to be a technological infrastructure that brings the answers off the backroads on onto the organizational interstate.

Organizational structure is important in leveraging technological architecture. While structure is intended to rationalize individual functions or units within an organization, structural elements have often had the unintended consequence of inhibiting collaboration and sharing knowledge across internal organizational boundaries. For example, structures that promote individualistic behavior in which locations, divisions, and functions are rewarded for "hoarding" information can inhibit effective knowledge management across the organization. If the same people have all the answers all the time, if every report or project seems like it begins from scratch, if critical knowledge disappears when a member leaves, then there may be a structural problem. In the classic scene from the movie "The Pink Panther Strikes Again", Inspector Clouseau enters an Inn. He sees a dog resting in the lobby and asks the innkeeper *Does your dog bite?* The innkeeper replies *No.* The Inspector reaches to pet the dog. The dog ferociously bites him on the hand. The Inspector yells at the innkeeper *I thought you said your dog did not bite!* The Innkeeper replies, *That is not my dog.* Good structure should not only ensure accuracy of knowledge but should also facilitate understanding.

Along with standards of trust and structure, culture plays an important part in building capability. Interaction between individuals is essential in the innovation process. Dialogue between individuals or groups is often the basis for the creation of new ideas and can therefore be viewed as having the potential for creating knowledge. Employee interaction should be encouraged, both formally and informally, so that relationships, contacts, and perspectives are shared by those not working side by side. This type of interaction and collaboration is important when attempting to transmit tacit knowledge between individuals or convert tacit knowledge into explicit knowledge, thereby transforming it from individual to organizational level. In addition, employees should have the ability to self-organize their own networks of knowledge and practice to facilitate solutions to new or existing problems and to generate or share knowledge. Sometimes, the culture we make can kill innovation and knowledge transfer although we set up the culture in hopes of achieving the opposite. I remember attending an MBA graduation. I was the faculty member who was assigned the role of hosting our graduation speaker, Michael Armstrong, CEO of AT&T. I stood on the stage with Mr. Armstrong and our Dean as the graduates filed into the auditorium. Mr. Armstrong commented on how distinguished our graduates looked. He then asked our Dean if they were innovative. Without hesitation, our Dean said, *Well, they were when they arrived here!* This bit of self-deprecating humor had an important message. We all hoped that the MBA experience had not harmed or taken away their natural urge to be creative and to dream.

Graduate business study is not designed to do so, but one can't help but wonder.

Process Capabilities

Part of managing knowledge and creating trust within the organization is developing processes that acquire knowledge. Two primary means for collecting knowledge are (1) to seek and acquire entirely new knowledge and (2) create new knowledge out of existing knowledge through collaboration between individuals and between organizations. This is an important part of discovery. Individuals, groups of individuals, and organizations actively create knowledge for a shared purpose. This is something very identifiable in super projects such as the Event Horizon Telescope, New Horizons, and OpenAI. The network of collaboration is robust and extremely cooperative, particularly along the dimension of knowledge creation and transfer. Acquiring knowledge is costly and time consuming. It must be identified, shaped into a useful form, and then authenticated. Sharing this process across a community builds efficiency and pockets of unique specialization. Knowing where the wellsprings of knowledge are within a community and how to access them is to create extra knowledge capacity. The wheel is not reinvented every time there is an identified need for knowledge or expertise. New knowledge is only created when it is not part of the existing community of knowledge.

An organization must also acquire the ability to make knowledge useful (i.e. convert it into useful form). This process is characteristic in conversion. The organization must organize and structure knowledge, thereby making it easier to access and distribute it within the organization. By combining or integrating knowledge, redundancy can be reduced, and efficiency can be improved by reducing excess volume. As developed by Nonaka and Takeuchi,[17] organizational knowledge starts at the individual level with thoughts or understanding. It then evolves as individuals dialogue with

---

[17]Ikujior Nonaka and Hirotaka Takeuchi, *The Knowledge-Creating Company: How Japanese Companies Create the Dynamics of Innovation*, Oxford University Press, 1995, Oxford, UK.

their colleagues. The ideas are then articulated and converted to a form that can be widespread. As described, tacit knowledge, which is difficult to codify, evolves to some form of explicit knowledge which is easier to codify, as it diffuses throughout an organization. Conversion is a key process in taking what is known in concept and experience in individuals and making it accessible to the organization. In super projects, this is done through complex data visualization and presentations based on simulations, animation, and virtual reality. The noticeable aspect of this conversion is the interactivity and engagement that it encompasses. If a picture is worth a thousand words, becoming immersed in the picture and able to engage in its context is worth a thousand pictures!

Knowledge application processes are oriented toward the use of knowledge. This is worlds trickier than one might initially guess. We now live in a world of information. You might say we are in an age of exaggeration. Information and knowledge are bigger and more dramatic viewed through the lens of modern media and technology. The first step in navigating this landscape is to clearly separate what is known from what is not known and to accept that a great amount of knowledge is debatable. It is easy to develop a sense that knowledge is a dichotomy of what is known or what is not known. If something is not known, then we investigate it and then it becomes known. If only it were that easy! In science, politics, business, or religion, there is knowledge that is debatable. Before we apply knowledge, we must know its true state. Only then can it lead to good decisions. We must also know ourselves and we must not forget the important role wisdom plays in knowledge application. Research has shown that the *less* of an expert someone is in a field, the more they tend to overestimate their ability. Plus, there is a strong tendency by these same people to be a poor judge of the skills of others. Further, those that are *most* skilled tend to underestimate their abilities.[18] If you want

---

[18]Justin Kruger and David Dunning, Unskilled and Unaware of It: How Difficulties in Recognizing One's Own Incompetence Lead to Inflated Self-Assessments, *Journal of Personality and Social Psychology*, 77(6), 1121–1134, 1999.

to see an example of this, then just browse the comments section of any online news article or watch a panel of "experts" on any news channel. Therefore, there is a very steep human bias to overcome in applying knowledge successfully. Not all knowledge is understanding and there is a strong tendency to incorrectly estimate our ability to use it, expert or non-expert. Knowing the true nature of knowledge and our potential reaction to it is important to creating effective application processes. In ancient communities, wisdom filled in these important gaps. An outside set of eyes, someone who has no emotional stake in the decision, or someone who has been there before can be an important wellspring of wisdom. As stated in an Arapahoe proverb, *if we wonder often, then knowledge will come.*

The Flow of Knowledge

Along with capability, an organization must create a robust, consistent, and predictable flow of knowledge. This flow should be both "pull" and "push". Members should be able to easily seek, identify, and "pull" the knowledge they need from the organization. They should also be able to receive knowledge "push" from the organization about new science, events, or environmental changes that may impact their work. As illustrated in Figure 3, there are four major types of knowledge flow that occur in an organizational setting. These flows are from Member to Member, Community to Member, Member to Community, and Community to Community. Each plays a critical role in building trust and coordination. This discipline-based perspective is useful in determining where knowledge roadblocks occur and where there are clear highways of knowledge flow. Ideally, there are robust flows across these four domains. If this is true, and knowledge capabilities are intact, then the probability of bigger and better ideas is very high.

Procedural Knowledge flows from member to member. This knowledge content is based on "know-how" about how to accomplish a task, how to assess outcomes, and how to solve problems. It is a critical flow that cannot be encumbered by incentives or prior experiences that motivate

Figure 3: Flows of Knowledge

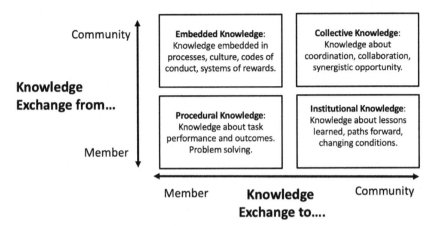

members to stop sharing "what they know". The principle of chemistry as well as roles combine with the principle of trust to create a context for rich knowledge flows between members. This flow is based in fact, is demonstrable, and is directly applicable. Knowledge that does not meet these standards is discouraged and often deemed more of a hazard than a help.

Embedded Knowledge flows from the community to the member. This is knowledge content that conveys culture, process, codes of conduct, and systems of rewards. It aligns closely with the principles of ambition and chemistry to keep members focused and rewarded. In traditional settings, this flow is too often ignored or heavily codified in strategy documents and other policy/procedure. In addition, the flow might only occur sporadically, at the beginning of a project, or when a crisis hits. In the groups of this study, this flow along with institutional knowledge (discussed next) is a constant stream of guiding principles, adjustments, and contingencies that create quick adaptability.

Institutional Knowledge flows from the member to the community. Again, good team chemistry and roles help to make this a robust flow. One role in particular seems crucial in developing institutional knowledge. The role of *seeker* formally assigns the activity of gathering and exchanging knowledge from within the community and between communities to a member. This is a powerful mechanism when teams of people are working on various aspects of a shared project. It is also powerful when teams are not working on shared assignments as projects, however diverse, will have common problem sets and coping strategies. Bringing to the community lessons learned, promising paths forward, and the collective knowledge that exists outside the community creates velocity in moving forward, eliminates duplicity, and takes better advantage of available resources.

Finally, *Collective Knowledge* is rooted in collaboration, cooperation, and synergistic opportunities between communities. Again, the formal role of a seeker within each community can facilitate this exchange. Another tactic that has great effect is cross assignment of members between communities. The concept of a "tribal council" is also a noticeable coordinating structure in this flow. Leaders of tribes (architects) meet not only to provide updates on their progress but also to share stories about their tribes' challenges, victories, and the journey. In these councils, ceremony and storytelling become important avenues of creating rich flows of community knowledge. Like knowledge, other flows of resources (time, money, technology) move openly and fairly between communities and members when the principle of trust is present. These flows, along with honest communication and stories about what is prized, what is feared, and what might be done, are key aspects of building the principle of trust.[19]

Trust is a very complex concept, and this chapter has framed it in a bit of a different way. Given that breakthrough innovation is something bigger, more meaningful, and more personal to members, there is a deeper and more cerebral aspect of trust. It is a central piece of inspiration. This is captured in the standards of trust. This can be thought of as the

---

[19]Liz Ryan, Ten Ways to Build Trust on your Teams, *Forbes*, March 17, 2018.

socialization aspect of the concept. Values, norms, and codes of conduct are applicable and address relationships between members and between members and the organization. However, there is also an operational aspect of trust. Surprisingly, this is the more dominant, discipline-based aspect of the principle. It addresses how the organization acquires, converts, and distributes knowledge. This creation of this knowledge marketplace is grounded in capabilities and the flow that creates a fluid, coordinated, and adaptable organization. The organization is smart. Knowledge is a resource that is created, shared, and filtered to meet known and unknown challenges. Guiding standards and knowledge capabilities work together to build the principle of trust. If you are a leader or a contributor, it is important to constantly assess this unique duality of trust within your organization. Its absence can explain why good initiatives stall. A simple misinterpretation or lack of understanding can kill the best ideas. Its presence opens a wide frontier of possibility. A shared understanding of why new ideas are needed, how they benefit everyone, and why old ideas are harmful is the fuel for driving real innovation. The key is to recognize trust as something that is driven by discipline as well as inspiration. Again, this seems very contradictory in a principle that has been based solely on psychology and cognitive science. Yet, trust is based on knowledge and knowledge is based on creation, access, and interpretation. All of these features are rooted in the process, technology, and methods of the organization.

Chapter

07

Lean on Data

Numbers have life; they're not just symbols on paper.

—Shakuntala Devi

As suggested by the insightful quote of Shakuntala Devi, numbers have life. They tell stories and they take us places. They have taken people to the moon, they have helped us navigate the seas, and they tell us when things are going well and when they are not going so well. As a principle of breakthrough innovation, the ability to capture, formulate, and interpret data that is collected and experienced is critical. It also moves us further into the frontier of discipline. There are three important aspects of this activity: (1) *Linking* and aligning numbers, analytics, and performance indicators, (2) *Causal* interpretation of the linkages, and (3) *Determination* if the linkages are moving the organization toward the intended outcome. Innovative teams are well equipped for this activity because of their deep appreciation for stories (interpretation) and knowledge (numbers and context). Plus, the trait of resourcefulness places emphasis on gathering only the signs, data points, or stories that are most relevant while leaving unneeded information behind. Leaning on data is rooted in the ability to identify systems of numbers and relationships that link the efforts of the group to success measure and then to the intended objective. It can be thought of as choosing the compass that not only signals direction but also signals how well you are doing in progressing toward the objective. I conceptualize the activity as a "chain of logic". This chain links the initiatives of the organization with intended objectives. As developed, it is a system that may be viewed differently in theory and in numbers, its logic may shift over time, and organizations may or may not reconnoiter these chains as conditions change. Recalibrating a chain of logic is not easy. As I saw on a bumper sticker one day, "Change is good, you go first!" Yet, to be innovative is to know when shifts occur and how they impact the organizational chain of logic. Let's develop these concepts in more detail.

Chains of Logic

Organizations and individuals build chains of logic for a number of endeavors. For example, an outcome of professional success might be linked with the initiatives of performing well in K-12, scoring well on college admission tests, gaining admission to a great university, earning an undergraduate degree, and maybe earning a master's or Ph.D. Along the way, you gather and generate data such as grades, rankings, and other endorsements. That data then becomes a system of analytics which are patterns of statistics and insights. Some of these analytics and other knowledge become key performance indicators. As long as that chain is valid, then you can accurately calibrate your initiatives with your intended outcome. More so, you can measure your progress against others seeking similar outcomes. Universities should also observe this chain among learners and align their chain of logic accordingly. This is important; chains of logic live within codependent ecosystems. As long as there is harmony, then all is understood and all is predictable. This is illustrated in Figure 1.

To be fair, I have taken a very general view in describing and illustrating a chain of logic. The amount and sophistication of psychology and the amount and sophistication of numbers are far greater than that depicted. When interactions between numbers and psychology are added, then the equation gets very complex. However, the key point to remember is that

Figure 1: A Chain of Logic

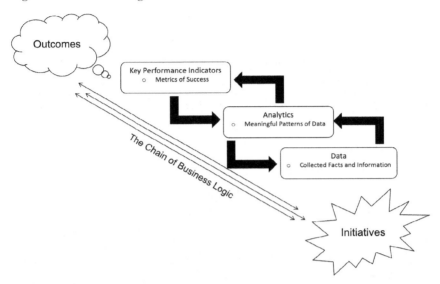

individuals and organizations develop targeted outcomes. To achieve the outcome, they create and launch a set of initiatives. They then set up a system of measurement to calibrate what they do (initiatives) with what they want to achieve (outcomes). How this is done is sometimes the work of genius and, sometimes, not so much. A story will illustrate the point.

Recently, the National Football League experienced a labor dispute with the NFL Referees Association. This resulted in a "lockout" of regular referees. In their place, "replacement" referees were used to officiate the first three weeks of the NFL season. As the replacement officials began missing calls, a powerful chain of logic began to take shape. If the owners would settle with the union, then the regular officials could return to the field and the excessive missed calls would stop. The outcome, better officiating, would be realized if the owners seized the initiative to settle with the union. The performance part of the chain is simply correct play calling. I became intrigued and wondered if the chain and its interpretation were valid. The logic seemed to indicate that the chain was intact and predictable until replacement officials were introduced. It was not difficult to get data on NFL officiating. Granted, it was not perfect data, but it was possible to see definitive trends in officiating (1970 until 2018) and if the change in officials resulted in a dramatic increase in bad calls. The results were very telling. Officiating had steadily become worse over the years. In addition, the number of questionable calls by replacement officials was not statistically different from what would have been expected from regular officials.[1] Why? My guess is that the game has become more sophisticated over the years. Again, an artifact of adding rules, replays, and other distractions to the game. In addition, players are now superathletes. Coaches are very sophisticated in creating offensive and defensive schemes. This has made the additive rules difficult to apply. Basically, the sophistication of the game has made it very difficult to officiate. Yes, the replacement officials may have had a higher predisposition to miss a call, but the storm of news coverage that demonized them missed the underlying problem that still haunts the game. The NFL owners settled the lockout, but the bad officiating continues to this day.[2]

Setting a valid chain of logic begins with defining the right outcome. As noted in the chapter on being ambitious, it is tempting to define an outcome that is too localized and too small. For example, it was not Apple's intention in the iPod project to build a device. Instead, the outcome was to revolutionize the experience of listening to music.[3] Through their process of breakthrough innovation, this experience manifested itself in the capability to acquire, store, and listen to any music you wanted wherever you wanted — ten thousand songs at your fingertip, wherever you might be. Once you have the right outcome, then initiatives and objectives are easier to put into place. The logic of the chain starts to build and come into focus. Finally, systems of measurement tell you if the progress is efficient and if you are on course. This sequence is very important. Too many times, organizations will start with initiatives, set

---

[1]Kevin Clark, The NFL Replacement Ref Audit, *Wall Street Journal*, September 19, 2012.
[2]Jason Gay, Is This a Stolen Super Bowl? Well...., *Wall Street Journal*, January 27, 2019.
[3]Leander Kahney, *The Cult of iPod*, No Starch Press, 2005.

systems of measurement, and then acquire the target. Ironically, this sometimes works. However, it is not a viable strategy for true innovation. Although it is tempting to declare victory once you develop a perfectly aligned chain of logic, the idea chase is not fully over. The final lap in the mile is to build adaptability into the chain. Sometimes, the once dependable outcome will shift, or the recipe of initiatives that achieved an outcome no longer works, or the system of measurement is no longer reliable. Similar to the emergence of superathletes, sophisticated coaches, and complex rules in the NFL, a fundamental shift occurs. This may lead to a need to reconfigure a chain of logic.

Shifting Outcomes

The school of disruption provides a great perspective for understanding dramatic shifts in outcomes.[4] This innovation idea is one we want to keep but we will modify it just a bit. The basic idea is that established organizations can lose their place to unexpected competitors. Borrowing from these ideas, let's shift the focus away from new competitors to outcomes. In any organizational situation, there is the possibility that a perfectly aligned chain of logic can be shaken by a shift in outcome. This shift can be due to technology, preferences, or newly discovered ways of working. This is illustrated in Figure 2.

The story begins in a very positive way. An incumbent organization has identified an outcome that is ambitious and has launched a set of initiatives that enable it to achieve the outcome. Systems of measurement are accurate and reliable. As the organization achieves more success and perfects the chain of logic, the outcome becomes almost mythical. It is impossible to imagine other outcomes and other chains. Yet, on the radar screen appears an alternative chain of logic. The alternative sequence operates in the incumbent's sphere of influence but seems nonsensical. It may hit a different outcome with

---

[4]Clayton Christenson, The Innovators, Dilemma: When New Technologies Cause Great Firms to Fail, *Harvard Business Review Press*, 2015.

Figure 2: Shifting Outcomes and Chains of Logic

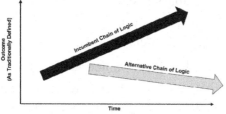

An incumbent Chain of Logic improves over time. Initiatives appear to be aligned with outcomes and systems of measurement. Alternative Chains of Logic that exhibit different patterns of alignment and chase different outcomes appear inferior and foolish.

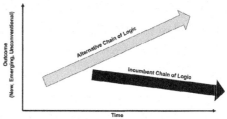

The Alternative Chain of Logic matches an emerging, important, and new outcome. The chain improves dramatically over time as the outcome gains momentum. The Incumbent Chain of Logic is an ill fit for the new outcome. The more it is fortified the worse it performs.

a very different alignment of initiatives and measurement systems. Think of a soda such as Coca-Cola as the incumbent and a bottle of water as the alternative. In this case, sugar, caffeine, and formula are the targeted outcome of Coke. Water seems strangely inadequate and nonsensical when measured against this outcome. The magic is that water is hitting a new, emerging, and important alternative outcome. That outcome is hydration. When we replace the incumbent outcome of sugar, caffeine, and formula with the alternative outcome of hydration, then the alternative chain of logic dominates the incumbent chain. This represents a fundamental shift in logic or disruption. The ability to sense these dynamics and adapt accordingly is part of the innovative perspective. These shifts can occur in almost any aspect of commerce, medicine, or life. The key is to keep an eye on outcomes and not technology, media, or other embodiments or vehicles of outcome. The critical question is as follows: What is the fundamental outcome that drives this organization and is it important?

Three Deadly Responses

As illustrated in Figure 3, when a significant shift in outcome occurs, it becomes necessary to recast the chain of logic. The theory of disruptive innovation suggests that chains are more easily invented than adjusted. Therefore, it will be the new, entrepreneurial organization that sees the new outcome and orchestrates the chain of logic to meet it. However, it is also possible that incumbent organizations assemble or improvise a chain of logic for an outcome that suddenly appears. This is the magic of information symmetry. Also, remember the school of fast following we discussed earlier? It sometimes works! That said, reading the tea leaves of a shifting outcome is tough and, yes, maybe in the past it was tougher for established organizations. Today, the balance is different. The margin of error for finding the next breakthrough is not as low for the start-ups and not as high for established organizations. Plus, once the new frontier is discovered, holding it exclusively for a long period of time is not guaranteed. This is a new artifact of information transparency, big data, and artificial intelligence. Market dynamics that were once hidden

Figure 3: Shifting Models of Logic

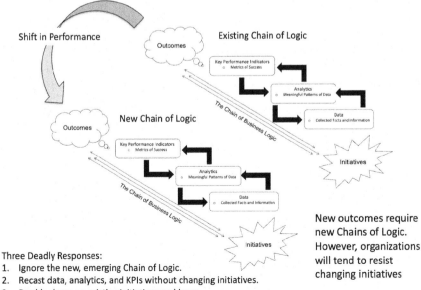

Three Deadly Responses:
1. Ignore the new, emerging Chain of Logic.
2. Recast data, analytics, and KPIs without changing initiatives.
3. Double down on existing initiatives and hope.

New outcomes require new Chains of Logic. However, organizations will tend to resist changing initiatives are now revealed for all to see. So, there is now a more even playing field for the start-up and the established organization; a more equal chance to miss or hit the next wave of shifting outcome. That is tough news for innovators and incumbents. It builds in a tendency to follow and correct mistakes rather than lead and make mistakes. Particularly, when all the world is a stage. Therefore, there will be a strong gravitational pull toward staying with the familiar and resisting the new, emerging chain of logic. In those instances, three deadly responses are likely.

The first deadly response is to ignore and maybe ridicule the new chain of logic. Leadership might even go so far as to say that organizations, customers, and employees love us so much that chasing a new outcome would be more dangerous than staying the course. I call this the "Sears Mistake". Sears was a powerhouse of U.S. retail for many years, an incredibly profitable business. The symbol of their prominence was the "Sears Tower" in Chicago. However, despite the success, changing demographics, styles, and the emergence of online retail created an outcome that Sears was unable to chase. Leadership was not blind to these changes; Amazon is a very hard business model to miss. However, they dramatically underestimated the magnitude and direction of the shift. Plus, to be fair, they were "coaxed" into keeping their chain of logic by employees, suppliers, and industry experts. The signs were in clear sight, the principle of leaning on data was not in place. Kodak, Nokia, Blockbuster, Commodore, Borders, Sony Walkman, Yahoo!, and Hummer are all examples of this deadly response. It is easier to fall into this trap than one might imagine.

The second deadly response is to recast the data analytics and performance indicators so that they tell you things are great. The contradiction between what has worked and falling performance is overwhelming for some organizations. To resolve the contradiction, they adjust the metrics. The initiatives and the faltering outcome of the chain remain the same; however, the organization thinks it is doing well. I call this the "Nortel Mistake". Nortel was a world leader in telecommunication technology. However, when the network revolution took shape, voice and data converged into digital signals, and new network technology dominated the marketplace. The leader of the new revolution was Cisco. Rather than adopting the new logic, subtracting old ideas, and adding better ones, Nortel recast its compass such that its way of doing business still seemed solid. In essence, the organization changed the schemes of measurement to make alignment of initiatives and outcomes seem logical. The contradiction is seemingly resolved. The problem is that the financial markets did not buy the rationale and Nortel lost all of its market value, a dramatic fall from grace. Again, leadership was not blind. There was no surprise. The company lost its sense of direction and more importantly its ability to adapt. Facebook has done this repeatedly in developing new features for its platform.[5] It is so bad for Facebook that its best new innovations (Instagram and WhatsApp) were invented somewhere else and then acquired. Facebook seems unable to grasp and focus on the shifting outcomes of users of social media. Yet, its system of analytics tells it that all is well. IBM (PC), Toshiba (electronics), Coca-Cola (water), and even Google (Google Glass) have fallen into this same trap of recasting analytics in the name of justifying a faltering chain of logic.

A third deadly response is to believe that more throttle on the existing chain will produce results. I call this the "Xerox Mistake". I saw this mistake firsthand when working with Xerox as a consultant. Xerox was losing its share in copiers and printers. Cloud networks, Adobe Acrobat, and digital storage were shifting the outcome of document management. Instead of competing against this landscape, the company doubled down on pushing its sales force. This tactic had no effect. Even the best salespeople could not sell into the declining marketplace. Companies simply did not want the equipment. They were looking for digital and software solutions. Adobe had shifted the marketplace of documents, electronic signatures, and contracting — a world that Xerox was not created for and a world for which Xerox would not recreate itself. This

---

[5]Farhad Manjoo, Facebook Has an Innovation Problem, *The New York Times*, February 10, 2022.

response is more prominent than one might believe at first glance. As I experienced, if someone points this out to a hard-charging leader, it is not easy and brings a very swift rebuke. Yet, whipping a dead horse is no recipe for making it run faster.

A team or community with the right mentality for finding the breakthrough will avoid these mistakes. Adaptation is part of the fabric woven into all aspects of the chain of logic. Even in the best of times, there is an undercurrent of belief that nothing lasts forever. Adding, subtracting, modifying, and recreating are always on the radar. In fact, this belief is a foundation for finding new and exciting sources of opportunity. Evolving science, new ways of exchanging data, and the creation of knowledge are seen as something very necessary to evolve and adapt chains of logic. This is not something to be feared. It is something expected, welcomed, and shaped. It is the adjustment made at halftime when the game plan is not working. The search for a new job when the one you have is not meeting your financial or career aspirations. The request for a second opinion to make sure you get the medical care you need. It is an important principle. So, how do we see the new outcome? The obvious answer is in the data, analytics, and performance indicators. They should signal trouble if we believe them. However, there is something more than numbers that makes the task tough. There is the prevailing body of conventional wisdom. This is the collection of beliefs about the chain of logic that is based on experience, credentials, and sometimes outright opinion. The comingling of numbers and conventional wisdom is complex and can often lead to strange decisions. Let's take a closer look.

Conventional Wisdom and Numbers

One of the most interesting aspects of leaning on data is the marriage of *conventional wisdom* (expert opinion, accepted practice, commentary) with *numbers* (data, metrics).[6] Every chain of logic will have numbers that

---

[6]Joan Magretta, Why Business Models Matter, *Harvard Business Review*, 80(5), June 2002.

attest to its effectiveness and relevance. These can be measures of voter approval, growth in market share, winning percentage, etc. In essence, any quantifiable measure of performance. There is also conventional wisdom. This is the opinion, view of the world, or perspective of experts, academics, and leaders in the field. It can also be a stream of beliefs that run through an organization. It is not entirely based on fact and sometimes involves a lot of extrapolating from the past, building on fading ideas, and a lot of speculation about the future. It can also emerge over time without formal validation. There is nothing wrong with conventional wisdom as long as it is recognized as such. It is fascinating and it is many times a part of knowledge that is debatable. However, it is also powerful and something that can be shaped to create a context for poor decision-making. Together, numbers and conventional wisdom frame the perception of effectiveness for a chain of logic. However, there is a paradox. Conventional wisdom does not always align with numbers. Experts may praise and promote a chain of logic that does not perform well in numbers. They might also condemn an emerging chain of logic that is performing well by the numbers. To add to the complexity, conventional wisdom will tend to trail numbers in yielding an accurate assessment. In other words, the chain of logic will show promise or problems in the numbers before it shows promise or problems in conventional wisdom. This can create uncertainty in assessing the validity of the chain.

To help shape this frontier, let's frame these possibilities as a matrix of wisdom, numbers, and logic. It is called the "Paradox Matrix" and it is illustrated in Figure 4. Using this tool, it is possible to get a better sense of what is working and what is failing in conventional wisdom and numbers. The principle of leaning on data is rooted in understanding the potential alignment and disconnect between these two frames of performance. The disconnects can be dramatic. One of the disconnects is a path toward opportunity that is revealed in numbers but not in wisdom. The other is a path of failure revealed in numbers but not in wisdom.

Figure 4: The Paradox Matrix: Conventional Wisdom, Numbers, and Logic

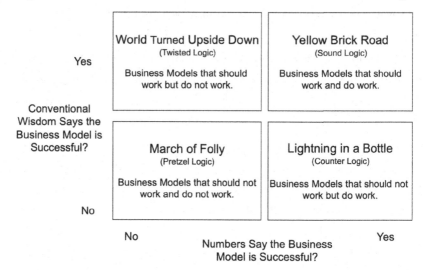

When wisdom and numbers indicate that a chain of logic is successful, then *Sound Logic* prevails. As illustrated, this frontier is called the *Yellow Brick Road*. This space represents the current "state of the art". Professors in MBA classrooms will praise these businesses, and the stock market also rewards them with strong valuation. Certain political campaigns will be lauded by the political pundits, and those candidates will win elections. Professional sports teams follow chains of logic in acquiring players and coaches, and developing ways of playing that are heralded by sportswriters, and those teams win championships. In short, there is a strong alignment between the experts and the realized numbers. This does not mean it will last forever. However, in the present environment, these chains of logic are sound and solid.

At the other extreme, chains of logic in which wisdom and numbers indicate a lack of success are called a *March of Folly*. Although it seems illogical, some wayward organizations will attempt to implement these chains. The reason for this is *Pretzel Logic*, a system of logic that supports a nonsensical conclusion, primarily, a belief that the outcome will be somehow different for the perpetrator because of special insights or capabilities. This is very seldom true. Custer's last stand against the Lakota Nation is a vivid example of this logic. The U.S. housing bubble, and subsequent recession, is another great example. This crisis was caused by the inability of a large number of homeowners to pay their mortgages as their low-introductory-rate mortgages reverted to regular interest rates. Risky lending, easy money, and fraud were known to be trouble, the numbers backed it up, but the train kept rolling until the bubble burst.[7] Some believe the mistake is now being repeated. Even very innovative organizations can make this mistake. Apple's attempt to add music by the rock band U2 to the iTunes account of all their customers without their customers' consent is a shining example.[8] Whenever you hear the phrases *it will be different for us, they did not know what we know*, or *the world has changed since then*, be aware. A March of Folly might lie ahead.

When wisdom signals success but the numbers signal trouble, the result is a *World Turned Upside Down*. This is a very dangerous frontier. Yet, some organizations will attempt this chain believing the signal of conventional wisdom is more accurate than the numbers. The organization is "coaxed" into staying with a chain of logic that is fading. In this context, *twisted logic* prevails. Everything that once worked for an organization begins to work against it or *all you know is wrong*. The typical origin of this situation is the belief that a yellow brick road chain is transferable to any context. The use of World War II fighting tactics in the jungles of Vietnam was a very stark example of this logic for the United States Military. Wal-Mart's unsuccessful entry into Germany and other European countries is an example of this twisted logic in today's context of business. Steaming media which basically turns the old model of news and entertainment upside down still creates challenges for traditional broadcasters. The

---

[7]Alan Greenspan, The Roots of the Mortgage Crisis, *Wall Street Journal*, December 12, 2007.
[8]Erik Sherman, Apple's $100 Million U2 Debacle, *CBS News*, September 17, 2014.

song "A World Turned Upside Down" was played by the musicians of the British Army as they surrendered to Washington at Yorktown. If you hear the phrases *it worked then so it will work now, it works here so it will work there,* or *this should work,* you may be embarking upon the strange frontier of the Upside Down.

The most interesting context of shifting chains of logic is *Lightning in a Bottle. Counter logic* prevails in this situation because wisdom suggests failure while the numbers signal success. This is the favored frontier of the most innovative organizations. This is also where the decoupling of wisdom and numbers is most important. As Wilber and Orville Wright experimented with their flying machines at the turn of the century, many leading experts ridiculed and scoffed at their efforts. Yet, their experiments yielded data and results that defied much of conventional wisdom. Although they were two brothers from nowhere, bicycle makers, and not part of the intellectual elite, they demonstrated every aspect of the innovative principles in their process of invention — particularly, a mastery of logic that matched their initiatives to outcomes.[9] Something as simple as a bottle of water or as grandiose as a website that allows you to purchase anything you want from anywhere you might be is a powerful reminder that "lightning-in-the-bottle" types of initiatives can completely recast prevailing chains of logic. From running a four-minute mile to the exploration of Pluto, many great feats are built on belief in the numbers and the audacity to challenge conventional wisdom.[10]

This paradox matrix, and its way of framing the logic of performance, is a very powerful tool for rationalizing numbers, analytics, and emerging business models. It incorporates realized numbers (what we see) and reconciles them with prevailing wisdom (what we interpret). This can then lead to critical introspection of chains of logic and the context in which

---

[9]David McCullough, *The Wright Brothers*, Simon and Schuster, 2015.
[10]Bill Taylor, What the Four Minute Mile Taught Us About the Limits of Conventional Thinking, *Harvard Business Review*, March 2018.

they live. After all, it is very easy to assume that conventional wisdom leads data. It is not true. The signal will show up first in data, but it is up to the innovator to believe what they see. This is particularly true if an expert or senior leader is cheerleading an idea that is fading or has failed. Data is not the most glamorous part of the innovation story, but the most innovative organizations and leaders gather it meticulously. They develop alternative interpretations for the data, gather more data and expertise, and finally determine the right set of cause-and-effect relationships. It is easy to collect data. Almost any organization can do this well. The secret is to interpret it. This is where the additive effect of the principles discussed earlier comes in to play. Ambition, chemistry, roles, and trust leverage the collection of data so that the stories it tells are revealed, believed, and form the basis of an effective response.

In this chapter, we have viewed the principle of leaning on data from the perspective of logic. Organizations set up chains of initiatives, systems of measurement, and targeted outcomes as a means of rationalizing their existence. When these chains are in harmony, then the organization is on the right course and it can have confidence that any adjustments that need to be made will be signaled and quickly implemented. To do more than average is to seek the right outcome, choose initiatives that are logically consistent with achieving the outcome, and create a compass that keeps the organization on the course. It is also the ability to adapt new chains when they are needed, abandon chains when they are failing, or modify a chain that is struggling. Wisdom and numbers interact in strange ways to confound the building of good logic. Yet, there is huge opportunity for those organizations that realistically assess current logic and can envision the prevailing logic that will be needed in the coming waves of technological, scientific, and business innovation. Numbers tell stories and play a very important role in the idea chase. This interplay of numbers and stories is a perfect manifestation of the harmonic power of inspiration and discipline.

Show Perseverance

We fight, get beat, rise, and fight again.
— General Nathanael Greene,
United States Continental Army, 1778

The small town of Camden, South Carolina, is not a place many people can find on a map. It is an old city by United States standards with parks, squares, a city hall, kind people, and lots of beautiful trees. Although it might not be as famous as Boston, New York, or Philadelphia, an incredible event that helped Americans achieve their independence took place about six miles north of the town in August of 1780. It is known as the Battle of Camden. A significant force of the Continental army and militia led by General Horatio Gates met a well-trained British Force led by Lord Cornwallis. It was a miserable defeat for the Continentals. Many tactical mistakes were made and the grand army simply disintegrated. General Gates abandoned the field and rode horseback seventy miles without stopping. Whether his ride was a result of fear, cowardice, or good horsemanship is still a topic of debate by historians. So why was this so important? Because after the debacle, General George Washington named Nathanael Greene the Commanding General of the southern forces. Greene was a master of tactics, a detailed planner, and a realist — the perfect profile to find the needed breakthrough. Unlike Gates, Greene knew that the key to eventual victory wasn't to win grand battles, it was to endure. This was particularly true because the British were operating far from home in a very inhospitable part of the world. Practicing unconventional warfare, Greene harassed the British, yet lost several battles. However, in doing so, he weakened the British army. Lord Cornwallis said of Greene, "No General has gained more by losing Battles!". His army's endurance and tactics pushed Cornwallis out of the Deep South. This eventually led to the capture of Cornwallis' army at Yorktown. Greene's mindset was out of the ordinary, his accomplishments were extraordinary, he found the constellation in the stars, and the principle of breakthrough innovation that was in action was that of perseverance.

Perseverance is well placed on the discipline side of our innovation continuum. This does not mean inspiration is absent. It does mean that discipline is a bit more dominant. The reason for this is that breakthrough ideas are inherently risky. The more risk that is added to the organization, the greater the tension. The greater the tension, the more perseverance that is required to keep the initiative moving. Therefore, the leadership mandate is to manage risk and, in doing so, drive out organizational tension. The initial part of a project and its concluding part are easy. The most difficult part of a project and where perseverance is most critical is in the middle. Many times, what is desperately needed in the middle is faith. It is when times get tough, the odds seem long, and minutes seem like hours that "faith in the middle" keeps the energy flowing. This faith has two foundations. The first is a disciplined method for managing risky projects. Projects have sequences, priorities, and critical paths. They also have risk factors that make them more likely or less likely to stray from the plan. A shared understanding of these operational characteristics and risk factors is critical for creating a predisposition for success. The second foundation is more psychological. Breakthrough projects have numerous impacts on people, processes, and other projects. Being familiar with perseverance as means of setting expectations, handling the unexpected, and improvising set the stage for instilling faith when trouble appears.

And, when you are working on bigger ideas, it will appear. Again, we see the wonderful interplay of inspiration and discipline. The rigor of managing the project and the art of managing the people create a spirit of perseverance which, in turn, protects the momentum. Let's look first at the dimensions of perseverance and then the practice of risk management.

Dimensions of Perseverance

As illustrated in Figure 1, perseverance is built on three interrelated principles: *persistence, endurance,* and *patience.* This is the part of the idea chase that is almost never discussed. It does not fit the attractive story of quick ideas and instant success. The reality is that ideas are elusive. Ideas hide in the noise and distraction of everyday life. They are threatening and they may challenge assumptions. In their early forms, ideas are more like ugly ducklings than beautiful swans. Unlike conventional paths, non-conventional paths are full of winding turns and unexpected detours. Victory is not easy. The breakthrough idea is something that is hard-won and earned. All of this speaks to the attribute of *persistence.* Continuing forward in the face of difficulty is tough for any organization or individual. It is easy to lose faith, to turn back, or to simply give up. African-American track star Wilma Rudolph suffered scarlet fever, whooping cough, and measles, survived infantile paralysis, and required a leg brace until age nine. She went on to win three Olympic gold medals and was considered

Figure 1: Dimensions of Perseverance

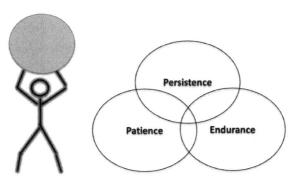

the "Fastest woman on Earth". J.K. Rowling became the world's best-selling children's author despite living on governmental benefits as a single mother. Initially, her manuscript for Harry Potter was rejected by several publishers. The lessons from these amazing women are the same as those of successful marathon runners and mountain climbers. Develop a clear picture of the destination, develop a well-defined path toward its achievement, and develop a set of milestones to gauge progress. In the most innovative organizations, setbacks are not only expected but are also welcomed. Hardship is a chance to demonstrate the full capability of the organization and make it stronger.

Endurance is the ability to not "break" under pressure. It speaks to the strength and grit of an organization or individual as they face hardship. It also speaks to the "grace" or "style" in which the hardship is handled. Even today, with advanced foods, radios, and insulated clothing, a journey on foot across Antarctica is one of the harshest tests a human being can be asked to endure. A hundred years ago, it was worse. Then, wool clothing absorbed snow and damp. High-energy food came in an unappetizing mix of rendered fats called pemmican. Worst of all, extremes of cold pervaded everything. During a scientific expedition in the Antarctic in 1912–13, Douglas Mawson lost his colleagues 300 mi from safety. Frostbite and starvation caused his hair, nails, skin, and the entire soles of his feet to fall off during a grueling two-month trek back to camp. At one point, Mawson fell down a crevasse and was left dangling in the abyss from a rope. He dragged his crippled body up and continued on the trek. Mawson's journey has gone down in the annals of polar exploration as probably the most terrible ever undertaken in Antarctica. Yet, when he returned to camp, he sent a message back to his fiancée in Australia. A short message, but one so understated it could only have been written by one of those epic heroes of the age of Antarctic exploration.[1] There was no complaint or self-pity. No mention of the horrors he had just endured. It read, *Deeply regret delay, Only just managed to reach hut*. So, what are some of the lessons

---

[1]Bear Grylls, *True Grit*, Bantam Press, 2013, London, UK.

of endurance from Mawson? First, be prepared. There is no way he could have survived without being prepared for the ordeal he never dreamed would happen. His stamina, know-how, and tenacity were all there before he undertook the journey. Second, have slack resources available. Clothing, ropes, and tools that met the anticipated and unanticipated pieces of his ordeal were on hand and critical to his survival. The final lesson is calm. Not only is endurance part of breakthrough innovation, but also the way it is handled in terms of fortitude, grace, and control is important in achieving elusive outcomes.

Patience is perhaps the most understated yet important characteristic of any innovative effort. Great victories take time and that requires patience. Yet, we live in a world of fast results, express shipping, and video on demand. There is nothing wrong with any of those things, in moderation. However, because of those things, we may all be losing the ability to practice patience and the situation may only get worse. We do not like to wait. In fact, patience is often viewed as a sign of weakness. Yet, patience is a hallmark of finding great ideas.[2] Like endurance, patience speaks to how we respond to delay or an undesired consequence. However, with patience, it is the emotional response that is in focus. An individual or organization demonstrates patience when it responds to delay or adversity without getting angry or engaging other negative emotional consequences. In an episode of Mr. Rogers' Neighborhood, Fred Rogers wanted viewers to hear what it sounded like when the fish in his on-set aquarium ate their food. He called in a marine biologist to install a microphone in the tank, but the biologist grew impatient when the fish weren't eating. They could have re-recorded the scene, but Rogers kept it in as a lesson in patience and the appreciation of silence. Patience requires an ability to see things from several perspectives, to remain calm in the face of calamity, and to quickly adjust expectations. Experimentation, scientific problem-solving approaches, and great knowledge flow can assist in developing

---

[2]Christina Bielaszka-DuVernay, The Balance Needed to Lead Change, *Harvard Business Review*, September 16, 2008.

organizational patience. Also, it is important not to mistake patience for lack of speed. Patience improves speed. Rather than redoing reckless decisions, the organization gets it right the first time.

So, if obstacles are going to appear, is walking through them the only remedy available? Actually, the answer is "no". There is the reactive part of persevering that deals with enduing an obstacle and there is a proactive part that identifies potential obstacles and develops coping strategies. The proactive part is risk management. It is possible to foresee challenges ahead, real and imagined. There can be very obvious gaps in the requirements of an endeavor and an organization's capabilities. It is also possible to see dragons and fire ahead when such things are not a threat. The goal of risk management is to objectively reconcile the requirements with the capabilities and develop a way to cope. This is not easy. There is a tendency to overestimate the capabilities of an organization and underestimate the difficulty of an endeavor. There are countless stories of failed software implementations to back up this claim.[3] To persevere, an honest evaluation of an endeavor's riskiness must be established. This serves three purposes. First, the organization can prepare for the challenges ahead. Second, through this process, we can understand more about the organization's propensity for taking on risky endeavors. If the only endeavors that are attempted are low risk, then there is a strong likelihood of low-innovative outcomes. Finally, developing risk profiles of projects allows the organization to track them over time. This gives insight into the organization's capacity to mitigate risk. In the following section, let's explore a framework for developing and tracking the risk profile of projects. It is the place where innovative discipline is critical.

Risk Management

Risk is an unfortunate but likely consequence of any ambitious endeavor. While there are many stories and articles that tout "fast innovation" and

---

[3]A.H. Segars and D. Chaterjee, Diets that Don't Work: Where Enterprise Planning Goes Wrong, *Wall Street Journal*, August 23, 2010.

"failing fast", the experiences observed in highly innovative organizations are different. Breakthrough initiatives are tedious, cumbersome, and involve many setbacks. However, in keeping with the principle of ambition, setbacks are not cast as "failure" and there is no discussion of accepting failure as part of the journey. Rather, it is known by the group that there will be tough patches in the road and that patience and perseverance will be required to stay on course. Big ideas and new frontier rarely appear as a beautiful swan; instead, they are ugly ducklings. It is the goal of the group to turn the ugly ducklings into swans. To help in this process, it is useful to categorize an endeavor or project in terms of its predisposition for setbacks. Three broad dimensions of riskiness are as follows:

(1) *Structure*: How well understood is the problem? Are there paths of prior success? Has this been done before?
(2) *Technological Experience*: Do we have skills, resources, and "know-how" to address the problem?
(3) *Scope*: How big is the project? How encompassing is it to the organization? How much resource will be required?

Structure

Structure is a very tricky aspect of riskiness. In many endeavors, the bulk of time and effort is spent solving the problem and a minuscule amount of time is spent in defining the problem. It is also possible to believe that the problem is understood and a recipe is obvious when it is not.[4] In other words, there is a strong predisposition to overestimate the understanding of the problem to be solved. Some organizations may define the problem based solely on the recipes that they know. Further, there is also the mistaken belief that the sooner the project is started, the sooner it will be finished.[5] Speeding toward a solution or defining a problem based on an inventory of known solutions can actually waste time

---

[4]Dwayne Spradlin, Are You Solving the Right Problem? *Harvard Business Review*, September 2012.
[5]Strefan Thomke and Donald Reinerstsen, Six Myths of Product Development, *Harvard Business Review*, May 2012.

Figure 2: Problem Structure: Proof of Concept and Design

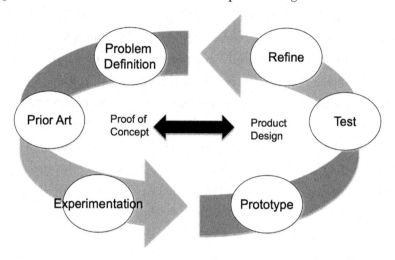

and resources. The magic in structuring the problem is knowing that you need to collect data to define the problem, not define the problem then collect data. It is a small but important nuance. There are a number of tools and techniques that help in this process. I will describe the approach commonly taken in innovative organizations; it is illustrated in Figure 2. In the innovative spirit of adding, subtracting, and modifying, the model has features of other frameworks, eliminates some cumbersome features, and simultaneously combines the important problem-solving phases of "proof of concept" and "design".

The process begins with building a "straw man" or first iteration of the problem definition. Quite likely, this will be stated in terms that are wordy or too complex. I see this all the time in my consulting endeavors. When I ask an organization what they are trying to achieve, the answer is usually a long narrative built on the words such as "change", "transformation", "velocity", "emerging technology", and "process". There is nothing wrong with any of these terms, but it becomes pretty obvious that there is no definitive problem definition, just buzzwords and a lot of PowerPoint slides. A good problem definition is stated in simpler terms. For example,

Apple's rally cry for iPod and iTunes was to "revolutionize the experience of listening to music". The device and download platform were avenues to achieve the objective but they were not part of the problem statement. Next, the organization should search for prior art. *Who has done this before? Are there examples we can follow?* Too often, the organization assumes that it is the only one to attempt the feat. Also, there is a strong tendency to localize the search for prior art. The search should include other contexts, other organizations, and similar situations that are far afield from the home base. There is a lot of knowledge and a lot of experience that is lost when the search from prior art is localized. Experimentation is the next phase. Here, cause-and-effect relationships are tested. Various versions of prior art are assessed. Myth is separated from fact. Together, problem definition, prior art, and experimentation provide a proof of concept. Questions such as *Is this the right problem?*", "*Is this important?*", and "*Is this achievable?* are addressed and come into focus.

In the design part of the process, the problem definition is operationalized as a project. Tasks, deadlines, and sequences of events, all the essential pieces of the puzzle, are developed. Prototyping is a critical aspect of this activity. A trial project may be launched, a test product built, or a collaborative arrangement tested. This not only brings an aspect of visualization to the project but also formally tests assumptions and assists in sharpening or redefining the problem statement. Testing extends prototyping by combining and subtracting attributes of various prototypes. The prototypes are also tested against a variety of conditions and constraints. Refinement is the process of improving and clarifying based on the results of testing and prototyping. Existing and new knowledge are then combined to sharpen or reshape the problem definition. Here, you can see clearly the important interplay between inspiration and discipline. This should not be a long or laborious process. However, it should be rigorous and should constitute a significant amount of the innovation effort. The give and take between "proof of concept" and "design" provide a useful context for conceptualizing, visualizing, and testing the structure and organizational understanding of any given problem. Solving this is not easy. However, success in the endeavor greatly lowers the risk of the project and creates important avenues in addressing the remaining two risk factors.

Technological Experience

Similar to structure, it is very easy to overestimate the organization's experience and capability to meet an innovation challenge. This is particularly true if the challenge lies outside organizational expertise but the organization does not recognize it as such. Likewise, it is easy to underestimate capability if the challenge is within the organization's expertise but is not recognized as such. Boundaries of expertise change over time and it is possible for an organization to lose and/or gain expertise unwittingly. If the organization has accurately developed proof of concept and design, then some idea of the skills, technologies, and resources needed should come into focus. Of course, the most readily available source of technological experience is within the organization. *Internal* capabilities can exist or they can be developed or acquired. Some of the world's most incredible inventions were the result of evolved internal capabilities. Flight, electricity, telecommunications, and automobiles were born from the efforts of self-trained inventors and invented organizations. Therefore, it is important to assess what current capabilities are and what they might become. *External* capabilities are those that exist beyond the organization's boundary. It is a collaboration or joint venture with organizations that might have the knowledge or capability to push a project forward. In its best form, collaboration can speed up project progress and reduce risk. However, it can also be an impediment if the external organization is not cooperative (i.e. not following the principles) or the project is so specialized that creating shared understanding is difficult. A third source of technological expertise is *combinatorial*. This can be internal or external. It is the resulting expertise or capability that results from combining capabilities. This may be the most difficult to define but the most powerful if it is identified. In super projects, where the goal is to deconstruct the human genome, explore Pluto, or photograph a black hole, combinational expertise is critical. Astronomers combined with Astrophysicists who are then combined with experts in Artificial Intelligence create knowledge and expertise that is beyond any individual person or group. Without it, the technical expertise needed for the Event Horizon Telescope cannot be realized. The same is true in projects that develop advanced robotics, genomics, or new treatments for the worst diseases. The right portfolio of internal, external, and combinatorial experience is a critical avenue for reducing the riskiness of the most innovative endeavors.

Scope

The final factor of risk is scope. This is the magnitude of the project in terms of budget, time, people, and impact. A great way to think about scope is in terms of *reach* and *range*.[6] This is illustrated in Figure 3.

Figure 3: Scope as Reach and Range

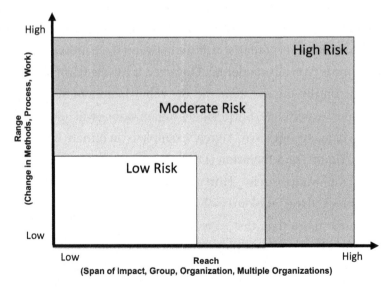

---

[6]Peter Keen, *Shaping the Future: Business Design Through Information Technology*, Harvard Business School Press, Boston, MA, 1991.

If a project encompasses multiple organizations, multiple boundaries, and multiple lines of authority, then *reach* is high and so is the level of risk. It becomes more difficult to coordinate and build needed systems of technology and process to successfully manage the project. Again, it is easier than one would think to mistake a project that has high reach for one that has low reach. Sometimes, coordinating two autonomous organizations is difficult. In addition, it is easy to underestimate where boundaries of autonomy exist within a large organization. Many software implementations have failed miserably because this aspect of scope was not understood. That said, it is also a mistake to scale a needed project because of obstacles in reconciling reach. *Range* can be thought of as the magnitude of change or adjustment in methods, work, or process needed to meet the challenge. If existing ways of work will not be unsettled, then the dimension of range is low and so is potential risk. However, if methods, processes, and ways of work will be changed to accommodate the endeavor, then range is high and so is risk. When reach and range are combined, then a portfolio of possible scope possibilities is revealed. Of course, when reach and range are high, then scope is high and so is potential risk. Conversely, when reach and range are low, then scope is low and so is potential risk. In between is a cautionary frontier where scope is typically moderate. However, it can also drift low or high depending on the organization and the other factors of structure and technological experience. Surprisingly, organizations will underestimate the scope of a new initiative. A great example is an initiative to improve Diversity, Equity, and Inclusion (DEI). It is very easy to frame such an initiative as a hiring exercise. Hire more people from underrepresented communities and the problem is solved. However, as a form of innovation, DEI is much more than that; it is transforming the organization such that true meritocracy is visible, consistent, equitable, and available to all. The reach and range of DEI are high as are the potential benefits. Yet, in many organizations, the reach and range are cast as low, leaving the most transformative aspects of the initiative and its breakthrough benefits unrealized.

Once an assessment of scope, structure, and technological experience is complete, then it is possible to understand the overall riskiness of the project. Not only is it a good idea to determine where an individual project falls in terms of risk but is also useful to plot the project within the portfolio of other organizational projects so that the amount of total risk becomes known. As mentioned earlier, one project will impact other projects. A high amount of total project risk creates tension, yet it is also a sign of true innovativeness. The key is to know this and actively manage it. Conversely, the organization might see that it carries little risk. This can be a sign of complacency or an inability to handle a project that creates tension. Most importantly, plotting the riskiness of a project sounds the alarm for interventions and preparation needed for eventual success. This is the heart of perseverance. It is the same thought process of individuals and teams that explore the Antarctic, the depths of the seas, and bring breakthrough products to life. Leaning more on the disciple side of innovation, let's use the three dimensions to create a Project Risk Portfolio which can then be used for anticipating and managing risk. It is presented in Figure 4.

Figure 4: Project Risk Portfolio

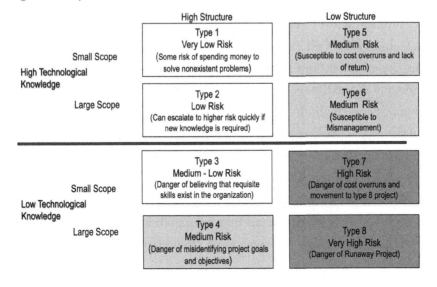

As illustrated, a project will take on a certain "Type" from 1 to 7 based on its position with respect to Technological Knowledge, Problem Structure, and Scope. A very noticeable characteristic of innovative organizations is their careful attention to this aspect of the process. There is consistent monitoring of a project's status and its progress through the matrix. Also, all projects and even pieces of projects are known and understood in terms of their riskiness. The inspirational touch from the analysis is these seven important rules:

(1) Too many Type 7 or 8 Projects are Trouble.
(2) Too many Type 1 or 2 Projects are Trouble.
(3) Type 7 and 8 Projects need to be managed toward Type 1 or 2.
(4) Type 1 and 2 Projects should not become Type 7 or 8.
(5) Type 5 and 6 Projects are potential opportunities to leverage know-how.
(6) Type 3 and 4 Projects require a "helping hand".
(7) Numerous projects clustered Northwest, Northeast, Southeast, or Southwest may indicate a project management problem.

Keeping the rules in mind, let's take a tour of the Project Risk Portfolio. If a project measures low on problem structure, high on scope, and low on technological skill, then it is the riskiest. We call these Type 8 projects. The organization does not have requisite skills, the problem is not well understood, and the scope is broad. If we change the dimension of scope from large to small, then it becomes a Type 7 project. Scope is smaller but the organization still lacks technological skill and problem definition. The project is still very risky. Both of these projects live in the Southeast part of the portfolio. Too many of these projects may tax the endurance of an organization. Tension mounts and uncertainty may set in. Also, if a project "spins" in the Southeast for too long, then it may drain resources from other endeavors. Runaway projects and tied-up resources become a serious threat.

It is quite likely that many organizations will "pass" on such projects, opting instead for something less risky and more of a sure bet. The assumption is that risk is something to be avoided. Ironically, this reasoning may not always be sound; by passing, the organization may be yielding good ground to a rival. Most breakthrough endeavors begin as a Type 7 or 8. Of course, a rival will also see the project as a Type 8 but, rather than run, they will actively take it on and then reposition it so that it is less of a threat. For example, the iPhone would have initially appeared as a Type 8 project to Apple. At that time, Apple was not clear about what the market valued (low structure), Apple had few partners or little know-how in telecommunication (low technological skill), and the scope of the project was large. The device was a sea change for the organization. Yet, the company was extremely efficient in deconstructing each risk factor and eventually moving the project to safer ground (Type 1 or 2). In the case of Apple, the structure of the problem seemed to be addressed first. This involved developing an outcome for the project in terms of how people use information and how technology was converging. They then leaped over the technological hurdle by partnering with AT&T. Finally, the project was divided into logical phases and prioritized to meet the challenges of scope.[7] Importantly, there is no single prescribed path in moving a Type 8 project to a Type 1 or 2 project. At least I did not see it in my research. However, there is always a concerted effort to "manage" a risky project to safer ground by directly addressing the three dimensions of risk. Even if the Type 8 project is creating tension, the active signs that leadership is managing away risk will create the persistence, patience, and endurance that are needed to keep going.

If a project measures low in scope, has high structure, and the organization has high technological knowledge, then it is a Type 1. These projects are the least risky. If the scope is changed from small

---

[7]Brian Merchant, *The One Device: The Secret History of the iPhone*, Little, Brown and Company, 2017, Boston, MA.

to large, then the project is a Type 2. In this instance, the scope has become riskier, but overall project risk is still low. The home of these projects is in the Northwest frontier of the portfolio. The Northwest is a magnet for any organization. It is known as the "home run ball", "the low-hanging fruit", or "the no brainer". The organization is skilled, the problem is known, and the scope is manageable. In many less innovative organizations that I have consulted with, this part of the portfolio is heavily populated, and the drive is to keep adding more. The obvious problem is that at some point the real innovation lies elsewhere. Too many Northwest projects are a manifest sign of complacency and, quite simply, a lack of organizational courage. Interestingly, when there is a dramatic shift (new chain of logic), these projects can turn into Type 7 and 8. This is a definitive outcome of organizations that find themselves in a "World Turned Upside Down" situation. For example, the projects in retail that were low-risk Type 1 and 2 for Sears became increasingly risky when online retailing shifted the marketplace. To be fair, Type 1 and 2 projects can be great endeavors. Sometimes, just a tweak or a minor adjustment is all that is needed for a great strategic endeavor. However, too many Type 1 or 2 projects may narrow the vision of the organization and the skill sets needed to take on more difficult endeavors. This creates a very strong predisposition to keep adding Type 1 and 2 projects rather than subtracting them. Again, this form of additive innovation builds on old ideas and it is not likely to lead toward something that is breakthrough.

A project that measures high in technological knowledge, low in scope, and low in problem structure is a Type 5. If the scope turns from small to large, then it is a Type 6. These projects occupy the Northeast part of the portfolio. This space is a conundrum for organizations. The technological know-how exists but the problem definition is not clear. These projects can be considered moderately risky. However, they can be really important if you are the first organization to shift the project from the Northeast to the Northwest. I saw a lot of these instances in a research project

I conducted on technologies remaking the world.[8] Some firms had extreme know-how but were unable to fully use it because the application cases were unclear. This was particularly true in the area of artificial intelligence and blockchain technologies. The dot-com bubble and crash of 2000 were largely result of technical know-how seeking an unclear problem definition.[9] However, once the problem definition was solved, then the project became a strategic strike. This is commonly found in the field of medicine. Dr. Jonas Salk successfully combined and extended the efforts of other research teams in the search for a vaccine for polio. In the 2 years before the vaccine was widely available, there were more than 45,000 cases of polio in the United States — this number dropped to 910 in 1962.[10] His main contribution was shaping the problem such that know-how could be applied. This same process came into play during the pandemic of 2020. Teams of researchers had to bring structure to a problem that was never seen before. The know-how was there, which is something we can all be thankful for; the breakthrough was decoding the virus and its unique transmission capability so that it was understood.[11] Once this was accomplished, then vaccines could be developed. Interestingly, the vaccines were also novel in their use of mRNA to teach cells to produce a protein that triggers an immune response. And, that is the key — problem definition; if it is wrong or remains undetermined for too long, then mismanagement, uncertainty, and excessive costs can occur. In the case of COVID-19, more lives could have been lost. However, if the problem definition is shaped correctly, then an organization can find new avenues to transfer and further wield its technological know-how.

If technological knowledge is low, problem structure is high, and scope is high, then the project is a Type 4. Again, this has moderate risk. The

---

[8]Albert H. Segars, Seven Technologies Remaking the World, *Sloan Management Review*, March 2019.

[9]Ben Geier, What Did We Learn from the Dot Com Bubble of 2000?, *Time*, March 12, 2015.

[10]Salk Institute for Biological Sciences. History of Salk: About Jonas Salk. Salk Institute website. https://www.salk.edu/about/history-of-salk/jonas-salk/. Accessed June 27, 2019.

[11]COVID Research: A Year of Scientific Milestones, *Nature*, May 5, 2021.

project is not something consistent with organizational skills and the larger scope adds to the complexity. If we shift the scope from large to small, the risk is reduced, and the project becomes a Type 3. As implied, when working in the lower end of the technological skill frontier, a great avenue in reducing risk is to scope the project smaller. However, repeatedly applying this strategy may result in projects with limited impact. A better approach is to reduce scope with an eye toward gaining requisite skills and then moving the project to a Type 2. Together, Type 3 and 4 projects occupy the Southwest frontier of the portfolio. Again, this is a paradoxical and sometimes frustrating area because the organization understands the problem definition but does not have the know-how to proceed without risk. The organization also faces a temptation in believing they have the skills just because they understand the domain of the problem. Perhaps the best way forward is to recognize these projects as needing a "helping hand". Collaboration with other organizations can quickly move the project to the safer ground of the Northwest. However, if the partnering organization adds complexity and does not share the same understanding of the problem, then the project can quickly shift to the risky frontier of Southeast or the Northeast. Skills can also be developed within the organization to move a project to safer ground. If this can be done quickly and effectively, then the technological know-how line can shift down trading the risky frontier of the South for the safer frontier in the North. The Wright Brothers followed this approach. They were self-educated, methodical, and moved the technological experience line downward. Samuel Langley, the Wright Brothers' rival, moved the technological know-how line upward with his efforts and approach. The more he experimented, the less he knew! This was ironic, given that Langley had the resources of the Smithsonian Institution and well-trained scientists at his behest. Through what they learned, the Wright Brothers were able to bring definition to the problem, deconstruct the project, and realize success.[12]

---

[12]David McCullough, *The Wright Brothers*, Simon and Schuster, 2015, New York, NY.

Patience, persistence, and endurance are the tougher side of the innovation conversation. Yet, the psychologists tell us that during those trying times, we are experiencing the times of our lives. Somehow, we persevere. Organizations may also experience key inflection points in their progressions. In such times, it is tempting to run or ignore the challenge. A breakthrough approach to innovation not only faces adversity but also expects it and welcomes it. That is certainly different from a perspective that cultivates a subtle fear of environmental uncertainty, high-velocity environments, and the unexpected. There is an unmistakable aggressiveness in tackling challenges and an unmistakable sense of honor in meeting the challenges within a very innovative community. Knowing that innovation is risky is the first step in building organizational courage. This can be done very methodically by examining scope, problem structure, and technical knowledge. Then, coping strategies and interventions can be developed to move a risky endeavor to a less risky frontier. This greatly enhances the predisposition for a successful outcome. Sometimes, change requires more than authority, a vision statement, or PowerPoint slides. It requires the "gut check" of an organization's perseverance and a strategy for moving projects through the Project Risk Portfolio.

Embrace Sacrifice

The choices we make get their weight and meaning by the things we sacrifice for them.

— Bruce Springsteen, Columbus, Ohio

acrifice is likely the most personal and deeply emotional of the principles. Almost everyone has a story of sacrifice — a loved one who lost their life in war, a parent who worked two or three jobs to provide, the time we gave up our place in line for someone who needed it more. In my opinion, these selfless acts may be the most beautiful part of life and living. They are also extremely innovative and very courageous. This is because sacrifice is the ultimate act of subtraction in pursuit of something greater. It is a wager; something now possessed is given away for the promise of something more. It is not natural, it can be a contradiction, and it is not the first thing that comes to mind. Yet, the impact is profound. Those that have truly mastered sacrifice willingly embrace it. It's not something to avoid or ignore, it is a playground of breakthrough ideas. The story of Maya Lin and her design of the Vietnam Veterans Memorial is a fantastic example of this magical exchange.

As an 18-year-old student at Yale University, Maya Lin was always impressed by the powerful aura of the University's Memorial Rotunda. The Memorial contained the names of alumni who died in service to their country. Each name is beautifully etched into the marble walls. That impression was unforgettable when she designed a walled monument to veterans of the Vietnam War as part of an assignment for an architectural seminar. Although she received a "B" for the work, her professor encouraged her to enter it in a design competition held for a Veterans Memorial to be built at the National Mall in Washington, D.C. Lin's submitted design included every name of the nearly 58,000 American servicemen listed in chronological order of their loss. These names would be etched in a V-shaped wall of polished black granite sunken into the ground. As monuments in the capital of the United States go, this is a drastically different design. The Washington, Jefferson, and Lincoln Memorials are very additive in their design. They tower above existing landscapes and resemble a Greco-Roman sculpture in communicating their powerful messages. Lin's design was subtractive. It would be placed within the landscape; in a gathering of earth, sky, and remembered names. It would be a memorial that created space where one's imagination and personal feelings of remembrance would be reflected in the polished stone. The panels within the monument would seemingly gaze back at the visitor. Lin's design was selected from over 1,400 submissions, including one submitted by her professor. Not surprisingly, the selection was met with much controversy. Some critics claimed the design was a subliminal anti-war symbol. Others called it a "monument to defeat", a representation of the nation's guilt and culpability. Even the Secretary of the Interior blocked the project and demanded changes. However, after the site was unveiled, the ill feelings and doubts quickly vanished. The memorial was immediately seen as an architectural marvel and an important place of healing and reflection. By subtracting, Lin gained more. Every name is represented at the site, and the reflections of visitors on the stones with the names of those lost create a very powerful feeling of unity.

The classic schools of innovation are built on creating additive innovation such as the grand memorials we find in cities around the world. There is nothing wrong with this perspective. However, subtraction and modification are also innovative approaches that often lead to new breakthroughs. Lin's approach did not build on the design concepts of the memorials that already existed in Washington, D.C. Her design captured the essence of the Vietnam War as a breakthrough idea built on the beauty of simplicity. Less was more and the sacrifice of the grandiose structure gained a new place of engagement and introspection. The Vietnam Veterans Memorial fulfills its mission to this day. It gives context and meaning to suffering that is otherwise incomprehensible.

In the pursuit of breakthrough innovation, individuals and teams willingly sacrifice in order to gain something greater. This is personal sacrifice. On a larger level, organizations must also sacrifice old ideas to make way for new ones. This is organizational sacrifice, and it is the hardest demand of innovation to meet. Yet, it is also the most important. It is impossible to do everything. Choices must be made, and those choices are not easy. That is why sacrifice lives on the discipline side of the innovation continuum. It is critical to take a meticulous and data-driven approach in deciding what we chase, what we leave behind, and what we spend to chase it. Many organizations simply can't reach this lofty hurdle. It is easier to simply add rather than subtract or modify. So, let's look first at personal sacrifice and then the more difficult frontier of organizational sacrifice.

Personal Sacrifice

From an individual perspective, there is a duty and an expectation to sacrifice for the community or organization. This is important; sacrifice is reciprocal, one lays aside their interests for the greater good, and it is also expected that others in the community will do the same. As part of the research for this book, interviews and surveys were used to identify these sacrifices. In some sense, you can think of these as the "cost" that individuals as part of innovative organizations willingly pay to realize something greater — the breakthrough idea. They are as follows:

(1) **Time** — Spending time to complete tasks, helping others, helping yourself.
(2) **Wealth** — Sharing rewards, working for purpose, alternative rewards.
(3) **Plans** — Working on the teams' schedule and not your own.
(4) **Talents** — Giving your talents to enrich others, bending your talents.
(5) **Energy** — Giving your best physical and mental effort to the task.
(6) **Pride** — Letting go of opinions, humbleness, earning the conversation.
(7) **Fame** — Sharing credit, spotlight accomplishments before people.

Let's discuss these attributes within the context of some extraordinary examples of personal sacrifice. Dashrath Manjhi is known as the "Mountain Man". He was born in a Musahar family, at the lowest rung of India's caste system. He ran away from his home at a young age and worked at Dhanbad's coal mines. After many years, he returned to his village and married Falguni Devi. Tragically, she died while trying to cross a rocky mountain that separated her village from the village that had medical facilities. Because he did not want anyone else to experience such a fate, Manjhi decided to carve a path through the Gehlour hills so that his village would have easier access to medical care. Using a hammer and chisel, He carved a path 360 ft long, 25 ft deep, and 30 ft wide to form a road through the rocks in Gehlour hills. He completed the work in 22 years (1960–1982). Though mocked for his efforts, Manjhi's work has made life easier for people of his village. The sacrifices of time, wealth, and energy are paramount in this example. A 22-year endeavor is an amazing amount of personal sacrifice just to ensure that fellow villagers have a path to the nearest hospital. There is also a sacrifice of personal gain because the time pursuing other enriching endeavors is eclipsed by the time needed for the task. Of course, it takes an amazing amount of physical energy to chisel away at the rock but it also takes an enormous amount of psychological energy to keep going. Granted, this is an extreme case, but it illustrates the depth and types of sacrifice that some make for a task they truly see as important. Of particular note is the amount of time, psychological and physical energy needed for things beyond the ordinary. Sometimes, these unglamorous aspects of innovative efforts are often not highlighted in books or in motivational speeches. Yet, for those who do sacrifice, it is often done without fanfare and, if it is recalled, it is said to have been well worth it.

Often noted in interviews and very prominent in surveys is the notion of humbleness and sharing the spotlight. In a sense, the pursuit of individual fame or of recognition is seen as harmful to a community effort. Again, an example highlights this important point. Although he eventually achieved a well-deserved place in history, Martin Luther King Jr. was not on a quest for fame or fortune. From the earliest weeks of the Montgomery bus boycott (1955–1956), he saw his role as one of personal sacrifice. He was drafted by the other black civic activists in Montgomery to be the spokesperson for the bus boycott, primarily because he was brand new in town and wasn't aligned with any of the existing black civic factions in the city. Throughout his time as leader, Dr. King framed his life and his role in a self-sacrificial way. "Bearing the cross" is the phrase that he used on at least four or five occasions that are recorded on audiotape — where he is explicitly or implicitly talking about how he coped with the role he was given but did not seek.[1] Dr. King gave his talents, time, and energy fully and willingly and endured the ultimate personal sacrifice for an extraordinary cause in a very difficult time. One of his underlying themes was that of humility. He knew that a humble person does not compare themselves with others. It is the expectations of one's self and self-improvement that are the most important gauges. Having a realistic sense of one's position relative to other people is important. As practiced by King, humility devoid of any arrogance is liberating and powerful.

---

[1]David J. Garrow, *Bearing the Cross: Martin Luther King Jr., and The Southern Christian Leadership Conference*, William Morrow & Co., 1986, New York, NY.

As noted by the gestalt therapist Fritz Perls,[2] *I am I and you are you; I am not in this world to live up to your expectations, and you are not in this world to live up to mine.* This perspective is a critical part of sacrifice and essential for climbing emotional, political, and organizational mountains.

As both of these examples illustrate, sacrifice begins with a commitment of time. Accomplishing worthwhile goals will likely take more time than one would like to give. It takes time to accomplish your goals and there is also the time that you spend helping others and the time you spend improving your own skills. This certainly does not imply that time as a quantity is the answer. It is the amount of "quality" time that is important. So, while there is an expectation of a time commitment, innovative groups understand that the time must be used efficiently and effectively. As Dr. King knew, spending energy in a way that promoted humility and reconciliation was more effective than open warfare. It was a quicker means to the mark. Wealth is also something that is sacrificed for bigger ideas. Now, I am not talking about socialism or a complete lack of concern for wealth and well-being. I am talking about the recognition of limited resources and the benefits of being rewarded fairly and having those who play critical roles being rewarded fairly. As quarterback for the Baltimore Ravens, Joe Flacco was part of a Super Bowl-winning football team and the most valuable player of the Super Bowl. He was rewarded with one of the most lucrative contracts in professional sports. Unfortunately, the aftermath was not so glamorous. Flacco and the team began a free fall after the Super Bowl win. The high price paid to Flacco left limited room for the acquisition and development of other key players, mainly an offensive line to protect the quarterback and a defense to prevent the other team from scoring.[3] The inability to embrace sacrifice locked up resources needed to continue the success. This is an ongoing story in the world of professional sports. Like professional sports teams, there are stars in

---

[2]Frederick Perls, *In and Out the Garbage Pail*, Gestalt Therapy Press, San Francisco, CA, 1969.

[3]Tom Perrotta, Joe Flacco's Awesome Mediocrity, *Wall Street Journal*, December 11, 2016.

innovative organizations; however, they recognize the key contributions of other members and the benefits of sacrificing some short-term wealth for the long-term benefits of greater accomplishment. In everyday life, we can see the same form of heroic sacrifice. Frontline healthcare workers, fire fighters, and police officers sacrifice financially and place their own safety at risk for the greater good. The world is fortunate to have essential workers with a spirit of sacrifice; it was a key piece of getting through the pandemic of 2020 and 2021.

Willingness to change or completely eliminate one's plans is a subtle but important part of sacrifice. As noted earlier, Martin Luther King Jr. had no aspiration for leading an effort such as the Civil Rights movement. Dashrath Manjhi had no original aspiration to build a road. The willingness to be adaptable and flexible with your own sequence of timelines and desired destinations is in keeping with the spirit of discovery. It is not easy to accomplish and it may run counter to our own "being", but it is necessary. Events rarely adjust to your schedule. In one of the projects of Pixar researched for this book, there is a wall mural of the expected path. The depiction is neat, logical, and very organized. On the next wall is a mural of the path as it has unfolded. This depiction looks more like a spiderweb or a tangled fishing line. It is a point of humor and a fun reminder of how plans are sometimes sacrificed.

Talents and energy are also personal sacrifices that build the overall capability of the organization. Sacrificing talent is taking the things in which we excel and using them to help build the talents of others. Mentoring is the activity associated with this sacrifice. Conveying wisdom, know-how, and experiences face to face in field conditions is perhaps the best transfer of knowledge and talent between two individuals. If we elevate this activity to interchange between groups of individuals or communities, then the benefit is multiplied. It takes time and a willingness to share one's talents for this to happen, but it is something very innovative. I certainly benefited from mentors who were willing to share their skill and insights with me. I never thought about that as a sacrifice until I began doing the same for my students. Yet, I never regret the time I spent and, hopefully, those experiences were beneficial; I know they were for me.

Along with talents, energy is a needed sacrifice. Great feats are tiring no matter who you are and no matter what your age. It is important to be "present" with mental energy and active in terms of physical energy. There is the heavy lifting in the accomplishment of one's own task and there is the heavy lifting in helping others accomplish their tasks when needed. William Harvey Carney was the first African-American awarded the United States Congressional Medal of Honor. He was born a slave in Virginia, but eventually made his way to freedom in Massachusetts. When the Union Army began accepting volunteers, he joined the 54th Massachusetts Infantry Regiment, the first African-American unit organized by the northern states. The 54th Massachusetts Infantry Regiment, led by Robert Gould Shaw, was tasked with taking Fort Wagner, a beachhead fortification that guarded the southern approach to Charleston Harbor. A previous attack on the fort failed, and the 54th was chosen for the next attempt. As the soldiers stormed the fort's walls, the Union flag bearer was killed. Carney grabbed the flag and held it for the duration of the battle. Carney, along with the rest of the 54th, was forced to retreat. Throughout the battle, Carney never lost possession of the flag, despite suffering multiple injuries. *Boys, I only did my duty; the old flag never touched the ground!* he said after the battle. Carney was awarded the Medal of Honor in 1900.

Pride is a difficult sacrifice. Yet, Dr. King rallied people in the streets, suffered indignation, and encountered ridicule. Fellow villagers mocked and ridiculed Dashrath Manjhi as he built a road for their benefit. Innovative organizations are filled with incredibly talented people. They are also people that gladly sacrifice pride for the benefit of the community. This means supporting the idea that is not your own, looking past the mistakes of others, knowing there is always more to learn, and earning the conversation. It is tempting for all of us to believe we are worthy of more than we receive. As educators and researchers, we see this from time to time. MBA students who feel that the degree and their insights make them immediately ready to be the Chief Executive Officer. Academics who believe their research unlocks the key that is unseen by even the wisest politicians or judges. In the broader context of media and news reporting, the panel of talking heads searching for the catchphrase that launches their own show. It's life. However, in an innovative organization, there is a strong theme of "earning the conversation". This means having accomplishments, experiences, and trials that qualify a person to be a part of the "conversation". Your works give your words "iron". It has nothing to do with age, rank, or years of employment. It is based on the record of accomplishment. Tribal councils of old were populated by elders and young warriors who had "earned the conversation". This along with tolerance and a strong sense of advocacy for the best ideas, wherever they come from, forms the bedrock of sacrificing pride.

Fame is the final sacrifice noted in the interviews. Importantly, this is not to say that people in innovative organizations do not want fame; they do. However, the fame they seek is for the project, for the project's goal, and for the team, not for themselves. This can be difficult to accomplish because the great innovation narrative is that "someone" came up with the great idea, created the innovation, and will likely, once again, "walk on water" in the near future. We love our heroes and we love the myth of the lone genius. Even in one of the projects researched for this book, a young scientist, Katie Baumon, became the unwitting face of the Event Horizon Telescope. Social media posts by uninformed politicians, media jocks, Internet influencers, as well as dramatic and exaggerated news stories went "viral" amplifying her role and de-amplifying the role of other project members.[4] Importantly, Dr. Baumon did not ask for any of it; in fact, she has always been steadfast in her claim that the effort was collective. Most importantly, in the best example of the principle of chemistry,

---

[4]Marina Koren, The Dark Saga of Katie Bouman, *The Atlantic*, April 15, 2019.

her colleagues at MIT quickly came to her defense, acknowledging her important contributions and also echoing the sentiment that the feat could only be accomplished with a collective effort. Therein lies some of the elusive story behind big ideas. It is typically a collective effort of very intelligent, innovative, and humble minds that are bound by the drive and thrill of chasing the impossible.

Organizational Sacrifice

Now, let's raise the level of difficulty just a bit. How do organizations embody the principle of sacrifice? While we all have experienced or witnessed some form of individual sacrifice, organizational sacrifices are not as well documented or as well understood. Yet, they do occur. Plus, they occur much more naturally and much less painfully in innovative organizations. To them, organizational sacrifice is part of the idea chase. The principle can be found in a phone conversation between Steve Jobs of Apple and Nike CEO Mark Parker. After assuming leadership of Nike, Parker asked Jobs if he had any advice. *Well, just one thing*, said Jobs. *Nike makes some of the best products in the world. Products that you lust after. But you also make a lot of crap. Just get rid of the crappy stuff and focus on the good stuff.* Jobs paused and Parker filled the quiet with a chuckle; however, Jobs didn't laugh. He was serious. *He was absolutely right*, said Parker. *We had to edit*.[5] Long ago, Napoleon practiced this same mode of organizational editing in his military campaigns. Napoleon's forces traveled with small logistical trains to improve mobility. His soldiers learned that marauding was a more reliable source of food, horses, and provisions than the traditional supply system. They endured the hardships of traveling light for the advantage for mobility and adaptability. Often hungry, they were eager to fight for the glory of France and were the most feared force in Europe.[6]

---

[5]Carmine Gallo, Steve Jobs: Get Rid of the Crappy Stuff, *Forbes*, May 16, 2011.
[6]Andrew Roberts, *Napoleon: A Life*, Penguin Group, 2014, London, UK.

Sacrifice is not a term that is typically associated with exploring new frontiers or generating fantastic ideas. However, it is a critical component of a successful idea chase. Sacrifice is the ultimate act of organizational selflessness; rather than do what is best for a powerful member or an influential sub-group, decisions are based on benefiting the entire community. Beyond this, decisions are based on what will make the community viable in the future rather than what has made it viable in the past. Therefore, it is this act of sacrifice that sheds or deescalates non-performing initiatives and replaces them with new, more promising initiatives. Organizations without this principle may add new initiatives or programs of change, but they never sacrifice the original initiatives that these new projects are designed to replace. This results in a "crowded house" of failed, fading, uncertain, promising, and performing initiatives. Such crowding can create the dangerous paradox of *Everything Is Important, and Nothing Is Important.* In this context, crowding may starve off resources needed for the successful launch of new initiatives or the required upkeep of performing initiatives. In turn, non-performing initiatives may receive too much resource. When this occurs, the organization may lose its focus and sense of direction as it plants one foot firmly in the past while the other foot timidly steps toward the future. Organizations that embrace sacrifice think of breakthrough innovation not only as the launch of new initiatives but also as the subtraction of "non-performing" initiatives. This is out of the ordinary, difficult, and highly creative.

Organizations in Context

So, now that we have established a definition of organizational sacrifice, the question becomes the following: *How do we accomplish it?* Glad you asked. This is something that I have spent over twenty years helping organizations accomplish. From governmental organizations, to media concerns, to cutting-edge technology companies, it is a difficult task. Not because it is difficult to know what is "crappy", to use the terminology of the late Steve Jobs, but because it is difficult to say "goodbye". It is

Figure 1: An Organization in Context

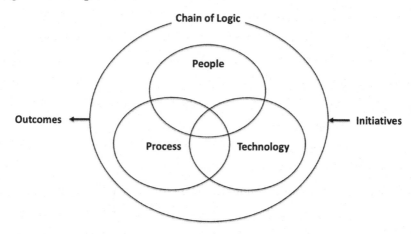

never easy to "vote" something off the island, even if it is to make room for something everyone knows is needed. What can be helpful is a tool and technique to frame the difficult conversation: a way to examine the working parts of the organization in context and then assess if those parts are "crappy", or "repairable", or "strategic". First, let's build a view of an organization in context.

As illustrated in Figure 1, an organization in context consists of two main parts. One of those parts is tangible and observable. It can be thought of as the "engine" of the organization. Organizational theorists call it structure.[7] This engine is depicted by the three interlocking rings of *process*, *people*, and *technology*. The second part of an organization is more cerebral and strategic, the Chain of Logic. As developed earlier, these are the initiatives, outcomes, and system of analytical coordination of the organization. Outcomes are embodied in products/services, initiatives are embodied in strategies, and the compass is embodied in a system of measurement or guideposts. Together, these cerebral parts drive the engine forward and

---

[7]H.J. Leavitt, Applied Organisational Change in Industry: Structural, Technological and Humanistic Approaches. In J.G. March (Ed.), *Handbook of Organisation*, Rand McNally and Company, Chicago, IL, 1965.

navigate its path. Ideally, there should be complete consistency between the chain of logic and the engine. However, as we saw in Chapter 7, conditions often change as new and improved chains of logic prevail. These shifts often require a sacrifice of parts of the engine to make space for needed additions. For example, new technology such as Zoom or Teams brings videoconferencing and collaborative work to a greater number of people at low cost. Suddenly, assumptions about geography, work, and services are forever altered. A world of "tele-everything" replaces or modifies the old way of doing things. In the new world, telemedicine, telework, streaming media, and user-produced content radically alter systems of value. An organizational engine and chain of logic may not have been created with that future in mind. Therefore, it all must be reexamined to generate a new organization that is capable of competing. As noted earlier, for some of today's most successful organizations, the new organizational form is portfolio based. Let's take a closer look at the three main pieces of the organizational engine.

Processes

A process is the sequence of actions or required steps to achieve a particular end. Of course, it is something we are familiar with, but in this context, it takes on a slightly different interpretation. In an organizational context, it is a collection of practices, policies, rules, and coordinating structures that drive activity. In some sense, it is how we are organized for competition. How decisions are made, how functions are organized, how reward systems, hiring, procurement, payments, rules, policies, procedures, and anything that coordinates the work and activities of the organization are part of the "process". To simplify the depiction of processes, it is sometimes useful to classify them in broader terms. For example, a manufacturing organization might have broad classes of procurement, logistics, inventory, and manufacturing processes.[8] In addition, it might have a back-office

---

[8]Albert H. Segars, William Kettinger, and Warren Harkness, Process Management and Supply-Chain Integration at the Bose Corporation, *Interfaces*, June 2001.

process of accounting, human resources, and payroll as well as a front-office process of selling and administration.

There are many ways to identify and classify processes; the main point is to build some framework for understanding this important part of the engine. For many innovative organizations, process is a fruitful area for subtraction. As time goes by, it is easy to add processes, rules, and procedures. However, many of these coordinating mechanisms may not age well. In some instances, they are non-inclusive, unfair, and harmful. Ironically, egregious violations of Diversity, Equity, and Inclusion are often not the result of people breaking rules; they are the result of people following them! The same can be said of toxic workplaces. By following the rules based on faulty ideas, everyday people can become part of a problem that they might not recognize. Further, these same people are horrified when it is revealed to them. Many devastating wars and awful atrocities have as their foundation the act of blindly following terrible and out-of-date rules based on bad ideas. This in no way excuses the dreadful behavior of rogue actors. However, processes as well as rules (written and unwritten) are powerful enablers. Rather than add more, innovative organizations will first subtract away processes that create tension. It is many times better to purge a process that has not aged well rather than layer another process on top of it. This is particularly true in building a modern workplace. Better to "clean the house" of out-of-date processes and then thoughtfully add processes or rules where needed. In doing so, the organization brings on the new without being burdened by the old. Adding more processes on top of bad processes in the name of innovation only results in a costly and confusing old organization.

People

People are the most important part of the engine. Of course, we can organize people by their specialty. Doing so is organizationally easy but also potentially harmful. The categories and the assumptions behind the categories build in a wall of expectation that may work against diversity and inclusion. It also implicitly limits organizational capabilities. Yet, this is the traditional way of organizing in many organizations including academia. Each member has a "department" that "fits" their background and specialty. In a business school, these departments are typically Marketing, Finance, Accounting, Operations, and, a catch all, Management. To keep family peace, every department will have an equal number of people and the same budget. Over the years, I have noticed that this mode of organizing is very beneficial to academics but non-beneficial to students. It also excludes many academics that work between boundaries. Not surprisingly, many of these boundary-spanning academics are also members of underrepresented communities. It makes sense; we would expect such faculty to have a different viewpoint and we would expect that they would not fit neatly into an organization that was built over decades by an entrenched community. Breakthrough topics such as international business, entrepreneurship, wellness, healthcare, technology management, and innovation have no natural home in the structure. In those instances, there will be stress between the organization and needed outcomes. In universities, this usually results in a committee which is a sure-fire way to kill any innovation. In my consulting and life outside of academia, I have seen the same fate befall many organizations. Perhaps the better way to think about people is in terms of their capabilities and perspectives. *What talents, background, experiences and potential contributions does this person possess? What roles can they play? What new roles are possible because of this person's talent and perspective?* The following is the wrong question to ask: *Does this person "fit" neatly in a particular department?* It is easy to ridicule Disney for its reliance on roles and casting in identifying talent and creating its workplace. However, their approach works, and it is something you will readily observe in innovative organizations.

More and more, individuals are creating identities for themselves beyond formal degrees and classroom training. Everyone wants to find a meaningful place in the parade. Therefore, it is important to examine all aspects of a parade. Its destination, its organization, its participants, its coordination, its length, its ability to engage, what can be added, what can be taken away, its impact, and its spirit. Doing so harkens back to the principle of roles and responsibilities. The organization should put people at the center of the talent hunt rather than predefined job titles and rigid guidelines for how work is done. When rigid descriptions of work are placed ahead of people, then the organization limits itself and risks a real danger of not being inclusive or diverse. If the organization is a collection of initiatives that are optimized for their purpose, coordinated laterally, and focused on a mutually beneficial objective, then, by definition, it is more inclusive and more innovative. The "one-size-fits-all" type of organization is no longer a necessary default. People and technology have created a new frontier of possibilities. Therefore, how we view and organize the "people" part of the engine is critically important in assessing its predisposition for finding breakthrough ideas. Again, it is likely there are capabilities and perspectives that should be subtracted and some that should be added.

Technology

Technology represents the tools used to create "leverage" within the engine. In other words, it includes those things we use to extend the capabilities of the people and the process. Digital technology, buildings, infrastructure, ground/air transportation as well as how they are used are part of this domain. Technology is tricky because it changes faster than the other parts of the engine and its impact can be unpredictable. In addition, as illustrated in Figure 1, the three parts of the engine are interlinked. Therefore, as technology changes, people and process must adapt, and vice versa. Therein lies one major problem within an organizational engine. Adoption of new technology may not guarantee realization of its fullest use. Processes tend to benefit organizational members and sacrificing those when new technologies dictate such a change will likely be resisted. Again, this may build in obstacles to achieving a more inclusive workplace. Not everyone works with technology the same way and some of those differences are rooted in the sociocultural differences, cognitive preferences, and collective experiences of people. So, it is important to shape technology so that it can accommodate a range of learning styles and preferences. It is not hard to do.

Google is a master of technological inclusion with its combination of search engine technology and machine learning. The technology adjusts itself to the preferences of users. Apple also pioneered this approach by leaving room for its users to customize their iPhone experience. Apple sells the technology incomplete. The user completes the design by adding apps, photographs, music, and other features that synchronize the technology with their cognitive and social preferences. Asking people to adapt to technology is potentially exclusive and may limit creativity. Building technology so that it adapts to people is inclusive and opens a wide frontier of new ideas and possibilities. This is a subtle but very important design principle of great technology. Also, the strategy of subtraction becomes important. Sometimes, old technology must be "voted completely off the island" to make way for the new wave. To simply add is to take away the very potential of what new technology can do. Most IT managers will emphatically proclaim that their organizations have too much technology. Rather than adding more, simplicity is the path for realizing the full capabilities of new technology. Invest in technology with an eye toward eliminating more technology than you add. Simplicity is a very beautiful outcome of breakthrough innovation.

Chain of Logic

The second part of an organization in context is the compass or the Chain of Logic. This concept was discussed in Chapter 7, *Lean on Data*. Now, we can combine the ideas of shifting outcomes and adapting chains of logic to the underlying engine of the organization. In some instances, a shift in outcome not only requires a new chain of logic but also requires that some processes, technologies, and people be sacrificed or modified. It is a burden to carry failing chains of logic and organizational engines as a "safety". Doing so taxes the resources of the organization and causes confusion. As stated by the Roman philosopher Seneca, *If a man does not know what port he is steering for, no wind is favorable*. If a new and beneficial chain of logic is discovered and communicated, it is much easier to adjust the engine. In fact, if the organization is adaptable, the engine may begin adjusting itself. However, if conflicting yet coexisting chains are prominent in the organization, then the engine has no chance of adjusting. This is analogous to hiking toward two conflicting destinations. You can spend time trying but you will likely never arrive at any destination. You just continue hiking. Therefore, it is important to link the engine with the chain of logic.

Okay, we just spent a few paragraphs identifying the main pieces of an organization and emphasizing the importance of identifying and categorizing the component parts. There are three reasons for doing so. First, it is important to see the interconnections between the chain of logic and the engine of an organization. My experiences lead me to believe that organizational leaders sometimes focus on one or the other rather than the combination. Second, categorizing the parts of the engine helps shape a picture of how the organization has invested its resources in order to achieve outcomes. Every part of the engine is an investment that enables or limits both initiatives and outcomes. Time, money, and the opportunity cost of other paths are embedded in these investments. Finally, it is important to build a portfolio that assesses the strategic importance today and in the future of the component parts. Here, we determine what is critical in terms of investment and strategic importance. Once the portfolio is built, it is then possible to start the process of determining where to invest resources and where to take away resources. The hard task of sacrifice begins in earnest; I call it *Investment Triage*.

Investment Triage

A useful way to unlock the *Everything Is Important, and Nothing Is Important* paradox is to think about organizational sacrifice as a form of investment triage. An organization must determine what is most important for achieving its goals. The organization must also realistically determine what is less important, what might need a refit, and what may need to be sacrificed completely. Processes, technologies, and people (the capabilities) as well as initiatives and outcomes (the logic) must be assessed in terms of "strategic importance". Strategic importance speaks to the criticality of the capability and/or logic in achieving significant and important objectives. This assessment is done against the backdrop of emerging and established chains of logic and capabilities within the marketplace or ecosystem. So, it is important to assess our outcomes, capabilities, and initiatives as well as those of others. Any of these things may measure "low" in strategic importance, meaning that it is not that critical in achieving breakthrough performance. Alternatively, it may measure "high", meaning that it is extremely critical. Further, this judgment should be made based on today's landscape as well as the landscape of the future. This results in two axes of measurement, strategic importance today and strategic importance in the future. Depending upon the appraisals, processes, technologies, and capabilities along with initiatives and outcomes will fall into one of four categories:

(1) **Legacy**: Low Strategic Importance Now, Low in the Future.
(2) **Falling Star**: High Strategic Importance Now, Low in the Future.
(3) **Rising Star**: Low Strategic Importance Now, High in the Future.
(4) **Star**: High Strategic Importance Now, High in the Future.

We will take a deeper dive into each category further down. True to the spirit of breakthrough innovation, let's fly a little higher for now before digging into the details. First, it is extremely useful to depict the categories as a visual, a visual that is designed and used to generate discussion and debate rather than capture the "right" answer. Remember our discussion on chemistry? We are not looking to build the kind of chemistry where everyone thinks the same. We want to build space to unleash differing perspectives and give everyone a chance to participate. Counterview points are welcome; however, bring some data along to make your case.

Figure 2: Investment Triage Matrix

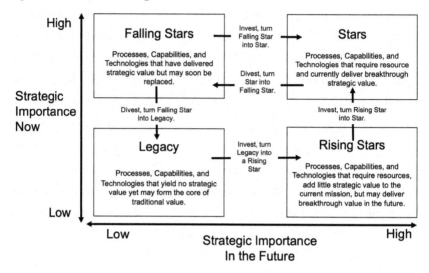

A visual representation of the "Investment Triage Matrix" is presented in Figure 2. Draw it on some poster paper, grab lots of yellow sticky notes, and have teams of people categorize the items of interest. It is very useful to have different teams categorize the same items. In my experience, there are almost always differences that form the basis of spirited and healthy debate. Again, a great measure of chemistry is how people address and resolve conflict, not just how well people get along. Exercises like this leverage the talent, open up the conversation, and hit both the discipline and inspirational aspects of innovation. Once the matrix is populated, it is then possible to have meaningful conversations about current and future investment.

Of course, the obvious question is as follows: *Where to start?* A great starting line is with outcomes — the products/services and things that are done to create value. Most organizations I have worked with like to start there. The central question is as follows: *How are our products and services positioned in the marketplace, now and in the future?* Categorizing your products and services along with those of high-performing competition or emerging competition can be very revealing. It also generates critical discussion points between what the marketplace values and what the organization offers. Leaning on data can help with this task. Rates of growth, profitability, and future growth have a place in the conversation. These measures should not crowd out conversation or thoughtful projection, but they should drive out pure speculation and selective memory. In addition, it is important to frame the frontier ambitiously. It is easy to ignore a *Rising Star* that does not look or function like a traditional product. Sony's Walkman was dominant in the marketplace, a true *Star*; alternatives such as MP3 players did not look like a Walkman and relied on downloaded music rather than cassettes or CDs. Initially, the bottleneck for MP3 players was bandwidth. It could take hours to download just a few songs. Sony thought this would not change fast or very soon. This is very unambitious thinking for a known innovator. The sudden emergence of broadband technology cleared the innovation bottleneck and gave MP3 players the final pieces needed to wipe out the Walkman. This also happened to Coca-Cola. Water, vitamin water, and sports drinks were *Rising Stars* but went initially unseen because Coke framed its marketplace in a very unambitious way. It was a serious mistake that Coke miraculously recovered from, but the lesson was clear: A *Rising Star* may not look like your favorite *Star*, but it may also be the very thing that could wipe it out. Plus, once you think you are safe, you are likely the most vulnerable. Today, reusable water bottles by Yeti, Takeya, and other outdoor fitters are disrupting the plastic bottles and distribution models of water leaned on heavily by Coke and Pepsi. Again, this is an "off-radar" Rising Star born in the industry of hydration (not soft drinks). Of course, the logic works in reverse. The best way to break into an industry is to create a new industry. It is very easy to weaponize a product or service that does not neatly appear on the "established" radar screen.

Should the outcomes of the organization be sure or fixed (governmental work, military, or a commodity business), then a great place to start is technology. Here, the question is as follows: *Are our technologies and assets aligned with efficiently achieving our outcomes?* As mentioned earlier, technology changes fast and it is easy to fall in love with it. Even in organizations that are not dynamic, breakthroughs are highly possible by adding and/or subtracting technology. Automation, data as a service, edge computing, analytics, and digital tracking are all points of potential breakthrough. FedEx, UPS, and other shippers have built empires on the breakthrough use of technology. UBER completely revolutionized transportation by recognizing the power of an app and the inconvenience of finding a taxi. Weather apps recognize that you likely need their information when you are outdoors, not in front of your monitor or television. IT managers love this type of analysis because it will demonstrate how much money is locked into technologies that are not strategic. In some organizations, it is not uncommon to see 75 to 80% of investment in these *Legacy* systems. Yet, the drive is to create more customer-facing innovation through technology. These *Rising Stars* are almost impossible to achieve if duplicated or antiquated technology chews up the vast majority of resources. For these reasons, technology is a great starting line for investment triage or a quick follow-up after products and services have been placed in the matrix.

People and processes are a great place to start if you are looking for internal breakthrough opportunities. As mentioned earlier, to innovate out you must innovate in. Sometimes, the people you have today are not the people you need tomorrow. I know this can sound harsh. It does not have to be. People are innately adaptable. When presented with a clear and logical case for capabilities the organization will need and a clear path to get there, it is amazing how people will respond. I have experienced this firsthand. When the pandemic hit in 2020, many of us professors and professional speakers were faced with possible extinction. The university as well as speakers' bureaus called upon us to develop an online presence and capability. They also asked us to do it quickly. No more classrooms, no more slideshows, no more face-to-face conversations. Everything we relied upon in education was now gone. Many of us quickly shifted to online presentation. There were tools, there were technologies, and there was a way to create a new form of engagement. We did it but not all of us did it. Some retired, some quit, and some wanted to wait out the pandemic. While all of it was happening, the world changed. What became clear is that an online capability is now a permanent part of the mix for being a professor or professional speaker. Remote learning opens more frontiers for educational engagement. Assumptions about place, time, and content are radically shifted. So, the following is an important question: *What capabilities, roles, talents, and people do we need to achieve great outcomes?* It does not mean that every capability or person must be strategic. However, it does mean that the organization should have a strong mix of talent to meet the challenges of today and tomorrow. As mentioned earlier, there are no more easy problems to solve. Adaptability, initiative, diversity, and improvisation are certainly four people-based capabilities that have become important in the post-pandemic marketplace.

An Example: The U.S. Navy and Naval Assets

Let's walk through the process with a real example from my research and consulting. The United States Navy found itself at a strategic crossroads in the mid to late 2000s. The assets and technologies of the service were some of the best in the world. However, the engagements these assets were built for were quickly giving way to a very different theater of warfare. The shallow water of the Persian Gulf and the need for mobility and quick strikes were not in the traditional design vision of Navy architects. The traditional vision relied upon large assets, lots of people, and dramatic strikes. It was the modus operandi of the Navy, but it was not aging well. Using investment triage, flag officers categorized ships, submarines, and a host of other technologies based on their strategic importance today and in the future. I moderated the discussion and occasionally hid behind the podium; it was a very professional but heated discussion. After hours of debate, it was determined that everything the Navy owned was a *Star*, and that it was the Army that really needed this exercise. This was not a surprising outcome. It is very tough to acknowledge that the aircraft carrier you commanded or the first jet you flew might be a *Falling Star*. After a week of cooling off and with encouragement from very senior command, the officers returned and did an incredible job of building the portfolio. Not only did they determine that a lot of investment was locked in non-strategic assets but they also recognized that the needed strategic projects were underfunded. Consensus was reached, an ambitious program of reinvestment was created, trust was built, and it was all driven by data. This effort is still underway in the Navy and has now spread to the Marine Corps.[9]

I tell this story to illustrate three points: First, this aspect of sacrifice may be the hardest part of innovation. These are tough discussions and not something that resolves itself in one meeting. However, with the help of the triage matrix and some general criteria, these discussions can be organized and productive. The common language of *Star*, *Falling Star*, *Legacy*, and *Rising Star* is useful in framing and thinking about organizational assets. We will further define these terms shortly. Second, the triage matrix links patterns of investment to the compass or chain of logic. Points of consistency and inconsistency are more easily identified. For the Navy, a different chain of logic was emerging, something that implied a different pattern of investment. Third, investment priority should shift from *Falling Stars* and *Legacy* to *Stars* and *Rising Stars*. In addition, some *Legacy* assets may need to be "voted off the island". This is triage and it involves very hard discussions. This is because funding needed for emerging *Rising Stars* and *Stars* typically comes from divestment in *Legacy* and *Falling Stars*. You can't do it all! This was certainly true for the Navy. It was not just a matter of money; the organization needed to focus and gain a shared understanding of priorities. As one Admiral noted, *We can only fit so many cars in the garage*. With that context in mind, let's take a closer look at each of the quadrants.

---

[9]James Stavridis, Growing Threats to the U.S. at Sea, *Wall Street Journal*, June 2, 2017.

Legacy

A product, capability, process, or technology (anything you wish to examine) that is low in strategic importance today and tomorrow is a *Legacy*. This does not necessarily imply that it is something that has been in existence for a long time. Rather, it recognizes that the asset or initiative will not yield a clear strategic advantage. Also, it does not mean that the asset is something that is undesirable. Many organizations have legacy products and legacy ways of doing business that are necessary and yield solid flows of cash. Some of these assets may provide a financial and operational foundation for the organization. It does imply that investment in *Legacy* initiatives should be closely monitored and their investment levels should not endanger more important initiatives in the portfolio. In many organizations, *Legacy* initiatives take on mythical status although they have long lost their strategic potential. Therefore, it is easy to miscategorize *Legacy* assets for *Star* or *Falling Star*. An example that comes to mind is professional athletes, in particular those in Major League Baseball. Because of past glory and star power, some players may be compensated as a *Star* when their current performance is that of a *Legacy or Falling Star*. This robs the organization of money to find the next Rising Star or keep the current Star.[10] Businesses make the same mistakes with products, political campaigns make the mistake with campaigning, and, as I am reminded by my daughter Kristen, dads make the same mistake with clothing. Legacy assets can be useful and, in some instances, they can be turned into a Rising Star with some investment. A professor who taught a Legacy course in an academic area under my watch once came to me seeking money to completely modify her course. The course she taught was Business Law: a useful course but not something that would distinguish our school from any other school. She wanted to build a course on international contracting and negotiation, with an emphasis on the Asia-Pacific. She had expertise in this area and was looking to do more with her class. I spent the money and her course turned into a Rising Star

---

[10]Brian Costa and Jared Diamond, Baseball's Comically Underpaid Young Stars, *Wall Street Journal*, March 8, 2016.

on the first offering. It is now a Star. On the other side of the equation, I am not hesitant to let some Legacy faculty "walk" when they demand an exorbitant "match" from a rival university. By voting them off the island, I can saddle a rival with an overpriced faculty and use the money I save to chase the next Rising Star. I promise you it works.

Falling Stars

A product, process, technology, or capability that is strategically important today but less strategically important in the future is a *Falling Star*. Because of their importance today, these assets often draw too much investment and a forlorn hope that their fall will be far off into the future. Too often, the fall occurs sooner than expected and investment that should be working toward more promising assets is locked into fading or strategically dead initiatives (the left-hand portion of the matrix). As mentioned earlier, Legacy and Falling Stars are the hardest to recognize because of their history within the organization and their past success. The minivan is a very recent example of a Falling Star product. The minivan's share of the overall U.S. market has steadily decreased within the past decade. SUVs, many of which now offer seating for seven or more people, are attracting many would-be minivan buyers who want a more ruggedly styled vehicle — something different from the "soccer mom" vehicle they rode in as a child.[11] True to form, automobile companies have attempted to make the minivan sleeker and more edgy, to no avail. Rather than pour money into a Falling Star, it may be better to divest, let the minivan fall to Legacy, then take the savings and find the next Rising Star. This highlights an important aspect of the matrix. Shifting outcomes cause assets to move. For example, changing tastes and emerging trends have moved the minivan from Star to Falling Star. Investment by the organization can also move assets around in the matrix. Sometimes, it may be possible to invest and move a Falling Star to a Star. Alternatively, the organization can divest of the Falling Star and let the asset fall to Legacy.

---

[11]Ben Foldy, The Minivan Is Out of Style; Sales Fade as SUVs Gain Traction, *Wall Street Journal*, August 1, 1019.

Rising Stars

Rising Stars are initiatives that are not strategically important today but they will become strategically important in the future. In contrast to Falling Stars, organizations will typically underinvest in Rising Stars. This represents short-term thinking and perhaps an unwillingness to take on new initiatives that may seem risky. Instead of moving investment from left to right in the matrix, it may seem practical to "double down" on Legacy and/or Falling Stars in the hope that they find past glory. In doing so, three negative consequences occur: (1) Rising Stars may never receive needed resources, (2) an important inroad of innovation is ignored, and (3) an important strategic inroad is left open to rivals. Rising Stars frequently do not appear as well-formed fantastic new ideas. In contrast, they may seem threatening, ugly, and risky (a Type 8 project). This makes investment extremely difficult; however, success in finding and building a Rising Star reaps many rewards. These are the future stars. A sure sign of a less innovative organization is the absence of Rising Stars. I call it the upside-down "L" pattern. There will be some Stars, more Falling Stars, and a lot of Legacy. In these cases, the organization may have a problem identifying important assets or initiatives on the horizon. Very innovative organizations will have a balance of assets throughout the matrix. In addition, the trigger for shifts in these assets will be foreseen investment and divestment rather than a reactive push from outside environmental conditions.

Stars

Stars are products, processes, capabilities, and technologies that are important today and tomorrow. Of course, every organization would like to have as many Stars as possible. However, Stars are hard-won, and when they reach their potential, they require resources to keep their luster. Unfortunately, it is also easy for a Star to drift into the zone of a Falling Star as rivals craft their own solutions to address a prevailing opportunity. Ironically, a Star may fade simply because the organization does not recognize it as a Star. It is not the success the organization wants.

Let me give an example. A global textile firm hired me to present the Triage Matrix to leaders of its multiple business units. After the presentation, the CEO wanted the executives to map the organization's businesses into the matrix. The first presenter was the head of "Flags and Banners". As he approached the podium to talk about the business and present his financials, a leader of another business unit, "Marine and Sailcloth", said, *We can skip this presentation, everyone in the room knows the flags and banner business is legacy.* This comment lit a fire under the seat of the head of "Flags and Banner". His animated response was, *I am very glad we are doing this analysis, for years we have been investing on impression rather than performance, my business is not as glitzy as others, but we have best numbers, and lots of room for growth!* He then presented very impressive financials and future growth prospects for the business. It was definitely a Star. Needless to say, after that presentation, the atmosphere in the room got very serious. The numbers of "Marine and Sailcloth" signaled a Falling Star at best. "Technical Fabrics" was a runaway Star, yet the overall organization was not investing to take advantage of that emerging and profitable marketplace. The irony is that the less glamorous businesses were the real stars of the organization. The next year, investment was adjusted accordingly, and the firm realized a commanding position in its Star markets. The moral of the story is that Stars may not always be "Hollywood" glamorous. Chasing the success where it is rather than where you want it to be can be a significant challenge. However, it is a critical part of the Idea Chase.

As discussed, the giving and taking away of investment dollars and resources are the keys to successful investment triage. *Stars* and *Rising Stars* require resource slack. *Falling Stars* and *Legacy* initiatives require resource control. There are instances when investment in a *Legacy* or a *Falling Star* can result in a new *Rising Star* or *Star*; however, it is typically the case that investment flows out of the left side of the matrix and into the right side. While conceptually easy, this is the toughest of the principles to implement. Sacrifice, personal or organizational, is deeply emotional and it is a principle that is earned through trial, difficult decisions, and the acquired ability to pioneer new paths. Sacrifice is not something you can turn "on" in an organization. It is an acquired capability that is earned over time. It requires discipline, yet it opens the door to a frontier of new inspirational possibilities. It is also the core of strategy. I have attended many courses and seminars on strategy. However, the most meaningful strategy course I ever attended was a course on finance and capital budgeting. This is because strategy is revealed in the financial choices that are made as well as the financial sacrifices made for those choices. Tell me how an organization spends its money, and I can tell you its strategy. It is the last and hardest lap of the innovation mile.

Turning the Principles into Action

Tomorrow belongs to those who can hear it coming.

— David Bowie, Heroes: Second of the Berlin Trilogy

I t is that place in the book where we put it all together. Let's begin with why the book was written in the first place. The world is now a very different place and many of the things that have made it different had their beginnings before the great pandemic of 2020. The pandemic simply amplified and accelerated their impact. The age of know-it-all executives no longer exists. Digital media now amplifies, distorts, and accelerates the spread of information. Good ideas and bad ideas now travel faster and farther. People have never been more informed or more misinformed. Organizations and workplaces that seemed strong and predictable now look woefully weak and chaotic. There is a growing misalignment between the workforce and the "work" organizations have to offer. All of this creates a growing context for leaders that is "out of sample". It is something that has not been experienced before. Yet, many solutions to these challenges are mistakenly crafted from prior "in-sample" experiences. Hiring people from underrepresented communities and simply placing them in an organization that is built for the majority is an example of an "in-sample" solution to an "out-of-sample" challenge. The same is true for hiring new college graduates who are aware of and accomplished at virtual work. Today, the workplace and work have a different meaning than they did five years ago. Organizations must transform and adopt modes of innovation to match new expectations, new systems of values, and new frontiers of possibility. However, to truly achieve it, leaders must first realize that they have not encountered this challenge before. It is often a mistake to frame a challenge and extrapolate solutions from what you have seen before. Incremental changes and approaches will likely fall short of the mark; breakthrough ideas are the path forward.

This brings us to the call for action, the idea chase. The object of the chase is the breakthrough idea. These "tough-to-find" ideas are often combinations of other ideas. They are analogous to the constellations in the nighttime sky. There is no shortage of models or schools of thought about how to chase them. Yet, today's world is different. We have entered a new age. So, we bring with us the pieces of the models that work, leave behind the pieces that no longer work, and invent what we need to face the challenges ahead. The chase must incorporate inspiration and discipline. As we discovered, this is the magic of great innovators and innovative organizations. The seven principles give us this unique symbiosis and provide a view of innovation that is measurable and manageable. Now, the time has come to apply it. First, we will use the principles as a means of developing a predisposition for finding the great idea. They can tell us the likelihood of a team or organization finding something more than an average idea. They can also explain the success or lack of success of past initiatives. Second, we will use the principles to frame and address one of the most pressing challenges for today's organizations: diversity, equity, and inclusion (DEI). The principles frame the challenge as one of transformation rather than simple compliance. As we will see, this leads to more impactful and longer-lasting outcomes. Finally, we will apply the principles to a modern form of organizational design. This form is built on social networks and communities of practice (CoP). It is new, it is dynamic, and it meets the challenges and opportunities of the Universal Revolution. The most innovative organizations have shifted to this organizing principle, and it has resulted in a workplace that creates, shares, and leverages knowledge.

The Principles as a Predisposition for Success: Glasses of Water

In assessing the predisposition of a team, community, or organization to achieve something beyond the ordinary, it is useful to think of the principles as seven glasses of water. If all the glasses are completely full, then all the principles are in full force and the likelihood of an extraordinary outcome is high. Both the inspirational and disciplinary aspects of innovation will be fully leveraged. It is quite likely that this symbiotic effect will lead to the discovery of that elusive idea of ideas. If some of the glasses are half full, partially full, or empty, then the likelihood of an idea that is better than average is much lower. The full force of the principles is not realized. You might achieve an end, but it will not be particularly impactful or, as a strategist would say, a strategic strike.

It is very eye-opening to measure initiatives, projects, or entire organizations that are less than successful against the principles. It becomes easy to see that the lack of achievement is because some of the glasses are less than full or completely empty. For example, the fall of the telecommunications giant Nortel Networks had its roots in the loss of the principles. As data and voice moved into mobile formats and across digital networks, the company remained steadfast in its traditional telephone business. Yet, all signals pointed to a new and different competitive landscape. Cisco and other companies embraced this new frontier with ambitious new products and services. They also believed and quickly acted on the new signals from the marketplace. The principles were in full force for these new and ambitious competitors. A popular narrative is that Nortel was caught completely unaware of the changes around it. However, this is far from the truth. There were pockets of businesspeople, technologists, and engineers within the company that knew the signals were changing and tried to relay the knowledge to senior management.[1] However, a lack of trust and many obstacles in the sharing of knowledge and information resulted in an "echo chamber" around leadership that doomed the company. To meet the new competitive challenge, Nortel would have to sacrifice old products and old ideas to make room for the new. It simply could not climb that mountain. For Nortel, the glasses of ambition, chemistry, trust, data, and sacrifice were quite empty. It was reflected in its initiatives, projects, and ultimately the organization. This was not always true; the company was invented and prospered with the glasses mostly full. Nortel built its empire on being very innovative but quickly disintegrated when the principles were no longer present. So, yes, it is possible to have the principles in full force but then lose them. It is also possible for the levels of water to sink or climb as an initiative, project, or entire organization progresses. Often, chemistry, trust, and perseverance will wane as projects, or the competitive landscape, become difficult. Quick and consistent managerial intervention is sometimes needed to maintain momentum and restore faith.

As illustrated in Figure 1, the most successful teams, communities, and organizations will have full glasses across *all* the principles. This is an important point; there is an incredible symbiosis between the principles which can only manifest itself if all principles are in force. The glasses do not have to be completely full, but any glass that is less than half full

Figure 1: The Best Predisposition for a Successful Idea Chase: All Full Glasses

Ambition	Chemistry	Roles & Responsibility	Trust	Data	Perseverance	Sacrifice

[1]Nortel Ex-Worker Says He Told Company of Revenue Problems, *Wall Street Journal*, May 6, 2019.

is a sign of trouble. It will likely create a "drag" on realizing the full force of other principles and of the collective. While it is certainly possible to repair a principle on the fly, it is far better to have the principles in place (glasses mostly full) at the beginning of an initiative. This is how innovative products, services, and businesses as well as the impossible come to life. The important thing to remember is that the principles take the very broad notion of innovation and make it measurable and manageable. They also provide a useful language for describing successful and less successful outcomes. You can measure the entire organization, parts of an organization, projects, or initiatives within the organization. In most organizations, some projects measure well across the glasses and some not so well.

Edgy Principles

I often ask participants in my executive development or consulting sessions to identify a project or initiative in their organization that is "stellar" and one that is just "ok". I then have them measure both projects across the principles. Comparing these initiatives and learning why they are different are fantastic means of revealing interventions that move projects forward and obstacles that hold them back. Viewing a collection of projects measured this way also creates a great proxy for developing an organization's profile across the principles. After all, an organization's profile across the principles is the sum of its profiles across projects and initiatives. Often, there will be two or three of the principles that are "edgy" for an organization. They will show up as empty or near-empty glasses on many projects and initiatives. The organization systematically fails to achieve these edgy principles yet easily achieves the others. This will lead to outcomes, as something gets done. However, the outcome will not be a breakthrough or real innovation. Some opportunity is left behind and the organization "settles" for the lesser idea. If this is the case, then the leadership mandate is clear; determine the cause of this edginess and develop the needed interventions to restore balance to the principles. Most often, the cause and needed intervention are easily recognized once the edgy principles are identified. Interestingly, through hundreds of these exercises, some common patterns in the glasses of water are easily identified across a wide array of troubled innovation efforts. Let's take a closer look at the "greatest hits" of these patterns.

The Idea Catapult

A very common pattern in troubled idea chases is an absence of chemistry, trust, as well as roles and responsibilities. All these principles fall on the inspiration side of the continuum. So, we know that the organization has some level of ambition, good discipline, but also exhibits some edginess in coordination and employee commitment. I call the pattern the "Idea Catapult". It is illustrated in Figure 2. The big idea revealed through data is launched over the wall without any thought of the shock and tension it might cause. The critical pre-work in preparing the organization will be done after the launch and as needed. However, like catapulting a projectile over a wall, the damage of an ambitious initiative that is "off the rails" occurs quickly, and it is often too late to repair it once it is realized. Many acquisitions exhibit this pattern. The acquisition does not have a home in its new organization and the acquiring organization is asked to house a stranger in its midst. Sadly, because of these flaws, the acquisition does not live up to the hype, further eroding trust, placing data into question, and dramatically lowering sacrifice. If perseverance remains high without correcting the other glasses, then the acquisition becomes extremely costly.

The interventions needed are obvious. Leaders must cultivate trust to reduce tension, carve out roles that help integrate the new idea into

Figure 2: The Idea Catapult

the organization, and identify the collection of talents that will create the chemistry needed to build and sustain momentum. In many ways, it is the work needed by a sports franchise when it adds a star player to a team. If the new star player shows up without the pre-work, then neither the star nor the existing team will be fully leveraged. To avoid this, a thoughtful and strategic process of onboarding is needed. Communicating the new vision truthfully; listening, responding, redefining, or creating new roles; and knowing how the new talent will impact the existing talent (and vice versa) are critical interventions. They avoid the trap of simply stacking new ideas on the old. They also turn an awkward situation into a coordinated strategic strike. Like people, ideas must be onboarded. When introducing the new idea to the organization, it is easy to underestimate the importance of inspiration and lean too heavily on discipline. Even if the data is clear in the creation and need for the idea, it only takes a few of these misfires to cripple an otherwise healthy organization. People must see the logic and place for the new idea. They must also understand their role and the roles of others in moving the idea along to its fullest potential. This creates the needed disposition to sacrifice, which opens a road to greater success.

Minimal Viable Innovation

Many organizations become masters of minimal viable innovation (MVI). They will make some incremental change or "tweak" in a product or process and then raise the innovation banner high. This will continue over time, and very soon it becomes a core competency and a favored mode of chasing ideas. The chain of events starts with an organization that is unwilling to sacrifice *any* old idea for anything new. So, we can say that sacrifice is edgy. The risk seems too high, the success has been too grand, and it has been on a long and prosperous ride. History and success combine to make the idea chase a search for something plain, predictable, and easy. This mode of innovation leads directly to low ambition. There is simply no incentive or organizational signal that being ambitious is desired or rewarded. In fact, the opposite happens, the organization rewards "leaps of certainty". Yet, there is some knowledge within the organization that

Figure 3: Minimal Viable Innovation

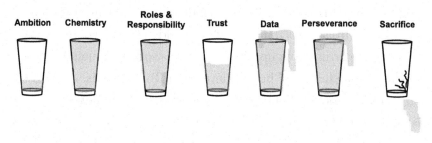

the ride cannot last forever. This leads to doubts and a silent and gradual eroding of trust in the leadership. Ironically, levels of chemistry, roles, data, and perseverance are high, perhaps too high. There is a way of working and level of grit that is consistent and recognized. So, there is some goodness in MVI. The overriding problem is that the extremes of inspiration and discipline are lacking. Anything breakthrough or better than average is out of reach because of the negative symbiotic effect of low sacrifice and low ambition. A meaningful idea chase has no chance and that is the way the organization prefers it to be. The collection of projects and initiatives will exhibit the pattern depicted in Figure 3.

Ironically, MVI does work to some degree. It is one of the artifacts of fast following and true grit. The danger is that overreliance on MVI closes many doors on an emerging frontier that will clearly reward more ambitious endeavors and the ability to vote old ideas off the island, in other words, the Universal Revolution in which we now find ourselves. So, the place to start in breaking down the complacency of MVI is sacrifice. The Investment Triage Matrix presented in Chapter 9 is a great way to assess how well or poorly ideas have aged and how new ideas are changing the landscape. This must be done objectively and with an eye toward cultivating new ideas as well as discarding ideas that no longer work. If this can be done effectively, then ambition will soon enter the picture along with trust. There is now a strong signal in the organization that real innovation and real transformation are on the rise. It is then possible to harness and realign the already strong principles of chemistry, roles, data, and perseverance to chase the bigger ideas. Ironically, moving from MVI to breakthrough is not quite the jump that one might expect. Trust me, I have seen it done. It just requires courage, some boldness, some realignment, and a willingness to "let go".

The Idea Hurricane

The idea hurricane is one of the most common and troubling patterns observed in some organizations. It is illustrated in Figure 4. The beginning of the hurricane is an idea or initiative that is ambitious, maybe overly ambitious. In fact, the inspirational idea is often far ahead of the discipline needed to make it work. The glass of ambition overflows. There is a drive to make the idea work with no supporting cast in place and no data to guide or rationalize the quest. Too much is promised, too much tension is placed in the organization and, as a result, the principles of chemistry, roles, trust, data, and sacrifice are edgy. They are empty glasses or worse. Yet, there is an overdrive of perseverance; the march goes on at all costs. In many respects, it is the idea or initiative pitted against the organization's will to implement it. These idea hurricanes are typically born out of the rock star school of innovation or out of the school of disruption. They are top-down driven, overly ambitious, off the rails, and untested. No one sees the cause for sacrifice, reasoning is based on hope rather than data, and the way forward is a forced march. This makes them different and more dangerous than an idea catapult. These initiatives and projects are like a

Figure 4: The Idea Hurricane

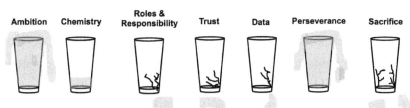

stalled hurricane lingering off the coast. They create a lot of destruction, chew up a lot of resources and they go nowhere. Ironically, they can also be found in both innovative and non-innovative organizations. No one is immune. This is because idea hurricanes often do have some merit, and sometimes they pay off. They are exciting, they are new, but they also lean too heavily on ambition and willpower. At some point, even the greatest idea needs a supporting cast, an identity in data, and a rationale for sacrifice.

The interplay between ambition and data is the best starting point for taming the idea hurricane. The inspirational fire of ambition must meet the logic and rationality of data to create an idea or initiative that does not overreach the organization's capabilities. This is a tough balancing act. It is possible to keep the ambition and extend the capabilities or lower the ambition and keep the capabilities. It is also possible to do a little of both. The key is that leaders must do something. Organizations do not have a magical ability to respond to "asks" that exceed their ability to deliver. Trust empties quickly, followed quickly by sacrifice. If there is any chemistry, it is redirected to fighting rather than supporting the initiative. This leads to very conflicted roles and responsibilities. The good news is that idea hurricanes cannot last for very long. Organizations eventually run out of resources or cannot tolerate the destruction. Yet, despite this, some organizations will have repeat performances. Once they recover from the last hurricane, they create another. Most notably, this can be seen in large-scale software implementations. Any technological initiative that impacts the entire organization can quickly become a hurricane. Prevention is the key; do not hope that the hurricane will miss you. It is not likely to happen and intervening when the hurricane hits is tougher than preparation before it hits. Use data to shape the ambition, develop trust in the benefits now and in the future, create a system of coordination, and be prepared to sacrifice. At some point, the organization must turn off the old technology for the new technology to reach its fullest potential. The same is true for ideas. The sooner the better. These interventions avoid the stacking of new on top of old and simplify rather than complicate their onboarding into the organization.

Idea Factories

A very interesting pattern, depicted in Figure 5, is the "Idea Factory". Here, the glasses of ambition, chemistry, roles and responsibilities, and trust are completely full. The organization is "full tilt" with respect to the inspirational side of the innovation continuum. However, the glasses of data, perseverance, and sacrifice are empty. In fact, they are less than empty; there are holes in the glasses so water cannot be contained. The discipline side of the continuum is completely missing and edgy. So, here is the story. Idea factories are built on the capability to identify lots of wonderful ideas. It is a place of extreme community and collaboration, very similar to the innovation mosh pit. Everyone has a place in the story, there is great knowledge flow among groups, and the organization has a distinct feel of ambition. Ideas flow but they also flow a bit recklessly. Data is viewed as an obstacle to innovation. Therefore, many ideas are untested and not completely formed. They are a product of overdriven creativity and imagination. When the first sign of trouble appears, the idea is cast out and a new idea takes its place. While coming up with ideas is the favored sport, sacrifice in terms of planning, scoping, and managing the initiative to fruition is a weakness. The hope is that the idea comes to the organization in the form of a Beautiful Swan rather than an Ugly

Figure 5: The Idea Factory

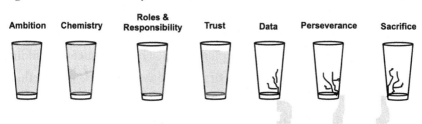

Duckling. If it arrives as a Swan, then the Idea Factory thrives. The breakthrough will be quickly recognized and moving it along the way will be easy. The hard work has already been done. However, if the idea arrives as an Ugly Duckling, then there is no discipline or grit to turn the Duckling into a Swan. That said, all is not necessarily lost. Sometimes, the Idea Factory can collaborate with another organization or project that is closer to the disciplined-based pattern of MVI. If successfully united, then, between the two organizations or projects, there is a set of full glasses. However, such partnerships are difficult to create and manage and the Idea Factory is typically a passive and temporary participant. They would rather leave the hard work to someone else and find the next idea.

It is easy to see the major flaws of Idea Factories. They lack the will and focus to take an idea and turn it into an initiative or project. The absence of sacrifice represents an inability to commit. The clumsiness of collecting, sharing, and interpreting data blinds any effort, and the favored response to difficulty is to run. Still, there is a fantastic capability for inspiration. So, what are the most cited interventions? The place to start is the interplay between data and sacrifice. The Idea Factory suffers from a lack of commitment. In refusing to make choices, it unwittingly makes the worst choice, to do nothing. Data can scope and shape the robust idea flow of the Idea Factory into a prioritized list of opportunities. It can also separate the actionable from the unreachable. This allows the sacrifice glass to begin filling. Now, it is possible to determine what is important and what should be cast aside or delayed. The rising stars emerge from the chaos. With this new focus, perseverance becomes easier to achieve. The riskiness of projects is understood and interventions for managing that riskiness are in place. Shocks are no longer that disruptive and needed remedies to those shocks are known and quickly implemented. This sequence of building discipline into overly inspirational organizations or projects is something that has gained much more importance as we exited the Information Revolution and entered the Universal Revolution. The challenges are more complex now and the cost of failing to meet those challenges is high. Idea

Factories are built on the belief that the flow of ideas will be constant and that somewhere in that flow there will be "low-hanging fruit". This was truer in the Information Age than it is today.

As any good mathematician knows, there are countless permutations of water and glasses. These are some of the most common and most interesting I have seen since using this approach to measure innovative predisposition. The glasses can change levels as projects and initiatives evolve. They can also change as organizations evolve. The changes in those levels are successful leadership interventions or terrible leadership mistakes. The main point is that the elusive construct of innovation is measurable and manageable through the framework of principles. However, this is not the only use of the principles. They are also very useful in framing difficult challenges. They can help identify the bigger question and the more insightful solution. With that in mind, let's use the principles to frame one of today's most important yet trickiest of challenges.

Using the Principles to Frame a Tough Challenge: Diversity, Equity, and Inclusion

One of the most challenging issues facing organizations is the achievement of DEI. Many organizations have launched organizational revitalization efforts under the banner of DEI only to find that the benefits, employee appreciation, and momentum fall short of expectations. Perhaps these efforts are clumsy due to a lack of "know-how" or unclear objectives. It is also possible that such efforts lack the ambition, vision, creativity, and energy that are typically given to launching new products or pioneering new marketplaces. In other words, the challenge is not framed within the principles of breakthrough innovation. An innovative DEI initiative should transform the workplace. It should open up a new frontier of perspectives and ideas. It should reinvent how an organization views work, roles, and talent. It should break down the rigid processes and sometimes toxic environment of the "factory" mentality central to scientific management and earlier revolutions. People should be happier, they should be more engaged, they should feel a sense of connectedness, communities of knowledge should emerge, and the organization should be transformed. Yet, the initiative is often treated with suspicion, skepticism, and, most dangerously, fear. Perhaps many organizations and their leaders are thinking about it in the wrong way.

The Challenge

Achieving DEI is perhaps different than any other organizational challenge leaders may face.[2] No one wants to believe there is a problem. If there is a problem, it belongs to someone else. The issue seems squarely rooted in the murky world of people and perceptions. It is easy to underestimate. It is incredibly important; yet, even some high-performing firms seem to fail at it. Ironically, it requires deep introspection, yet there is a strong temptation for leaders to believe that someone from outside can provide a quick "fix". It might be one of the few transformational propositions where everyone agrees that it is desirable while also having a different view of the desired end state and how to achieve it.[3] This complexity is further compounded by the arrival of consultants, experts, and boutique firms that offer seminars, interventions, analytics, or software to tackle the issue. Typically, the result is diversity training, hiring tests, performance reviews, and grievance systems that aim to limit bias in recruiting and promotion. While better than nothing, these process and policy overlays are primarily designed to prevent litigation. It is a reactive rather than proactive approach. Plus, it is not transformative. In many instances, nothing changes in the "heart and soul" of the organization or its deeply imbedded systems.[4]

Let's frame DEI within the context of the seven principles of breakthrough innovation; let's make it an idea chase. Doing so raises the stakes

---

[2]A. Mukherjee, *Leading in the Digital World: How to Foster Creativity, Collaboration, and Inclusivity*, MIT Press, Boston, MA, 2020.

[3]A. Bittner and B. Lau, The Key to Growing Human-Centered Businesses, *Sloan Management Review*, February 4, 2021.

[4]F. Dobbin, A. Kalev, and E. Kelly, Why Diversity Programs Fail, *Harvard Business Review*, 94, 52–60, 2016.

considerably. Rather than assuming that the current organization is fine and that we need to "tweak" people, let's take the view that we will need to transform the organization. In other words, we are out to build the workplace of tomorrow. Let's add to this mandate the belief that the organization we build will shape the people that work within it. So, rather than changing people and hoping the organization adjusts, we change the organization knowing that the people will respond to the organization we build. DEI provides a fantastic framework for building the organization of tomorrow. Within this framework, we seek to build an organization that accommodates many perspectives and people. We build processes that ensure people are engaged and included. We also build systems of reward that are equitable and reinforce the accomplishments of individuals and the communities they work within. Finally, we apply this perspective to the products/services we create, the communities we serve, and the profit we make. Such a view is transformational, not transactional. The principles are a great framework for escaping the trap of doing less in DEI. As illustrated in Figure 6, they frame the effort in a completely

Figure 6: Principles of Breakthrough Innovation and Transformative DEI

Seven Principles	Transformative DEI
Be Ambitious	→ Frame DEI as Transformative
Achieve Chemistry	→ Build a Moral Case for DEI
Define Roles	→ Make Sure Everyone has a Place in the Story
Build Trust	→ Encourage Willful Interrogation
Lean on Data	→ Create Systems of Accountability
Show Perseverance	→ Don't Underestimate the Challenge. Fine Tune Efforts Along the Way.
Embrace Sacrifice	→ Leave Behind Harmful Mental Models for those that are Beneficial.

different way. The organization is set on a path of transformation that will ultimately create a place and way of working that leverages talent and is focused on "the greater good". Let's see how the principles help uncover this exciting frontier.

Be Ambitious by Making DEI Transformative

Leaders can't simply mandate DEI; like any great idea, it must be earned. To earn it, you must be ambitious. It is easy to ask or expect too little of any endeavor. When leaders do this, it sends a message to the organization that the initiative is not important, not rewarded, and frankly, not worth the effort. Also, "fatigue" can creep in leading to a sense of hopelessness and bewilderment, particularly among those most passionate about the effort. When ambition is present, then these forces are reversed, and a sense of energy and forward momentum takes over. DEI is an opportunity to do things better, to be better people, to learn, to grow, to progress, and to maintain relevance. Endeavor to rethink the range and reach of the effort, it is likely not ambitious enough. Leveraging it to build products, pioneer new marketplaces, create new opportunity, and positively impact the community sets an ambitious tone and creates a place in the story for even the most skeptical. Thinking about employee well-being in terms of physical, mental, and professional success can lead to much-needed changes in work, workplace, and productivity. Within the organization, social gatherings, walking trails, sports leagues, company picnics, wellness programs, and other initiatives are visible reminders that an organization is safe, communal, and welcoming. Externally, sponsoring company tours for underrepresented communities, internship programs, visits to local schools, and community projects signal that an organization cares about the community and not just itself. It takes broad vision and a dose of ambition to realize that organizations are typically hardwired to be exclusive. Aim higher, think bigger, expand your viewpoint, ask bigger questions, expect more, and the DEI effort will be a new and prized resource rather than a burden to carry. As noted in recent research, organizations must think about DEI in terms of representation, participation, application, and appreciation.[5] All of these values are important when framing the transformational effort. Organizations should have a wider frontier of perspective represented, those perspectives should be engaged, the organization must be able to apply the ideas of the new perspectives, and there should be logical and meaningful systems to appreciate and value the contribution. This larger view of DEI is critical for achieving ambition and unlocking those great ideas that are elusive and well hidden.

Achieve Chemistry by Building a Moral Case

There are countless articles, research, and seminars that promote DEI as a "great business case".[6] The good news is that it is a great business case. The bad news is that a lot of atrocities and exclusive practices were also heralded in their day as a "great business case". The banner of "great business case" has been overused and overemphasized in board rooms and MBA classrooms. It has legitimized many exploitive actions throughout history and clouded the boundary of ethical and non-ethical behavior. Yes, it is good for everyone when organizations thrive. However, a better banner for organizations to march under is "honorable profit". Likewise, the case for DEI should not be primarily driven by profit; to do this is to lose a chance to build chemistry. DEI is a moral case that is centered on the purpose of meeting the needs of people, and society. It is human, not financial, and it is the right thing to do. This principle is critically important in achieving transformational change and it should be the language and philosophy behind the effort. The crux of chemistry is a cause or objective that is greater than the people that are pursuing it. Such causes take a "community" or a sense of "esprit de corps" to realize. Plus, they are usually achieved by ordinary people working in extraordinary ways to achieve something that was thought to be impossible. So, to create chemistry, a leader must move away from pointing fingers and move toward shaping an initiative that is inclusive. Ironically, many DEI initiatives are not

---

[5]A. Beach and A. Segars, How a Values Based Approach Advances DEI, *Sloan Management Review*, Summer 2022, 63(4).

[6]D. Thomas, Diversity as Strategy, *Harvard Business Review*, September 2004.

inclusive, they are divisive. As such, chemistry is an empty glass and anything that is achieved will be no better than average. It certainly will not be transformational. Create a worthy cause and put everyone on the solution side of the equation. Chemistry will then leverage your talent and you can watch the initiative reach new heights.

Define Roles: Everyone Has a Place in the Story

No discussion of DEI is complete without the important ingredient of leadership support. Like any important initiative, it is critical to have the support and "buy in" of senior leadership. However, it is also critically important that the initiative be "owned" by everyone.[7] This does not necessarily imply a "bottom-up" approach, but it does cast shade on a purely "top-down" approach. The best approach can best be described as "entrepreneurial". Rather than institute a series of edicts or control tactics, it is much better to develop a principle that all levels of management as well as frontline employees be engaged in problem-solving.[8] The key is community and contact. Rotating managers through departments and cross-training expose people to different aspects of the organization and to diverse people. It also creates conversations and opportunities that allow everyone to become part of the solution.[9] Mentorship and sponsorship programs engage managers, chip away at potential biases, and create useful networks for underrepresented employees. This is where *equity* enters the picture. Leaders should recognize the unique needs of individuals and tailor their approach to meet those needs. Equity is difficult to apply on a large scale. However, it is a powerful tool for mitigating challenges that hold back an individual. Equity can be thought of as a left-handed baseball glove; it allows everyone to play baseball (creating equality) without making everyone play right-handed. Senior leaders must avoid leaning too heavily on the "top-down" model of applying equity or shaping DEI

---

[7]Rosalind M. Chow, L. Taylor Phillips, Brian S. Lowery, and Miguel M. Unzueta, Fighting Backlash to Racial Equity Efforts, *Sloan Management Review*, June 8, 2021.

[8]D. Pedulla, Diversity and Inclusion Efforts that Really Work, *Harvard Business Review*, May 2020.

[9]Rob Cross, Kevin Oakes, and Connor Cross, Cultivating an Inclusive Culture through Personal Networks, *Sloan Management Review*, June 8, 2021.

policy. Instead, it should be diffused into the community so that people "own" the initiative and feel empowered to shape, implement, and refine it. Doing so creates a culture of roles and responsibilities for everyone. People have a place in the story in terms of character and contribution.

Build Trust through Willful Interrogation

An inconvenient, uncomfortable, awkward, and yet very necessary part in achieving DEI is willful interrogation. It is important for the organization to question *What is?* and *Why?* Organizations must adopt a principle that encourages frank discussions about race, representation, diversity, and inclusion. Many leaders would rather avoid such conversations for fear of saying the wrong thing. Because of this, camouflaged language, glowing generalities, and doublespeak are used to frame the issue. This is quite likely to do more harm than good. The grand announcement via email or executive town hall is also likely to raise suspicion rather than galvanize support. The immediate questions from the community are as follows: *Why did our leaders just recognize this problem? Where was this concern last year or the years before?* In some sense, the grand announcement suggests that leaders were somehow complicit or just completely naïve. The key is real conversation in safe places. This means small groups communicating with executives in a conversational and informal tone. For leaders, DEI is listening not talking. Leaders must also ask questions, be prepared to *not* have all the answers, and be prepared to see some unpleasant things that were always there but were somehow not visible. These conversations create trust. They also may reveal flaws in the organization that were once celebrated as strengths. As one senior executive noted, "we prided ourselves in only hiring from Ivy League Universities", "it was celebrated as a unique strength but it became our biggest weakness". Funny enough, this thinking also assumes that only people from the Ivy League can come up with new ideas, be a great leader, or have an entrepreneurial mindset. Statistically, this is not likely. Trust is having frank conversations about the past but more importantly open conversations about the future. It is also about scoring immediate "wins" by applying new thinking within the framework of DEI. The organization opens up a broader frontier of hiring or creates multiple avenues for achieving success. Action certainly speaks louder than words in building trust. Again, this is a glass that *must* be full to achieve something meaningful in DEI. However, it is perhaps the most "edgy" in terms of achievement. It takes time, it takes courage, and it takes quite a bit of humility.

Lean on Data by Creating Accountability

Another key to success is accountability. Here is where we lean on data. Importantly, this idea is not viewed primarily as a set of targets or a system of control. It is viewed as a means of detecting and correcting root causes of disparities. Discrimination and inequity can find hiding places in data that is too aggregated or not carefully analyzed.[10] For example, a recent study showed that there was a large difference in breast cancer mortality rates between black and white women in Chicago. This phenomenon was not seen in other U.S. cities. Further analysis pointed to three factors in the inequity: black women received fewer mammograms, the mammograms received were of inferior quality, and black women had inadequate access to quality treatment once their cancer was diagnosed.[11] Clearly, people are more than their health insurance records. In aggregated form, no difference may be detected in breast cancer mortality rates. The disparity is hidden so the problem is invisible. However, with deeper analysis, a more complete and unkind truth is revealed. The same phenomena can be found in data that captures promotion, salary, sick leave, and other metrics. Software can create a high-tech blinder to the context, systems, and other structures that reinforce the very things you are hoping to eliminate. Accountability is moving beyond "averages" and looking deeper into the data for cause-and-effect relationships and their linkage to mental models that are damaging to DEI. Taking this approach will help identify measurable and meaningful steps for transformation. But be

---

[10]E. Kennedy, Can Data Drive Racial Equity?, *Sloan Management Review*, December 3, 2020.
[11]V. Henderson, Implementation of an Integrated Framework for a Breast Cancer Screening and Navigation Program for Women from Underresourced Communities, *Cancer*, 126(10), 2020.

aware, some of these causes and effects may lie outside the organization. They may lie within educational systems, transportation systems, housing, and/or medical care. To be accountable is to understand the impact of these external structures on your DEI effort and endeavor to change or mitigate them. When this is done, the effort becomes credible, logical, and embraced.

Show Perseverance by Understanding the Magnitude of Change

You can't correct in a few meetings something that has been woven into an organization over several decades. DEI is complex, elusive, and it is easy to get it wrong. If fact, it is almost impossible to get it right on the first or second try. In addition, it is important to craft a path that fits the context of the organization. Improvisation becomes a key capability. This is why it is important to look beyond traditional boundaries for insights, clues, best practice, the unexpected, and future trends. Building robust knowledge flows outside the organization is a way to break out of old mental models and explore new possibilities. Sesame Street found an obscure puppeteer (Jim Henson) to create characters that communicated with all children. Even now, these characters deal with the tough issues that children face rather than a fantasy world of everything being totally easy or carefree.[12] Fred Rogers (Mr. Rogers) incorporated jazz into the context of his show rather than zany music that might create anxiety or distraction in young viewers. The point is that great initiatives in DEI often leverage things from outside of the traditional boundary. This is in the best tradition of innovative practice.[13] It is also a very critical part of overcoming obstacles. However, this is sometimes not recognized by leaders who feel that such conversations and associated efforts should be "kept in the family". It is far better to surrender the notion that DEI is something that we can understand and do in isolation. Expand the radar scope. Have the courage

---

[12]J. Vineyard, 9 Times Big Bird Helped Us Be Better People, *New York Times*, December 9, 2019.
[13]Albert Segars, *Ideas and Innovative Organizations: A Tribal Approach*, Peter Lang Academic Press, New York, NY, 2020.

to explore, borrow, and adapt from what has been learned and invented outside of your neighborhood. In other words, leverage DEI to become better at DEI. Most importantly, don't underestimate the obstacles, be present when the headwinds show up, and know that patience will be needed to truly realize something transformational.

Embrace Sacrifice: Leave Behind Old Mental Models

A mental model is the rationale for a thought process about how something works in the real world. People have mental models and so do organizations. Real transformation requires a rethinking of mental models as well as the processes, rules, and systems that flow directly from them. Racism, exclusion, inequity, and other atrocities are products of systems and structures built into organizations, governments, and ways of life. Yes, there are individuals that "hate", but it is institutionalized systems and their associated mental models that require the attention. This thinking led to the creation of Sesame Street. In the aftermath of the assassination of Martin Luther King, a professional group of Black Psychiatrists (Black Psychiatrists of America) became concerned about the growing influence of television. In particular, TV was a prime "carrier" of demeaning messages that stigmatized and undermined the mental health of vulnerable young black children. Sesame Street had originally been conceived as a novel way of bringing remedial education into the homes of disadvantaged children, especially children of color. However, through the influence of the BPA, a different kind of potential for the show was conceived: one that could directly counter and counteract the racist messages prevalent in the media of the time.[14] As a result, a new mental model in children's programming was born. The challenge is not to rely on the promise of changing people, which will meet with limited and sometimes counterproductive results. It is to design systems and structures to overcome inequities that result from flawed and outdated mental models. When those structures change, then the people that work

---

[14]B. Greene, The Unmistakable Black Roots of Sesame Street, *Smithsonian Magazine*, November 2019.

within them will also change. To realize transformation, old mental models must be sacrificed. This is true both at the organizational level and at the individual level. To attempt DEI without sacrifice is to change nothing. Yet, that is the "less-than-stellar idea" that seems so attractive to many leaders faced with this challenge. While sacrifice seems daunting, keep in mind that the other principles help clear the way. Glasses full of Trust, Chemistry, and Ambition create the right context for making needed sacrifices. The task of the leader is to make sure the glasses are as full as possible before the initiative begins and to keep them full as the journey unfolds. Doing so leverages the great power of DEI to design and shape an organization that is more compatible with the frontiers of knowledge, connectivity, and entrepreneurial workforce that will define marketplaces and commerce.

Hopefully, you can now see the value of the principles in framing a challenge. DEI is one of many challenges that can be reframed within this perspective. So, the seven principles are not only a way of measuring as we saw with the glasses of water but they are also a way of thinking — a way of asking bigger questions and getting bigger impacts. Now, let's look at the principles as a way of organizing, coordinating, and collaborating. A means to build an organization that works in the Universal Revolution of today — an organization that resembles a network, not a hierarchy. One that is inclusive values diversity and creates an opportunity for people to build an identity and story that is meaningful and impactful. Let's look at the workplace of tomorrow.

Communities of Practice, Social Networks, and Breakthrough Innovation

As I noted early in the discussion, revolutions are typically triggered by technology and then quickly impact people and organizations. It is like an earthquake at sea. The disturbance appears out of sight, but its impact is felt by the waves it produces. The new frontiers revealed by a revolution will almost certainly change the perspectives of people. Avenues that were once closed are now open and entirely new avenues appear. Prior ways of doing things suddenly or gradually give way to better options. These new frontiers also foreshadow brand-new possibilities for coordinating, organizing, and managing a workplace. The most obvious recent example of this phenomenon is the use of teleconferencing technology to work from anywhere. The pandemic of 2020 necessitated this shift and many assumptions about work were reshaped. People could be productive online, people valued working from home, there was no rush to return to the office, and virtual work was viewed as a perk not to be taken away. A new avenue of work was revealed and many assumptions about work changed. We learned more about human psychology. Some things we thought we knew about people were now wrong.

While it is easy to be distracted by today's incredible technology, virtual organizations, and digital nomads, they do not fully represent the deep change that has occurred in cutting-edge organizations. They are simply the enablers. There is a deeper and more substantive shift in the organizing principles of the workplace. These new and dynamic workplaces resemble the networks and communities of interest that were first made possible by social media. However, they do not mirror these virtual communities through technology only. They mirror them through the organization, coordination, and connectivity of people that are enabled and leveraged by technology. It is an organization that is built to be a social network. It is driven by innovation, knowledge flow, and diverse pools of talent. It has the key dimensions of inspiration and discipline as well as the ability to crowdsource ideas and know-how.[15] Innovation is driven from the network of communities and connections rather than from the hierarchy. There are still projects, teams, and some traces of hierarchical oversight. However, it is all connected, and it is coordinated. If this sounds revolutionary or

---

[15]J. Brunneder, O. Acar, D. Deichmann, and T. Sarwal, A New Model for Crowdsourcing Innovation, *Harvard Business Review*, January 31, 2020.

too much of a reach, don't be too sure of your assumption. It may not be possible or desirable to perfectly replicate a Social Network in every organization. However, there are aspects of it that can turn a very non-innovative organization into a forward-looking, ambitious, and proactive force. It is not a gigantic leap. Let's take a closer look at its essential parts.

As illustrated in Figure 7, the overriding attribute of a social network organization is CoP. A community of practice is a collection of people who share a concern or passion for something they do and learn how to do it better through their regular interactions.[16] By design, CoPs are not insular. They exist in an ecosystem with other CoPs to learn, share, and adopt different perspectives for solving problems. It is not something entirely new; however, many organizations lost sight of its value. A notable example of a CoP within an organization is the one developed around Xerox customer service representatives who repaired machines in the field. These Xerox reps began exchanging repair tips and tricks in informal meetings over breakfast or lunch. Eventually, Xerox saw the value of these interactions and created the Eureka project to allow these interactions to be shared across the global network of representatives. The Eureka database saved the corporation around $100 million.[17] Had Xerox expanded CoP-based innovation to sales, design, strategy, and other parts of the organization, it might have been more prepared for the revolution of digital documents brought about by Adobe and Microsoft. This is the fundamental difference in today's innovative organizations: CoPs are the main organizing principle and not a sideshow. These modern CoPs are ambitious, inward and outward looking, bonded by chemistry, havens of trust, and driven by data. It is a very safe place for people to build their skills and apply their know-how to solve tough problems.

---

[16]Etienne Wenger, *Communities of Practice: Learning, Meaning, and Identity*, Cambridge University Press, 1998, Cambridge, UK.

[17]John Seely Brown and Paul Duguid, Balancing Act: How to Capture Knowledge without Killing It, *Harvard Business Review*, 2000.

Figure 7: Innovation in a Social Network Organization*

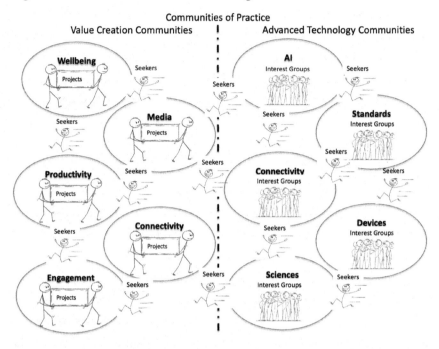

Notes: *Everyone is a member of a Value Creation Community (VCC) and an Advanced Technology Community (ATC). Most often, members keep the same roles in both groups. More than one person can have the same role within a group. Products/Services typically span and are "born out of" the VCCs and ATCs. The illustration captures a sample of VCCs and ATCs. The identity and number of communities should be based on the type, needs, and challenges of an organization.

Taking a page from the book of innovation in the scientific revolution, CoPs are split into Value Creation Communities (VCCs) and Advanced Technology Communities (ATCs). Like the duality of lab and factory in the scientific revolution, the VCCs are focused on creating products, services, and anything of value. They are inward looking and focused on now. In contrast, The ATCs are outward looking and focused on the future. They scan the frontier for new technologies, methodologies, and know-how that might be useful. They are lab-based CoPs that are constantly looking for "What Is Possible?". In Figure 7, I have used the organizing scheme found in some of today's most innovative technology-based organizations

(Life Science, Digital, and Robotics). Think of it as an amalgamation of the organizations researched for this book and not as a prescribed or ideal scheme for creating CoPs. They work well for these organizations. However, in the spirit of innovation, leaders should identify CoPs that work best for *their* organization. That said, I do recommend that organizations develop value-based CoPs as well as forward-looking CoPs. I also highly recommend that mechanisms are put in place to share knowledge freely between all CoPs. As illustrated, this can be accomplished very easily by assigning the role of "seeker" to a member of a CoP. The seeker's task is to visit other CoPs. While there, the seeker is an active member of the host CoP, not just an observer. The seeker should share what they know, learn from other CoPs, and then share back to their home CoP. Rather than assume this will happen organically, it is assured to happen by assigning the task to a member of the community. As illustrated, these seekers share knowledge across the CoPs: within the VCCs and ATCs and between the VCCs and ATCs.

Notice also that CoPs are assigned broader value-based identifiers rather than products or services. Within these broader categories, specific projects, initiatives, as well as products and services are housed. In Figure 7, the VCCs are organized by *Wellbeing*, *Media*, *Productivity*, *Connectivity*, and *Engagement*. These communities represent the main value-driving activities of the organization's offerings. They are the outcomes that their customers value and origin of new and existing projects and initiatives. The ATCs get their identity from technologies, standards, sciences, and devices that are important for future success. Should a technology that is not represented become important, a CoP will quickly take shape or expand to capture the new frontier. To reiterate, the illustration is a general representation of Social Networking as an organizing principle. There are many ways to organize and identify CoPs. The main point is the creation of an organizational form that acts more like a network than a hierarchy. That said, to create a social networked organization does not necessarily suggest that the hierarchy should be completely thrown away. Hierarchy can provide needed rationality. In many organizations, an investment committee oversees the CoPs. This committee is populated by senior executives and works directly with the architects of CoPs to manage investment, establish priorities, and facilitate the commercialization of ideas and initiatives. So, two things can be true at the same time: An organization can use hierarchy to rationalize and coordinate investment; it can also use social networking to generate the novel ideas. Again, we see the clever symbiosis of inspiration and discipline: hierarchical rationalization for investment and community sourcing for discovery.

Diving Deeper: Project Teams and Interest Groups

Let's dive deeper into the project groups and interest groups. As discussed in Chapter 5, a key principle of breakthrough innovation is clear roles and responsibilities for *all* members of a group or team. Everyone has talent gained from experience as well as talent that is a natural part of who they are. The goal is to engage all this talent when pursuing the elusive answer to a challenging problem. To reiterate, the trick is to unbundle attributes that are typically bundled together in the classic role of "leader". These unbundled roles should then be distributed to the group. After all, it is impossible for any leader to "know it all" or "be great at everything". So, instead of placing the entire burden on the mythical leader, we fully engage the range of talent and perspective of the community. As illustrated in Figure 8, the roles and responsibilities described in Chapter 5 are found in project groups and in interest groups. When these roles are assigned and known across the organization, it is easy to coordinate between projects and interest groups. It is also easy to identify specific people in a project or interest group that may hold needed data or answers. For example, as a project team designs a new therapy within the community of well-being, it might become interested in clinical trials of digital drugs. Within the ATCs of the organization are two interest groups — one in standards and one in devices — that are researching digital drugs. The scientists of those interest groups have experimental data and other research that might

Figure 8: A Deeper Dive: Project Groups and Interest Groups

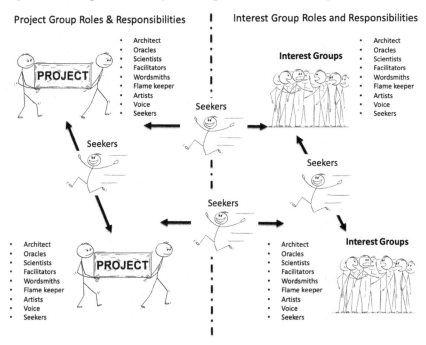

be valuable for the project team. Through roles as well as through the seekers that migrate between the communities, such knowledge will be more easily revealed. The project team and the interest group share and learn freely. This is the critical takeaway; the organization must function as a social network that is built to create and share knowledge. This is the new home of the best, biggest, and most impactful innovation. It is in the network.

As found in these three broad applications, the principles are a useful means for assessing the predisposition for innovation success, framing very tricky problems, and creating a networked capability to share knowledge and reveal the bigger ideas. There are certainly other applications that I will leave for you to discover. However, you use them, just remember that they capture a more ambitious form of innovation, an idea chase. They also capture the critical intersection between the inspirational depiction of innovation and its disciplined depiction. Finally, they are not a bridge too far. Yes, creating a social network within a classic organization may be a challenge. However, it is quite likely that a good number of these networks already exist, even in the most non-innovative organizations. The problem is that these hidden and informal communities are not formally leveraged, empowered, or woven into the process of innovation. In today's world, it is likely that the most impactful ideas will be born in these communities rather than in a traditional hierarchy or steering group. This is certainly obvious and welcomed in the most highly innovative organizations. However, most of these same organizations were not created as social networks following every one of these seven principles. Some were too inspirational, some were too methodological, and some did not know what they were. However, all migrated to this same place because the challenges they faced were growing more complex and the organization they had was not up to task. They innovated in to create the ability to innovate out. The trigger for the change was a dramatic shift in technology, people, and possibilities — the Universal Revolution. It began before the pandemic of 2020, accelerated as the pandemic unfolded, and hit hyper acceleration when the pandemic began to lift.

Concluding Thoughts

As a researcher and writer, it is certainly preferable to examine a phenomenon that is in steady state. As they teach you in a Ph.D. program, research is easier when the object of your study is not a moving target. Unfortunately, the most compelling things to study are almost always moving targets. To be honest, I thought chasing ideas was *not* quite a moving target. If it was moving, it was not moving fast. After all, great inventors have been chasing ideas for a long time. I was partially right. There is something to learn from people and organizations that chase the fantastic, past and present, particularly, when we expand the discussion to art, music, and science. However, I was also partially wrong. Innovation had taken on a different meaning and a very new form as we marched out of the late information age into the universal revolution. I felt it as someone who works and consults with very innovative organizations, and I heard it loudly from friends and colleagues. The stakes were higher, the challenges were greater, something was very different. Yet, the field of possibilities for confronting the tricky problems was never greater. The road ahead is a different innovation challenge but there are new tools in the toolbox to successfully find your way. There are principles, techniques, and organizational forms that align with the new frontier. They are measurable, they are manageable, and they are essential to chasing breakthrough ideas. Very soon in my own endeavors, I found myself researching, consulting, and experiencing innovation as a surfer riding a wave rather than a fisherman in a boat on a calm pond.

This book is about that wave and the people that are riding it. However, it was not the book I expected; it is much more. History has given us great clues about innovation, the present and the future ask us to keep the pieces that work, add the new pieces that are necessary, and apply innovation in more creative ways. For leaders, designers, and creators, it is time to ask and expect more from efforts to find new ideas. The goal is to shape innovation so that it is truly innovative. Communities innovate within networks. They also innovate based on principles that reflect inspiration and discipline. Organizations must be a friendly confine for those communities, and leaders must adopt a new mindset for their management. It is not a heavy lift and not a complete refit for any organization. It does require a rethinking of the frontier and a willingness to innovate in to innovate out. I sincerely hope this research and book are a bold step in that direction. That said, this book is not a complete recipe. The final step in the design is *your* imagination and creativity. You are part of the unfolding innovation story. Again, this is something that is new and different in today's world. Take these ideas and craft something that meets the needs and challenges of your idea chase. You will be surprised at the results, and you will likely find some ideas that were previously unseen.

As noted at the beginning of this book, it is tempting to say that chasing the fantastic is something that must be seen to be believed. However, it is more audacious than that; it is something that must be believed to be seen. Believe it, live it, pass it forward, and accept the new ideas and wonders that it will reveal. If you reach for the stars often, you will soon find the stars reaching back for you.

Appendix: The Research Methodology

The research gathered for this book took place over a five-year span. As noted in the book, during this time frame, it became obvious that the practice of innovation was changing. Problems were more complex, oncoming challenges were greater, and the world was reeling and recovering from a pandemic. In the beginning, site visits and my firsthand experiences with innovative projects provided the primary foundation of data collection. This was supplemented with secondary data provided by participating firms as well as surveys of their leaders. In 2020, the traditional avenues of gathering data were closed. Those avenues were soon replaced with numerous Zoom calls, Microsoft Teams Meetings, emails, and other collaborative technologies. As the pandemic wound down, a hybrid model of high-tech and high-touch data collection was developed. Therefore, the approach to research was itself an exercise in the new and emerging model of innovation described in this book. Luckily, the book is focused on very innovative organizations; therefore, the leap may not have been as long or as difficult for them as it would have been for less innovative organizations. In the following sections, the methodology and approach are described.

Phase 1: Primary Data, On-Site Visits, and Interviews

The main purpose of the *Idea Chase* is to uncover the secrets of the most innovative organizations in the world. Importantly, these organizations may be science projects, entertainment enterprises, healthcare, art, or more traditional businesses. The hope is that there is a consistency in these endeavors that informs the reader about breakthrough innovation. In other words, I am looking for a system of measurable and manageable principles that guide a variety of breakthrough innovations. The initial set of organizations and people studied include the following:

Entertainment

Sesame Workshop (the creators of Sesame Street)

Pixar

Disney (Star Wars, Disney Imagineering, Marvel)

Dream Works

Prince (Former band members and manager)

The Rolling Stones (One band member and management)

REM (Two band members and management)

Art

Lady Pink (Street Art)

John "Crash" Matos (Street Art)

Banksy (Street Art)

Industry

Google

Bose

Boston Scientific

Space X

Microsoft

Apple

Tesla

Amazon

Marriott

Siemens

Lego

Samsung

Healthcare
Johnson and Johnson
Genentech
Siemens
Mayo Clinic
Cleveland Clinic

Science
Event Horizon Telescope
New Horizons (NASA)
Mangalyaan (Mars Orbiter Mission of the Indian Space Research Organization)
Open AI

Each of these organizations or people is widely recognized for their "breakthrough" innovations. More importantly, they can claim multiple breakthrough achievements that have been accomplished over several years. This was the primary criteria for inclusion in the study along with the willingness of people and organizations to participate. Different from other research projects, this study spans industry, art, science, healthcare, and entertainment.

The outcome of the numerous interviews, site visits, and other forms of data collection in phase one was an initial definition of "principles" that led to breakthrough innovation. These principles can be thought of as preconditions for an innovative outcome that is much better than average. Through iteration, the seven principles became defined, commonly understood, and measurable. This was true across the diverse frontiers of innovation researched. From art to science, the principles were present, recognizable, and explained innovation outcomes. The principles were also tested for their validity in contextualizing historical breakthrough innovation such as the Wright Brothers' Invention of the Airplane, Martin Luther King's Civil Right Movement, and the inventions of Native

American Tribes. Again, the principles seem to provide a measurable and manageable framework for understanding the preconditions of innovation. When cross-referenced with initiatives that failed (e.g. Samuel Langley's attempt to build the flying machine), the principles also provided a rationale for the lack of success. Therefore, the principles were deemed robust in explaining both good and bad innovative initiatives. This was captured by the glasses of water exercise in Chapter 10.

Phase 2: Survey and Factor Analysis

The next phase of the study involved statistical analysis to measure the content and distinctness of the seven principles. The goal is to determine if the principles that were developed in the field studies and interviews are unique and novel when assessed by a larger sample. Using an online survey, non-interviewed members of the field sites assessed the presence and effectiveness of the seven principles in explaining breakthrough innovation. There are three goals here: (1) test the definition of the principles (shared understanding), (2) explore the interrelationships among the principles, and (3) link the principles to the discovery of breakthrough innovation.

The outcome of this survey was very positive. The principles are definitionally strong within themselves and definitionally distinct between themselves. The principles form a "clean" seven-factor model. Upon further testing, the model that explains the most variability is a two-factor model. The first-order factors (the seven principles) are governed by a latent second-order factor. This second-order factor is directly associated with breakthrough innovative discovery (a successful idea chase). Therefore, the data strongly suggests that the principles act collectively in explaining breakthrough innovation. In other words, it is not enough for one or two of the principles to be in force, they must all be in force for breakthrough innovation to occur. This is operationalized as "glasses of water" in Chapter 10. It is a very important scientific finding that has significant practical implications.

Phase 3: Broader Sampling of Innovative and Less Innovative Organizations

While the results of Phase two were very strong, they lack generalizability. The principles are derived from exemplars, which is the original purpose of the research project. To assess generalizability, the principles should be tested across a greater range of variances in the principles themselves and across varying levels of organizational innovativeness. In essence, it is important to determine if the model holds in organizations with varying levels of innovative success. Using Fortune 1000 Organizations as the sampling frame, general managers were randomly surveyed. The purpose was to explore the content of the principles, their interrelationships, and their relationship to breakthrough innovation. Again, the statistical results were very positive. The principles hold up incredibly well. There is now two-way validation. As measures of the *principles* improve, so do the measures of the *innovative outcomes.* Also, we now see the pattern in reverse. As measures of the *principles* decline, so do the measures of the *innovative outcomes.* There seem to be no confounding effects. Again, the results strongly suggest that all principles must be in place to achieve innovative outcomes.

Index

Printed in the United States
by Baker & Taylor Publisher Services